Migration, Minorities and Citizenship

General Editors: **Zig Layton-Henry**, Professor of Politics, University of Warwick, and **Danièle Joly**, Professor, Director, Centre for Research in Ethnic Relations, University of Warwick

Titles include:

Muhammad Anwar, Patrick Roach and Ranjit Sondhi (*editors*)
FROM LEGISLATION TO INTEGRATION?
Race Relations in Britain

James A. Beckford, Danièle Joly and Farhad Khosrokhavar
MUSLIMS IN PRISON
Challenge and Change in Britain and France

Gideon Calder, Phillip Cole, Jonathan Seglow
CITIZENSHIP ACQUISITION AND NATIONAL BELONGING
Migration, Membership and the Liberal Democratic State

Thomas Faist and Andreas Ette (*editors*)
THE EUROPEANIZATION OF NATIONAL POLICIES AND POLITICS OF IMMIGRATION
Between Autonomy and the European Union

Thomas Faist and Peter Kivisto (*editors*)
DUAL CITIZENSHIP IN GLOBAL PERSPECTIVE
From Unitary to Multiple Citizenship

Adrian Favell
PHILOSOPHIES OF INTEGRATION
Immigration and the Idea of Citizenship in France and Britain

Agata Górny and Paulo Ruspini (*editors*)
MIGRATION IN THE NEW EUROPE
East-West Revisited

James Hampshire
CITIZENSHIP AND BELONGING
Immigration and the Politics of Democratic Governance in Postwar Britain

John R. Hinnells (*editor*)
RELIGIOUS RECONSTRUCTION IN THE SOUTH ASIAN DIASPORAS
From One Generation to Another

Ayhan Kaya
ISLAM, MIGRATION AND INTEGRATION
The Age of Securitization

Zig Layton-Henry and Czarina Wilpert (*editors*)
CHALLENGING RACISM IN BRITAIN AND GERMANY

Jørgen S. Nielsen
TOWARDS A EUROPEAN ISLAM

Pontus Odmalm
MIGRATION POLICIES AND POLITICAL PARTICIPATION
Inclusion or Intrusion in Western Europe?

Prodromos Panayiotopoulos
ETHNICITY, MIGRATION AND ENTERPRISE

Aspasia Papadopoulou-Kourkoula
TRANSIT MIGRATION
The Missing Link between Emigration and Settlement

Jan Rath (*editor*)
IMMIGRANT BUSINESSES
The Economic, Political and Social Environment

Carl-Ulrik Schierup (*editor*)
SCRAMBLE FOR THE BALKANS
Nationalism, Globalism and the Political Economy of Reconstruction

Vicki Squire
THE EXCLUSIONARY POLITICS OF ASYLUM

Maarten Vink
LIMITS OF EUROPEAN CITIZENSHIP
European Integration and Domestic Immigration Policies

Östen Wahlbeck
KURDISH DIASPORAS
A Comparative Study of Kurdish Refugee Communities

Lucy Williams
GLOBAL MARRIAGE
Cross-Border Marriage Migration in Global Context

Migration, Minorities and Citizenship
Series Standing Order ISBN 978–0–333–71047–0 (hardback) and
978–0–333–80338–7 (paperback)
(*outside North America only*)

You can receive future titles in this series as they are published by placing a standing order. Please contact your bookseller or, in case of difficulty, write to us at the address below with your name and address, the title of the series and the ISBN quoted above.

Customer Services Department, Macmillan Distribution Ltd, Houndmills, Basingstoke, Hampshire RG21 6XS, England

Ethnicity, Migration and Enterprise

Prodromos Panayiotopoulos
Centre for Migration and Policy Research
Swansea University, UK

First published 2010 by
PALGRAVE MACMILLAN

Palgrave Macmillan in the UK is an imprint of Macmillan Publishers Limited, registered in England, company number 785998, of Houndmills, Basingstoke, Hampshire RG21 6XS.

Palgrave Macmillan in the US is a division of St Martin's Press LLC, 175 Fifth Avenue, New York, NY 10010.

Palgrave Macmillan is the global academic imprint of the above companies and has companies and representatives throughout the world.

Palgrave® and Macmillan® are registered trademarks in the United States, the United Kingdom, Europe and other countries.

ISBN: 978–0–230–22934–1 hardback

This book is printed on paper suitable for recycling and made from fully managed and sustained forest sources. Logging, pulping and manufacturing processes are expected to conform to the environmental regulations of the country of origin.

A catalogue record for this book is available from the British Library.

Library of Congress Cataloging-in-Publication Data

Panayiotopoulos, Prodromos Ioannou.
      Ethnicity, migration and enterprise / Prodromos Panayiotopoulos.
         p. cm.—(Migration, minorities and citizenship)
      ISBN 978–0–230–22934–1
         1. Minority business enterprises – United States – Case studies.
      2. Minority business enterprises – European Union countries – Case studies. 3. Entrepreneurship – United States – Case studies.
      4. Entrepreneurship – European Union countries – Case studies.
      5. Ethnicity – United States – Case studies. 6. Ethnicity – European Union countries – Case studies. I. Title.

HD2346.U35P36 2010
338.6'420890094—dc22   2010023977

10 9 8 7 6 5 4 3 2 1
19 18 17 16 15 14 13 12 11 10

Printed and bound in Great Britain by
CPI Antony Rowe, Chippenham and Eastbourne

This volume is dedicated to Abram Leon

Contents

Tables

Acknowledgements

There are too many acknowledgements to list individually. Clearly this book would not have been possible without the entrepreneurs, who assisted various research efforts over the years by giving their time and sharing their knowledge. Equally, this book would not have been possible without the work of other researchers who have made their work available. One general acknowledgement is to the pioneering and current work of Edna Bonacich and Ivan Light, who probably more than most, inspired the development of research on immigrant and ethnic minority enterprise as a significant field of study. The work of Saskia Sassen, Nigel Harris, Naila Kabeer, Floya Anthias, Annie Phizacklea, John Rex, Amanda Wise, AnnLee Saxenian, Ralph Grillo on a wide range of issues from race, ethnicity and multiculturalism, immigration, informalisation and employment have influenced the direction taken by the book. The contents have also been informed by the considerable research and published work produced by Frank Pieke, Greg Benton, Roger Waldinger, Alejandro Portes, Jan Rath, Robert Kloosterman and their associates, as well as, staff at the Institute of Migration and Ethnic Studies at the University of Amsterdam. Whilst none of the above are responsible for the contents, the book attempts to present their views accurately.

Preface

This book investigates in a comparative way the relationship between ethnicity, migration and enterprise. Ethnic minority enterprises are a highly visible phenomenon in the transformation of many inner-city neighbourhoods and run-down suburbs. Many of these areas have been transformed by ethnic minority entrepreneurs with little assistance – and in many cases considerable hindrance – from local and central government and the commercial lending sector. The book examines this process and presents material which indicates that immigrants and ethnic minorities, far from 'taking jobs' from native workers, are in fact creating large numbers of jobs in particular sectors, sub-sectors and localities. The book presents a study of the following strategic ethnic migrant groups, defined as such because of their numerical significance and also their actual and potential contribution to the (small) enterprise sector: Turkish migrant entrepreneurs in Europe, primarily Germany, Chinese-owned enterprises in Europe and the United States, Hispanic enterprise in the United States, and the more recent experience of Polish migration and enterprise in Western Europe.

The book uses the terminology of race, ethnicity and migration developed in the United Kingdom. It differs from that developed in both the United States and continental Europe in a number of ways. This can cause confusion, so it is worth explaining early on that by 'immigrant' we mean a person who was born in another country. By 'ethnic minority' we mean people who are born and raised in the country or countries they live in. It is the case that many members of an ethnic minority group might be immigrants, but they need not be so and indeed are not growing in numbers. It is important to understand this distinction and what it implies for a sense of belonging for young people growing up in the metropolitan heartlands of Europe and the United States who whilst they might, or might not, think of themselves as culturally different, do not think of themselves as 'immigrants'. This is quite different to the tendency in the United States to describe people as 'second-generation' or third- or fourth-generation immigrants. Switzerland voted in a referendum to deny 'third-generation' immigrants the right to vote. It seems that in some societies the label 'immigrant' cannot be escaped, despite the fact that it bears little relationship to the actual status of the person. Rather it serves to underpin, typically in the form of immigration controls and naturalisation policy, processes of selection by the political-institutional framework in the political ranking of human beings.

The book is the result of both academic and personal interests. It is part of a long period of research on the social dimensions of small enterprises, which included studies of refugee entrepreneurs in the Gaza Strip, informal sector artisans in Nairobi, youth entrepreneurs in the Commonwealth countries and immigrant and ethnic minority entrepreneurs in north London. One common strand in this research was how class society reproduces itself at the smallest scale amongst the self-employed and micro-enterprises. Another was how being shapes consciousness, and the relationship between the ideas held by economic agents and the changing material circumstances facing them. A particular and personal interest was the study of how immigrant workers and artisans became bosses in the clothing industry, or how a layer of petty employers emerged from the ranks of waged workers in the experience of the Cypriot community in north London. In many respects the book is a study of the development of ethnic capitalism and an examination of the extent to which social relations embedded in ethnicity can influence and shape economic action rooted in class. Even more challenging, as we shall see, is the way that many things we assume to be naturally 'ethnic' are in fact associated conditions of class.

One issue, which is perhaps clearer, is that writing a book of this nature is a proxy indicator of the tremendous changes that have taken place, both in terms of the presence and confidence of black and ethnic minority communities and in their relations with world around them, which, contrary to ethnic pessimists and the current 'backlash' against multiculturalism, they are very much part of. We are a long way from a dismal rainy evening during September 1969, when I stood outside Haringey Civic Centre, north London, where a protest against racism was being held. At the time I was a 17-year-old school boy who had recently arrived in north London from Cyprus and whose command of the English language left a lot to be desired. Somebody told me about the protest during the previous week's (largest ever) anti-Vietnam War demonstration of 200,000 people. The first thing that struck me was that there was nobody there. There were less than twenty people. I couldn't work out where everybody else was. All the protestors (except me) were Caribbean and African women who were up in arms against the 'Irish Catholic mafia-controlled council' which was 'bussing' their children outside the Borough of Haringey, because they didn't want 'too many black kids in the same school'. Some of these women went on to become genuine leaders inside their communities and were the backbone of support for Bernie Grant, who twenty years later became (Labour) Leader of Haringey Council and subsequently the first-ever African-Caribbean Member of Parliament for Tottenham in the London Borough of Haringey (Panayiotopoulos, 1992).

When I walk into the centre of Swansea, South Wales, where I have lived for the last thirty years, I usually make a point of walking along St Helens Road. It is a familiar enough sight in most cities in the UK and a microcosm of some of the changes taking place in local economies and described in the book. The area consists of a clustering of ethnic enterprises, mainly Bengali, Pakistani and Turkish owned. It is a centre which emerged over the last decade, relatively late when compared other large cities in the UK. It is a significant area of employment growth. This includes the direct employment of mainly fellow co-ethnics. A number of groceries also employ workers from other groups as porters for unloading deliveries and loading customer vehicles on what is a busy and narrow road. Most work as cooks and waiters in the many restaurants found on the road, as shop assistants in groceries, or in shops selling household furniture and fineries, garments, or in establishments which provide both material and temporal services to the Bangladeshi and wider community in the form of travel agents, barbers and the local Mosque. One recent development has been the establishment of three barbers' shops on the Road. Two of the owners are Kurdish and the other Turkish, and all began their working lives in the UK in doner kebab take-aways. It took them from two to four years to work out that their (apprenticed trained) skills as barbers could make them a better living, particularly from native working-class kids who like intricate hair shavings in addition to the more conventional haircuts, than selling doner kebabs in the middle of the night.

St Helens Road also generates employment through a wider and more discrete multiplier effect. Many native workers in industries producing plates, knives and forks for the restaurant trade, or who are self-employed as electricians, plumbers, painters and decorators, also have more work than they would, due to the expansion of minority-owned enterprises. Something like 300 jobs are generated directly, and another 200 indirectly, by the enterprises on St Helens Road (Panayiotopoulos, 2007). The entrepreneurs have transformed an area which was long abandoned by most businesses by raising their own start-up capital and with very limited assistance from Swansea local authority. This stands in marked contrast to the large sums invested by the same local authority in the development of the nearby Wind Street leisure complex which was modelled on the *Ramblas* walk in Barcelona as part of economic cultural regeneration, and to which it bears only an ironic comparison given that Wind Street and the nocturnal economy is mainly a place where people from Swansea and the adjoining areas go to get 'plastered' (to which I have no moral objections). What the example does illustrate, however, is that the Bangladeshi community in Swansea, far from taking jobs, has in fact created many jobs. The example also suggests that those who accuse ethnic minorities, ethnic entrepreneurs and ethnic economies of 'self-segregation' and condemn them as communities leading 'parallel lives', would perhaps be making better use of their time by directing their accusations at the nature and process of policy-making at local and national level.

Introduction

Ethnicity is a particularly messy concept and only the foolhardy would reduce the complexity of ethnic identity and minority status to overarching conclusions about all members of an ethnic or migrant group. At the same time, the studies illustrate a number of common themes which whilst apparent to all groups, seem to be amplified in particular migrant experience. Turkish and Polish entrepreneurs, despite their common origins as labour migrants, exemplify contrasting sets of relations with the political–institutional framework. The implication of the presence or absence of citizenship and political rights raises major questions for the development of sustainable enterprises amongst groups originally perceived by policy as short-term labour migrants, such as Turks in Germany and Mexicans in the United States. Much of the literature on Chinese migration and enterprise focuses on issues to do with 'irregular migration' and informal labour markets. This allows us to investigate the scissors effect and paradox found in much of the literature on ethnicity and economic action, between self-employment and small enterprise as an agency for social integration on the one hand and the tendency for many entrepreneurs to operate in informal economies which brings them into conflict with the regulatory framework on the other. The book points to the informalisation of production and the incorporation of ethnic minority and migrant entrepreneurs into flexible systems of production in which they adopt a range of strategies ranging from household survival to capital accumulation. Among Hispanic enterprise in the United States there are significant differences between Mexican and Cuban enterprise development, which raises conceptual questions about the validity of ethnicity as an analytical unit. The experience of the more recent migration from Poland to Western Europe, in particular the United Kingdom, raises new and familiar questions about the emergence of enterprise amongst a recent migrant group perceived as short-term labour migrants.

The book investigates the role of ethnicity as a common cognitive framework shared by owners of and workers in ethnic minority enterprises. At the same time it identifies processes of social and economic differentiation between and within ethnic minority enterprises in the shaping of diverse outcomes – winners and losers – amongst members of the same ethnic group. Gender differences are a case in point. Similarly, race is an important signifier of position which socially differentiates members of the same ethnic group. A breakdown of US Census data relevant to the Hispanic population and race shows that in residential terms, 'people of mixed racial ancestry are accepted by white Hispanics on the basis of shared ethnicity but are rejected by Anglos on the basis of race'. Further, that 'Anglos will view people of mixed race as black no matter how they see themselves' (Denton and Massey, 1989, pp. 790, 802). Similarly, research on the influence of race on Hispanic housing choices in New York City indicates that racial status determined where Hispanics moved and that 'white Hispanics are more successful than black Hispanics and other-race Hispanics in gaining access to predominantly Anglo sub areas, apparently by virtue of their non-black status' (Rosenbaum, 1996, p. 217). One implication of this line of inquiry is that it reveals the persistence of race in the structuring of American society. Racial minorities, like ethnic minorities, can be made up of immigrants but, again, this is not necessarily so. Indeed, in the case of the US Black American population, this is spectacularly not the case. At the same time a growing proportion of immigration to the United States is made up of Black Hispanics and for them the status of being a black immigrant in the United States adds another hill to climb.

The book investigates two processes taking place at the same time. Firstly, it considers the positioning and repositioning of many members of an ethnic group, typically from the ranks of wage-workers to those of the self-employed and petty employer, and sometimes the other way round. Secondly, the book examines the emergence from the ranks of the self-employed and petty employers of a smaller layer of larger employers, wholesalers, manufacturers and property developers. This indicates considerable fluidity in processes currently in formation.

Chapter 1 explains the development of thinking about ethnicity, from the crisis of modernisation theory and mainstream assimilationist thinking in the 1960s to the current 'backlash' against multiculturalism. The chapter provides discussion on the role of international migration and its manifestations, such as globalisation 'from below' and transnationalism. The chapter examines the development of ideas about ethnicity and enterprise and introduces key concepts used in subsequent sections of the book (a Glossary appears at the end of the book). Chapter 2 examines the role of the political–institutional framework in the incorporation of migrants from Turkey, who constitute the single largest ethnic group in the European Union. Many Turkish entrepreneurs began as labour migrants and were perceived as short-term *Gastarbeiter* (guestworkers). Economic recession and job-losses during the mid-1970s saw many ex-guestworkers and their children seeking alternatives in self-employment. Whilst most of these entrepreneurs have either worked in Europe for decades, or were born in Germany, the Netherlands or Britain, they lack citizenship, and this has important implications for the development of enterprise.

Chapter 3 presents a review of Chinese immigrant-owned enterprise, in order to examine the potential of enterprise as an agency for social integration. A related purpose is to consider the implications of participation by many of the entrepreneurs and workers in informal economies. The chapter points to ethnic adaptation and integration in local markets and informal economies, as contractors and sub-contractors as the visible end product of a process of informalisation driven substantially by economic restructuring rather than by attributes associated with any particular ethnic group. Chapter 4 considers the relationship between ethnicity, nationality, race and enterprise in a comparative study of the Cuban Hispanic enterprise in Miami frequently described in the literature as an 'achieving' minority, and the Mexican Hispanic community in Los Angeles. The chapter identifies significant intersections between ethnicity and race and ethnicity and class, and suggests that the interplay between these factors may be more relevant to understanding ethnic adaptation and segmented assimilation by Hispanic communities in the United States than attributes associated with national origins or ethnic identity.

Chapter 5 presents a study of globalisation 'from above' in a study of Polish migration and emergent enterprise. Poland and the other Accession 8 states joined the European Union following enlargement in June 2004. This migrant flow made up the second largest wave of migration to the United Kingdom and was significantly bigger than immigration from the New Commonwealth countries during the 1950s and 1960s. The chapter points to change and continuity in the incorporation of 'old' and 'new' migrants in the United Kingdom. Whilst Polish migrants were seen in instrumental terms as a labour market response to shortages in the workforce (like other groups), unlike other migrant groups, they did not experience a lack of political rights and restrictions to travel. The chapter examines the extent to which the political–institutional framework has facilitated a recognisable but selective pattern of independent, circular migration by large numbers of young men and women from eastern and central Europe, with not infrequently ethnic enterprise appearing in the form of the 'travel agent'. The chapter examines how Polish migration and enterprise has been impacted by the current recession.

Chapter 6 concludes that the studies of ethnic minority entrepreneurs challenge widely held views that ethnic groups and immigrants are 'taking our jobs'. The book concludes that ethnicity is an emergent and submergent phenomenon which needs to be contextually understood and, further, that an understanding of the relationship between ethnicity and enterprise (if there is one) needs to fully explain the processes of social and economic differentiation inside ethnic communities and between different types of ethnic minority enterprises. The book concludes on a note of optimism in the battle taking place against rampant xenophobia by pointing to multiculturalism 'from below' as a much more potent force in how sociability is reproduced and learned in everyday life amongst culturally diverse groups of people than is perhaps recognised by policy-makers and theories grounded in ethnic competition.

1
Ethnicity, Migration, Enterprise

Introduction

Analyses of ethnicity frequently make use of ethnic competition theories in order to explain relationships between what are assumed to be culturally distinct and relatively homogenous groups of people. To the contrary, it can be argued that ethnicity as a way people describe themselves and are described by others usually involves a relationship between an idealised conception of identity on the one hand and the changing practical lives of members of any group on the other. In this way stereotypes are often challenged. It is not unusual for the ideal and the practical to be pulling in opposite directions in the day-to-day lives of people independently of how they define themselves or how they are seen by others. Ethnic interspersion, multiculturalism 'from below' and historically unprecedented, but selective, levels of international migration and human contact are some of the factors which provide a material basis for challenging ethnic and racial competition theories. These factors have created the basis for new social hybridity and the formation of new social identities among culturally diverse groups of people in ways which were unimaginable even a decade ago. More importantly, ethnic competition theories fail to explain the reproduction of sociability in everyday life and the extent to which culturally diverse people forced to live, work and share public sector services together, learn according to prevailing norms in local neighbourhoods and communities to co-exist. The chapter examines the rise of ethnicity, the uneven development of multiculturalism as a social experiment in new ways of living and the current 'backlash' against multiculturalism. The primary purpose in this section is to investigate the development of interest in the economics of ethnicity.

5

The rise of ethnicity

The 1960s challenged many basic social assumptions and attitudes about race, ethnicity, gender, age and sexuality. The emergence of ethnicity as a cultural, political and economic basis of mobilisation posed particularly sharp problems for mainstream assimilation thinking: the United States was faced with the ghetto uprisings which began in Watts, Los Angeles, in June 1965 and which over the next few years generalised to involve most major black urban centres in the country. A study of the impact of the Watts uprising on a group of young people observed that the street youth had 'adopted seemingly overnight something called *Blackness*. They disclaimed what had been fought for by the older generation; they were no longer to be *Negroes*, they were now *Black*' (Glasgow, 1980, p. 2, italics in original). One year after the Watts uprising, Stokely Carmichael, a young black radical, was addressing a crowd of 3000 protestors in a park in Greenwood, Mississippi. James Meredith, who had integrated the University of Mississippi, was wounded on his solitary 'Walk Against Fear' from Memphis to Jackson, and other volunteers were marching in his place. Carmichael had previously taken part in the Freedom Rides and the campaign by the Student Non-violent Coordinating Committee (SNCC) during summer 1964 which sent hundreds of black and white volunteers to the South in a black registration drive (Zinn, 1964). As a field organiser in Lowndes County, Alabama, he helped raise the number of registered black voters to 2600 from a mere 70, or 300 more than the number of registered whites. Carmichael and other SNCC activists were arrested and jailed many times. He claimed to have lost count after 32. Carmichael was radicalised by the experience of working in the segregated South, where peaceful protesters were often beaten, brutalised and sometimes killed for seeking the ordinary rights of citizens. When they set up camp in Greenwood, Carmichael was arrested again and his frustration was evident.

'This is the 27th time', he was quoted as saying in disgust after his release. In a statement which was widely covered by US TV and radio he said, 'we have been saying "Freedom" for six years', referring to the chant that movement protesters used as they stood up to racist politicians and policemen pointing water hoses and unleashing snarling dogs. 'What we are going to start saying now is Black Power! What we need here is some Black Power!' The crowd (including some white participants) quickly picked up the chant with enthusiasm and started shouting with their fists in the air 'Black Power! Black Power!' (Kaufman, 1998, p. 2). This was the first time that the words 'Black Power' were used in the United States.

The demand for Black Power was repeated in a cry that would soon be echoed in communities from Oakland to Newark. But if Carmichael's call for black power galvanised many young blacks, it shocked White America with articles appearing in newspapers deploring the term as 'reverse racism'. Equally shocked was the integrationist leadership of the Civil Rights Movement: Dr King called it 'an unfortunate choice of words'. Roy Wilkins of the National Association for the Advancement of Colored People (NAACP), a bastion of black middle-class interests, scorned it as an example of 'the raging of race against race' (Kaufman, 1998, p. 3). In the book Black Power, which Carmichael wrote in 1967 with Charles Hamilton, the authors tried to explain the term. 'It is a call for black people in this country to unite', they wrote, 'to recognize their heritage, to build a sense of community. It is a call for black people to define their own goals, to lead their own organizations' (Carmichael and Hamilton, 1967, p. 3). By this point, Stokely Carmichael like other black American radicals had Africanised his name to Kwame Ture.

The rise of racial and ethnic solidarity and the idea that minorities have the right to act as agents in their own cultural, political and economic development challenged assimilationist 'melting-pot' ideas about human interaction which, as Glazer and Moynihan (1970, 1975) and Glazer (1997) noted, was most deeply felt in the United States, given its particular historical development as a country of diverse immigrant groups transformed into 'modern' Americans, typically within one generation. The rise of ethnicity in the United States revealed itself among the multitude of immigrant groups which make up its population, in the phenomenon of counter-migration back to their countries of origin, or perceived origin, as Greeks, Jews, Germans, Czechs, Poles and Italians emphasised their ethnic origins in a growing transnational relationship. King (2000) referred to the 'New Ethnic Politics', to describe the emergence of ethnicity in the United States and demands for a fuller political role. Rhea (1997) referred to a 'Race Pride Movement', which manifested itself amongst Asian Americans, Indian Americans and African Americans, which fuelled demands for 'equal respect for all cultural and ethnic identities in a political system' (King, 2000, p. 266). The United States saw the mushrooming of ethnic organisations lobbying the political establishment, with demands ranging from mother tongue language use in the education system to the redress of historic injustices. The rise of ethnicity in the United States contrasted sharply with the prolonged period from the early years of the 1930s recession until the early 1960s when, as Glazer (1983, p. 18) noted, 'ethnicity withdrew as a theme in American life'. To social conservatives, American Nativists, and paradoxically, modernisation advocates of mainline assimilation, the re-emergence of ethnicity challenged basic premises. For example, it challenged widely held views that 'a third-generation return to ethnicity is incompatible with the progressive decline across the generations in the salience of ethnic identities' (Alba, 1999, p. 306).

Ethnic mobilisations defied predictions made by the social sciences for the last 150 years about the expected demise of ethnicity. This expectation was applied equally to religion. The conventional sociological assumptions about the relationship between magic, religion and science was that just as religion had replaced magic, so science would come to replace religion and dispel irrational thinking. Max Weber argued that ethnic membership (*Gemeinsamkeit*) differed from the kinship group by being a 'presumed' identity, not a group with concrete social action like the latter. He pointed to the 'artificial origin of the belief in common ethnicity' and argued that the concept of the ethnic group 'dissolves if we define our terms exactly'. He did, however, point to a more potent role for ethnicity in that it 'corresponds to the concept of nation' (Weber, 1978, p. 391). Weber argued that the development of modern capitalism 'required a decisive break with traditionalism' and for this reason saw the Jewish diaspora as 'trapped' in tradition and incapable of playing this modernising role (Light and Gold, 2000, p. 5). Weber counter-opposed 'traditional' social organisation with a rational 'universalism' seen as the future trajectory for all humanity. In this analysis, ethnicity was seen as an artificial and at best a transient phenomenon, but also one intrinsically oppositional to the development of 'modern' capitalism.

The rise of ethnicity as a basis for invoking social, political, cultural and economic action created novel problems for the conventional social sciences and challenged its basic assumptions. Ethnic mobilisations and the wider construction of racial and ethnic identities presented particular problems for the Parsonian idea of modernity and assimilation which borrowed heavily from Weber and which dominated the discourse on race, immigration and ethnic relations in the Western world during the 1960s. The assumptions guiding conventional sociological thought both in the developed and developing countries were that we were involved in a trajectory, gradual or violent, which would see the subsumption of 'traditional' societies based on particular identities – such as kinship, religion, caste, race and ethnicity – into 'modern' societies in which rational individuals, sharing a universalist outlook, would interact (and transact) freely, liberated from the dark, irrational prejudices and loyalties of the past (Parsons, 1952; Parsons and Smelser, 1956).

The mobilisations during the 1960s suggested that race and ethnicity as particularist identities, far from retreating, were on the ascendancy. The (re)construction of cultural differences and boundaries between groups in ways which symbolised and actualised separate and possibly conflicting interests on the basis of a solidarity which did not conform with modernisation theory created, therefore, major conceptual problems for conventional (assimilationist) sociological thinking.

Barth (1969) in a study of ethnic politics amongst the Swat Pathan, argued that ethnic groups are defined by 'boundaries' based on shared values, customs and 'patterns of normative behaviour' and that the 'degree of conformity' to established patterns of behaviour acts as a key indicator of what defined ethnicity. Barth described the process of boundary formation with ethnic categories as 'organisational vessels' that may be given varying levels of intensity and contextual form in different socio-cultural systems: 'they can be of great relevance to behaviour, but they need not necessarily be so; they may embrace all social life, or they may be relevant only in limited areas of social activity' (Barth, 1969, p. 14). Abner Cohen, who studied the development of the nationalist movements in the ex-colonies, in response to this suggested that

> This [Barth's] approach raises a number of logical and sociological difficulties. Its central theme is descriptive and is essentially circular. What it says is that people act as the members of ethnic categories because they identify themselves and are sometimes also identified by others with these ethnic categories. How do we know this? The actors say so, or so they act. (Cohen, 1974, pp. xii–xiii)

The dangers of a one-sided, that is, 'culturalist' interpretation of ethnicity, are recognised by Cohen who notes that

> Ethnicity is a complex phenomenon … which involves psychological, historical, economic and political factors. A full study of its nature – if this is at all possible, will require giving due weight to these and probably many other factors and will call for the co-operation of many disciplines. But if we seriously attempt to do this at one and the same time, we shall not be able to go far in our analysis. (Cohen, 1974, p. xi)

Cohen (1974, p. xv), in trying to understand the rise of ethnicity in the newly independent countries and the cities of the United States during the 1960s, suggested that a political rather than cultural analysis of ethnicity may provide a more comprehensive framework in the study of the total social phenomenon. Similarly, though for different purposes, Weber also wrote that ethnicity 'is essentially a political phenomenon'. And, further, that 'in our sense, ethnic membership does not constitute a group; it only facilitates group formation of any kind, particularly in the political field' (Weber, 1978, p. 392). Adam Kuper similarly pointed to the limited role of cultural analyses in understanding the multidimensional process of ethnicity and argued that 'unless we separate out the various processes that are lumped together under the heading of culture, and look beyond the field of culture to other processes, then we will not get very far in understanding any of it' (Kuper, 1999, p. 247).

What is clearer is that ethnicity in much of the associated literature invokes the use of highly emotive language. Hutchinson and Smith (1996, p. 3), in an introduction to key readings on ethnicity, write that 'ethnic community and identity are often associated with conflict'. Frequently, 'ethnic' and 'conflict' are joined together to explain a multitude of disputes (Crawley and Hickman, 2008, p. 1223; Waldinger, 2000; Wimmer, 2008, p. 1026). Davidson (1999, p. 27) argues in paraphrasing Alastair MacIntyre that ethnicity 'is a term which no honest person should continue to use'. Explanations for ethnic competition and conflict frequently use a circular argument, whereby ethnic categories are presented as the revealed face of market competition and conflict, but at the same time it is argued that competition is a necessary precondition in the structuring of relatively intact and compliant ethnic communities which can be led by elites and brokers into a variety of ethnic conflicts. The idea of sociability, let alone social solidarity, is absent in this discourse.

It is perhaps important in an introductory discussion on ethnicity to note conflicting and contradictory processes taking place in the formation of ethnic identities. Ethnicity is frequently presented as coming to life in the counter-positioning of relatively cohesive and distinct cultural groups. At the same time much of the literature also suggests that ethnicity is an emergent and submergent phenomenon, which has to be contextually understood. The introduction cautions against seeing ethnicity as the natural property of any group. Migrants, for example, do not arrive with fully fledged ethnic identities ready to do battle with other ethnic groups, but on the contrary 'learn' how to be 'ethnic' in the host society, whether in response to institutional hostility and discrimination, or as a condition of association with an 'achieving' minority group. Ethnicity under these circumstances can appear as a defensive social position and survival strategy adopted by immigrants and their children with one consequence being that they look to the 'ethnic economy', self-employment and the small enterprise sector as alternatives to unemployment, low-pay employment and discrimination in the segmented labour market. Ethnicity can also appear as a weapon of the strong, in the development of transnational enterprises motivated by strategies of accumulation. Ethnicity has been thought of as a sharp knife which can be equally used to cut bread as to slice people (Hintjens, 2001). Perhaps an introductory concern about the term 'ethnicity' is the need to understand the conditions for the formation, persistence and transformation of ethnic identities over time (Brass, 1991).

More explicit manifestations of ethnicity appear in studies on the relationship between ethnicity, migration and employment. This often appears in the ethnicisation and gendering of particular occupations and trades. For example, in the United Kingdom one in seven Pakistani men is a taxi driver, cab driver or chauffeur, compared with one in 100 White British men. Over a quarter of Bangladeshi men are chefs, cooks or waiters, compared with 1 in 100 White British men. The proportion of Indian men working as medical practitioners, at 4 per cent, was around ten times higher than the rate for those categorised as White British. Among women, around one in ten women from the Black African group and one in seven women from the Other Asian group were working as nurses compared with around one in 30 White British women. Indian, Pakistani and Black African women were around four times more likely than White British women to be working as packers, bottlers, canners and fillers. Pakistani and Indian women were respectively around six times and four times more likely than White British women to be working as sewing machinists (Office for National Statistics, 2004c).

In trying to understand factors which explain ethnic minority concentration in particular sectors and sub-sectors, the work of Abram Leon (1998) about the relationship between ethnicity and class offers useful insight. Leon, a young Jewish Marxist who perished in Auschwitz, provided a useful starting point for analysis, which goes some way towards challenging the caricature of Marxist analyses on ethnicity presented by (Lord) Parekh (2004, p. 199), who writes that 'for Marxists [ethnicity] detracts from the class struggle, weakens working-class solidarity, and plays into the hands of the dominant class', or indeed Marxists such as Davidson (1999, p. 26) who equally conclude that 'the notion of "ethnicity" is ultimately a means of dividing people up into even more arbitrary classifications'.

Abram Leon (1998, pp. 79–80) in trying to explain the incorporation of Jews in the Medieval cities of Europe argued that 'Jews constitute historically a social group with a specific economic function. They are a class, or more precisely, a *people-class'* (Leon, 1998, pp. 79–80, italics in original). He pointed to the association of class with particular groups of people as not exceptional in pre-capitalist societies, and went on to argue that the enforced economic role of European Jews, driven by legal bans and social prohibitions from entering many occupations, was such an example of a 'people-class'. At the same time, however, Leon pointed to the impact of the first great wave of Jewish migration, not to New York, but to the interior of Russia, the Pale and Germany during the beginning of the nineteenth century, as resulting in Jews, for the first time, penetrating the industrial and commercial centres and playing important roles as managers of farms, merchants and industrialists. Under these circumstances, Leon argued, 'a Jewish proletariat was born', and that for the first time, 'the people-class began to differentiate socially' (Leon, 1998, pp. 90–91). Whilst Leon analysed how the emergence of capitalist relations impacted and socially differentiated the Jewish community in the early nineteenth-century Russian countryside, it can be argued that elements of the 'people-class' can be found in the incorporation of diverse ethnic groups in contemporary capitalist labour markets.

The role of ethnicity in the incorporation of minorities in labour markets is revealed in studies of the Los Angeles and the wider Californian labour market and the role of ethnic channelling and differences in the sectoral employment of Mexican, Korean and Chinese immigrant and resident groups. Ellis and Wright (1999) found during a twenty year period (1970–90) that the greatest concentration was amongst Mexican immigrants in agriculture. This is a sector in which Mexican residents were also highly represented, but amongst immigrants it was twice the level of residents. High concentration also exists for Korean immigrants and residents (one-third in each case) in the retail sector. At the same time, recent Korean immigrants were also concentrated in agriculture and construction, unlike resident Koreans. Chinese immigrants and native-born were both equally concentrated in 'non-durable manufacturing' (including the garment industry). One trend appears in the greater level of concentration and job-channelling of recent immigrants, with sectoral concentration most pronounced amongst Korean and Mexican immigrants. This indicates the role of ethnic networks in the channelling of immigrants and internal migrants into sectors where co-ethnics and co-nationals were concentrated. Another trend, however, is that employment distribution is also a function of individual human capital and skills and gravitation to sectors where their skills are in greatest demand. For example, 'unskilled workers are more likely to find work in the ethnic niches than the skilled'. Ellis and Wright (1999, pp. 29–31) further suggest that 'job placement of recent arrivals will depend on some combination of skills and network connection', but hypothesise 'that ethnicity will be more important determinant of sectoral employment than skill for recent immigrants'.

The role of ethnic job-channelling is illustrated in the historical and contemporary experience of women sewing machinists in the garment industry. In late nineteenth-century New York the social division and relationship between the 'uptown' German Jewish community, dominated by professionals and owners of large garment enterprises, and the 'downtown' Russian Jewish community, primarily made up of the ranks of contractors and workers in the garment industry, was reflected in the socialisation and channelling of young girls. Uptown Jewish New York 'made it a policy to steer young Russian-Jewish women into training courses and then into semi-skilled and unskilled sectors of the garment trades' (Glanz, 1976, pp. 27–30). By 1900, 77 per cent of Russian-Jewish women were employed in the garment industry, most of them as home workers. Similarly the expansion of Cypriot-owned enterprises in the London garment industry during the 1960s and 1970s saw a process (as potent as in late nineteenth-century New York) which for near on half a century saw the vast majority of Greek and Turkish Cypriot women channelled into the clothing industry as either indoor machinists or as homeworkers (Anthias, 1992; Josephides, 1988; Oakley, 1972).

The backlash against multiculturalism

Multiculturalism can be seen as a legacy of the ethnic mobilisations which took place during the 1960s and a contemporary manifestation of the crisis and loss of confidence by mainstream assimilationist thinking. It can be thought of as a convergence between political and cultural processes implied in an acceptance by the institutional framework that ethnic minorities have the right to engage in their own cultural development. It is both a means of institutionally accommodating diverse cultural, political and economic claims to recognition and inclusion in society, 'from above' and also a means of describing more discrete processes in formation which find expression in everyday life 'from below'. Multiculturalism and cultural diversity driven by migration have provided a growing focus for research in urban centres, not only in the metropolitan heartlands of London, New York and Los Angeles, but also Berlin, Toronto and Thessaloniki, a city with a long multicultural history, which has again become a centre of cultural diversity (Chu, 2007; Hatziprokopiou, 2004; Zeynep, 2004). Craig (2005) pointed to multiculturalism in the United Kingdom as the basis for social hybridity but also to the uneven development of multiculturalism and 'good' globalisation in the city of Leicester, when compared to the harsher environment for ethnic minorities in the city of Hull. Krogstad (2004) and Mung and Lacroix (2003), point to one popular understanding of multiculturalism in the form of transnational cuisine and fusion food. Ethnicity among minority communities in Berlin, London, Los Angeles and other urban centres takes a more practical form in the many schools, political, social, sporting, religious, cultural and home-country based associations catering to the needs of different members of an ethnic community. Frequently these organisations have or acquire a dual role, of on one hand maintaining the language and religion of members of an ethnic group tying them to events in the home country, and on the other acting as the basis of ethnic political mobilisation and in providing leadership in negotiation with local authorities and national policy-makers (Josephides, 1987; Panayiotopoulos, 1992; Pecoud, 2001).

The belief and practice, implied in multiculturalism, that ethnic minorities have the right to act as agents in their own cultural and economic development was never accepted by the social conservatives, either in the United States or in Europe. Schlesinger (1992, p. 43), predictably perhaps, wrote of the effects of the rise of ethnicity as a threat 'against the original theory of America as "one people", a common culture, a single nation'. Nathan Glazer (1997) argued that the rise of multiculturalism in the United States represented a fundamental rejection of the melting-pot ethos. A more typical position was that of ambivalence towards multiculturalism and rights to cultural autonomy by liberal thinking which argued with varying degrees of intensity that multiculturalism might be contributing, indeed may be the main factor, in the segregation experienced by ethnic minorities.

Antoine Pecoud (2001, p. 9) in a study of Berlin writes that whilst the existence of Turkish organisations and leaders is indeed a necessary element in multicultural politics, these leaders 'may arguably fail to represent the interests of the whole immigrant population'. Whilst this is by no means a quality associated only with leaders of immigrant organisations, it becomes doubly significant in a situation where these associations are among the few voices available to ethnic minorities. Pecoud argues that passivity is a characteristic feature of German emergent multiculturalism. This derives from German-Turks' and other immigrants' lack of citizenship, which renders them 'politically speech-less' and condemns them to remaining 'clients'. At the same time she points to 'self-ethnicisation' amongst migrants generally and Turks in Germany specifically, as a process of 'presenting their own problems as specifically "ethnic" in order to draw government or media attention' (Pecoud, 2001, pp. 11–12). In commenting on the growth in Turkish self-employment in Germany during the 1990s the conclusions drawn are that this 'may allow German-Turks to find ways to upward social and economic mobility and to express their particularities in accord-ance with the idea of a multicultural society'. However, one price of eth-nic self-reliance may be that there are fewer opportunities to engage in open labour market relations, as 'Turks would employ Turks, Germans would employ Germans, and so on. Multiculturalism may then become separation' (Pecoud, 2001, p. 13).

Parekh (2004, pp. 199, 201) pointed to multiculturalism as the pol-itics of recognition and redistribution, or the view that 'the state should take full public account of them [ethnic minorities] in laws, institu-tions, practices, and policies'. The danger in the politics of cultural recognition, Parekh (2004, pp. 201–202) argued, are that it 'assumes culture is more important than the economy'; that since identities are subject to change, therefore, any recognition of identities by the state 'would necessarily formalise and freeze them', thereby arresting their future development. For this reason it is argued 'the state cannot and should not recognise or have anything to do with identity' of any kind. Further, in offering advice to the oppressed, Parekh writes that since the pre-occupation is with 'difference' it 'undermines the solidarity of the oppressed and the marginalised' and 'makes it impossible for them to unite and act together' (see also Parekh, 2000).

The ambivalence shown towards multiculturalism by liberal think-ers has given way to what Grillo (2007) refers to as a 'backlash' against multiculturalism with Islamophobia at its centre. Grillo (2007, p. 980; see also Grillo, 2003), in trying to explain the backlash, points to the historical development of multiculturalism as undergoing three broad phases in the governance of diversity. The first phase, from the late nineteenth to mid-twentieth century, was a period in which diversity was constructed in the discourse of imperialism when (as Grillo argues), national and racial stereotypes 'were at their strongest' and the prin-ciple applied to dealing with ethnocultural difference was 'to abolish it', at best through assimilation. By the1960s the 'ideology of assimilation became harder to sustain'. The second phase, from the 1960s through most of the latter half of the twentieth century, saw the replacement of assimilation with 'integration plus' equal opportunities, signifying a greater recognition of social heterogeneity and drawing the conclusion that cultural diversity could be accommodated within a 'multicultural' framework. The third and current phase consists of an institutional backlash against multiculturalism and a return to cultural essentialism and nativism driven by cultural anxiety. Husbands (1994) similarly pointed to rising xenophobia in the Netherlands as a new kind of moral panic based in a 'crisis of national identity'. Grillo (2007, p. 993) suggests that the attack on a 'weak' multiculturalism in the United Kingdom and Western Europe has revealed the institutional fragility of 'an imagined (strong) multiculturalism' when the 'actually existing multiculturalism' is at best not well documented and its impact not clearly understood.

Ralph Grillo (2007, p. 979), points to the current 'cultural-diversity sceptical turn' as one underpinned by socially conservative assumptions about 'the incompatibility of different ways of living', or the view that multicultural countries have become 'too diverse'. Grillo (2007, p. 994) argues that the 'demonization of Islam' which followed 9/11 and increased support for anti-immigrant parties in Europe provided the political climate which has reinforced the 'backlash against difference' and produced dismal predictions, such as that 'the spectre that now haunts Europe is one of strident nationalism, ethnic self-assertion and the exultation of what divides people at the expense of what unites them' (Barry, 2001, p. 4). Hewitt (2005, p. 4) reminds us that the backlash against multiculturalism is above all a 'white backlash'. Sometimes the backlash is presented as an attack on 'political correctness'. As Scott (1995, p. 4) candidly puts it, 'if "political correctness" is the label attached to critical attitudes and behaviour, "multiculturalism" is the program it is said to be attempting to enact'.

The backlash against multiculturalism by social conservatives and far-right xenophobic anti-immigrant parties has been legitimised by liberal thinking which claims to see in ethnicity and multiculturalism 'the flight from enlightenment' or claims to universal rights (Barry, 2001, p. 9). Levi-Strauss (1967), who probably more than most advocated the real values of the Enlightenment and articulated a European perspective in attempts to reposition anthropology in the de- and post-colonial environment of the 1960s, argued that

Our science arrived at maturity the day that Western Man began to see that he [sic] would never understand himself as long as there was a single race or people on the surface of the earth that he treated as an object. Only then could anthropology declare itself in its true colours: as an enterprise reviewing and atoning for the Renaissance, in order to spread humanism to all humanity. (Levi-Strauss, 1967, p. 52)

The above sentiments shaped attempts to reposition the social sciences following the crisis of modernisation thinking and mainstream assimilation theories in the 1960s and influenced the development of ideas and values about multiculturalism as policy. John Rex (1996a) argued in the United Kingdom for an 'egalitarian multiculturalism'. At the same time, however, in Rex's framework and that of liberal thinking more generally, the recognition of cultural diversity was conditional on the fact that its development was 'compatible with and did not undermine, those institutions which were concerned with guaranteeing equality between individuals and classes' (Rex, 1996a, p. 243). Implied in this are ideas about 'balanced' communities and social cohesion. Rex and Tomlinson (1979) located the development of multiculturalism as policy in a statement made in 1967 by Roy Jenkins, Labour British home secretary, who defined 'integration' as not involving a 'flattening process of uniformity', but 'cultural diversity coupled with equal opportunity, in an atmosphere of mutual tolerance'. Paul Foot wrote that Roy Jenkins as Home Secretary 'brought to the Home Office a liberalism which it had not smelt for fifty years' and was responsible for strengthening the Race Relations Act to include housing and employment. He also noted that when Jenkins was moved to the Treasury in January 1968, his successor James Callaghan 'almost at once' caved in to opposition led by Enoch Powell against 'coloured' immigration and introduced the Immigration Act, denying Ugandan Asian British passport-holders entry into the United Kingdom (Foot, 1968, p. 255).

Qualified support for multiculturalism allowed the French government, and much of the French left, to argue that in the name of defending the secular values of the Enlightenment the *hijab* (headscarf) has to be banned in public spaces (Boulange, 2004). In the post 9/11 environment young Muslim women frequently bore the brunt of the day-to-day hostility against Muslims. Some had the *hijab* torn off their faces by patriotic thugs. The French Government banned the wearing of the *hijab* in schools and a number of Muslim girls were expelled for continuing to wear it. This has major implications for France's estimated six million Muslims. The Government also banned Sikh turbans, Jewish *yarmulkes* (skull caps) and large crosses, all falling under the heading of 'conspicuous' religious symbols. In Germany, five states made legislation to ban the *hijab* from schools but not *yarmulkes*, crucifixes and habits (Benoit, 2003; Graham, 2003). The backlash against multiculturalism in the form of a backlash by liberals and secular ex-leftists against a religious minority can be seen as a concentrated example of what Modood (2000) has referred to as the construction of a 'desirable' and 'essentialist' multiculturalism which found it difficult to institutionally accept the recognition of some religious groups.

Perhaps what is surprising about the backlash against multiculturalism in the United Kingdom has been the attack from people who are employed to promote equal opportunities. Trevor Phillips was appointed by Tony Blair as Head of the Commission for Racial Equality (CRE) with the brief of abolishing the CRE and integrating its activities into the new Commission for Equality and Human Rights (CEHR). This suggests a diminishing role for race in the equal opportunities agenda. Trevor Phillips is also on record as saying he wants to 'kill off multiculturalism' because it 'creates separateness' (Phillips, 2004) and has supported its replacement with 'national cohesion' policies based on 'an inclusive sense of Britishness' (Home Office, 2005, p. 20). In a subsequent BBC interview Phillips said that multiculturalism was leading to Britain 'sleep-walking into segregation' (Phillips, 2005; see also Black Information Link, 2006; Mahamdaillie, 2005). In response to Trevor Phillips and the Bishop of Rochester, who advanced the claims that there were 'no-go areas' in Britain which were a hotbed of 'Islamic extremism', Finney and Simpson (2009) argued in their study of friendship groups that they were 'becoming more mixed, not less'. Most ethnic minority young people said that at least half their friends are white. Less than 20 per cent of minorities born in Britain said they only have friends from their own ethnic group. If any group is ethnically isolated, it is white people – over half of white people say they only have white friends. In out of over 8850 electoral wards in England and Wales there are only fourteen in which a non-white ethnic group makes up over half the population. In none does a single ethnic minority account for over three-quarters of the population.

Wood et al. (2006) point to an evolution in multiculturalist thinking in the United Kingdom in the form of 'interculturalism'. It differs from multiculturalism in that it 'does not recognize cultural boundaries as fixed but in a state of flux and remaking' and 'aims to facilitate dialogue, exchange and reciprocal understanding between people of different backgrounds' (Wood et al., 2006, p. 9). It is also driven by the growing cultural diversity of the United Kingdom illustrated by recent mass migration from Poland and the relationship this implies between the 'old' (New Commonwealth) and 'new' (Eastern European) migration. This has raised new and novel questions about cultural diversity and the future direction of multiculturalism in the United Kingdom which initially developed substantially under the impact of New Commonwealth migration and as an attempt to change the vertical terms of engagement between black and ethnic minority migrant groups with the dominant culture. Interculturalism adds a different layer to analyses of cultural understanding by pointing to processes of horizontal negotiation between old and new migrant groups. More significantly, perhaps, the study by Wood et al. (2006, pp. 14–15) points to the uneven spatial development of multiculturalism in the United Kingdom. It makes use of an 'isolation ratio' to measure multicultural and intercultural relations. This is calculated on the basis of who is likely to live next door to a member of the Black, Minority, Ethnic (BME) or White population group in different cities. A BME Bristolian, for example, is 2.6 times more likely than a White Bristolian to live next door to someone who is BME; in the London Borough of Lewisham (which includes Brixton) this is 1.3 times more likely and, in Burnley, 8.7 times more likely. The White isolation ratio is even higher in working-class estates on the outskirts of towns (Wood et al., 2006, p. 95).

In trying to understand the uneven development of multiculturalism in the United Kingdom, it is worth reflecting on Rex and Moore's (1967) pioneering work in their study of Sparkbrook, Birmingham (the first study on 'race relations' in Britain). They pointed to how the local authority, the City Council's Housing Department and its officers were chiefly responsible for the reproduction of 'Twilight Zones'. They showed how the use of local regulations to exclude immigrants from decent council houses, or from particular areas (such as suburbs) forced them to live in inner-city run-down lodging houses. Similarly, white estate agents racially channelled people into particular areas of town. One novel conclusion by the research at the time was that racism is not just the product of individual minds but also of institutions. Another conclusion is that the accumulated impact of forty years of the above kind of policies, repeated by many local authorities, has been a significant factor in shaping the uneven development of multiculturalism in Britain.

Most studies of multiculturalism tend to focus on particular cities and neighbourhoods at the expense of workplace studies. In a study of the everyday experiences of a recent migrant group employed in London's low-paid sectors including care work, hospitality, cleaning, food processing and construction, Herbert et al., (2006, p. 2) considered the proposition by Amin (2000) that 'people spend the majority of their time at

work and that it is a key space where the micropolitics and daily negotiations of ethnic differences are played out'. They found that 'respondents conveyed the distinct sense that London and the spaces within the
city were not associated with white hostility'. Racism in their locality
was not presented as a major problem. Their main concerns were about
racist practices in the labour market with many stressing that they felt
'excluded from professional and white collar jobs' despite holding relevant skills and qualifications (Herbert et al., 2006, p. 3). They found
that for many of their respondents, multiculturalism from above, with
its limited focus on cultural integration, 'was a distant rhetoric that had
little bearing on their daily lives' and suggest that divisions, exclusion
and segregation 'had little to do with multicultural policies, and were
the result of older patterns of racisms' (Herbert et al., 2006, p. 12).

The argument by Pecoud, Phillips and Parekh that multiculturalism
retards the development of ethnic communities and reinforces separ-
atist ethnicities leading to the segregation of real or imagined communities would find it difficult to explain why people from diverse cultural
backgrounds come together. Theories which are dismissive of cultural
boundaries and identities do not find it necessary to explain how or
why large numbers of culturally diverse people transgress, transverse
and recreate cultural boundaries and form multicultural political alli-
ances round issues of concern to them: such as in the make-up of the
estimated one to two million people who took part in the biggest demonstration in the history of the United Kingdom on 15 February 2003
in London, against the oncoming war in Iraq, or in trade union action
involving a multi-ethnic multi-racial workforce. The election of Barack
Obama defied both political predictions that Hispanics would not vote
for a black candidate and academic analyses which argue that in the
United States 'a black-non black divide is taking shape, in which Asians
and Latinos are not only closer to whites than blacks are to whites, but
also closer to whites than blacks at this point in time' (Lee and Bean,
2007, p. 579; see also Glazer, 1997).

Similarly, approaches which are dismissive of multiculturalism do not
find it necessary to explain the difference between multiculturalism
'from above' and 'from below', with its more extensive recognition of
ethnic minority agency. Much of the backlash has been directed against
the politics and policies of recognition and redistribution or multiculturalism 'from above' in which, not infrequently, ethnic groups are reduced
to passive participants in processes where ethnic brokers, entrepreneurs
and association leaders substitute and act on behalf of real or imagined
communities. Wise (2007) and Wise and Velayutham (2007) in a study

of Ashfield, a multicultural suburban hub of about 50,000 people in Sydney with 43 per cent of residents born overseas, pointed to a qualitatively different kind of multiculturalism. In the 1950s Ashfield was home to large numbers of Italian and Greek migrants, later to migrants from Lebanon and the Philippines and, more recently, from mainland China. Participant observation in shopping centres, local pubs, clubs, parks and churches revealed a more expansive multicultural process 'from below' with strong capacities for 'transversal' intercultural crossings. By transversal, Wise (2007, p. 2) means the way people in their daily lives 'reproduce sociality', through for example 'gift exchange and reciprocity, kinship and social network, ways of talking, and place orientations' and more importantly, perhaps, in the way 'individuals in everyday spaces use these modes of sociality' to produce and negotiate at ease relations which cut across cultural difference 'whether or not this difference is a conscious one'.

Multiculturalism 'from below' parallels discussion by Werbner (1999) on 'working class cosmopolitanism' and the need to recognise how class influences emergent forms of cultural transnationalism, cosmopolitanism and multiculturalism and the way in which the status of being a professional, entrepreneur, or working-class Pakistani migrant, in this instance, influences, and in cases forces, new ways of dealing with everyday life. Attempts to investigate this line of inquiry have been frustrated by arguments, for example, that racism, multiculturalism and the development of ethnic identities 'cannot be reduced to class relations' (Solomos and Back, 1995, p. 419). This kind of thinking does not take us very far in trying to understand the development of classes and social-economic differentiation amongst members of a racial or ethnic group and how this influences the strategies used by them to deal with racism and adversity and how they respond to opportunities available to them. Frequently the strategies used by ethnic workers and entrepreneurs involve the use of some combination of ethnic and class resources (Light and Gold, 2000; Panayiotopoulos, 2006).

Ideas which are dismissive of class do not find it necessary to explain the role of class in the development of cross-cultural spaces provided by public sector services (education, education, housing and transport) which working-class people use independently of their ethnicity and in which many are employed. Public service provisioning forces people to come together and becomes a critical area for the reproduction of 'sociability', whether you are waiting to pick up your children from the local primary school playground, or randomly sharing a seat on a bus or train with another human being, or being a member of a multi-ethnic public sector union local.

At the heart of ideas about multiculturalism from below is what Fishman (1980, p. 87) called the ethnicity of 'being' or 'the untutored and largely unconscious ethnicity of everyday life' and 'the way various ethnic collectivities discuss and recognise that phenomenon'. In this lies the proposition that being shapes consciousness or at least influences the development of ideas and practices about ethnicity and multiculturalism. Both multiculturalism from below and the ethnicity of being address themselves to actual everyday life rather than, as Grillo (2007) and Modood (2000) noted, to an 'essentialist', 'desirable' and also malleable multiculturalism from above.

International migration

The backlash against multiculturalism is taking place at the same time as migration is changing the ethnic composition of the United States and Europe in both quantitative and qualitative ways. US immigration trends show that most migrants are as skilled and educated as native-born workers and that the proportion with a college education is similar. This makes immigrants theoretically highly substitutable for native labour. The proportion of immigrants classified by the US Immigration and Naturalisation Service (INS) as 'professionals' is in fact significantly higher than for the US population as a whole (Portes and Rumbaut, 2001). One factor which drove the US economy from the 1990s until the financial-led economic recession in 2007–09 was the convergence between high rates of economic growth and the highest ever rate of immigration recorded in the history of the United States. More than 13.5 million people immigrated to the United States during the 1990s, arriving in even greater numbers and with more diversity than the three decades of the 'First Great Wave' of immigration towards the end of the nineteenth century, when the Jewish ghettos of Eastern Europe and the villages of southern Italy, Poland and Greece provided the bulk of immigrants. Immigration during the 1990s accounted for 40 per cent of US population growth (Goldenberg, 2002;). The 'Second Great Wave' typified by the 'new' Asian migration is expected to fundamentally restructure race and ethnicity in the United States. US Census Bureau projections are that those categorised as 'White non-Hispanic' will decline from 73 per cent of the population in 1997 to 53 per cent in 2050. Hispanic Americans are expected to increase to 25 per cent and Asian Americans to nearly 10 per cent of the US population by 2050. Black Americans are expected to register a smaller increase, from 12 per cent to 14 per cent (Booth, 1998, US Census Bureau, 2004) (see Chapter 4).

The abolition of the US national origins system during 1965 – which militated against new immigrant groups – proved a path-breaking decision for new Asian immigrants and contributed significantly to the population increase of urban metropolitan regions such as Greater Los Angeles, from 9.9 million in 1970, to 14.5 million in 1990. The increase was made up 1.7 million additional native-born persons and 2.8 million who were foreign born. Asian first-generation immigrants made 911,130 (28.6 per cent) of the total increase amongst the foreign born (Sabagh and Bozorgmehr, 1996, pp. 95–96). The growth of the Korean community is revealing: from less than 10,000 foreign-born persons in 1970 to 155,500 by 1990. The Chinese community, although it has longer roots in California, similarly saw the number of foreign-born rise from less than 30,000 to 231,361 by 1990. Another 414,427 Koreans and 75,769 Chinese were born in the United States. Asians made up nearly 10 per cent of the population of Los Angeles by 1990 (Sabagh and Bozorgmehr, 1996, pp. 82–83).

Similarly, UK Census data show the impact of immigration and its consequences on reshaping, in particular, the population of England. An 'ethnic question' was included for the first time in the 1991 Census for England and Wales which asked people to define what ethnic group they thought of themselves as belonging to. They were given the choice of White, Black African, Black Caribbean or Black Other, Indian, Pakistani, Bangladeshi or Sri Lankan, Chinese, Other Asian or Other. At the time, this question was criticised by many as illogical and racist, for example in its implication that 'White' constituted an ethnic category, the statistical incompatibility of Black and British classification and the non-recognition of groups of mixed descent (Rex, 1996b). There were three main changes made to the ethnic categorisation used in the 2001 Census. The first change was the introduction for the first time of 'Mixed' as a tick box option. Secondly, the 'White' group was separated into British, Irish and 'other White' to take into account ethnic minority people born in Eastern Europe or the Middle East. Thirdly, the Census included a tick box of 'Black British' in order to allow people of Caribbean and Asian origins but born in the United Kingdom to define themselves more accurately (see Table 1.1, Ethnic Question in the 2001 Census for England and Wales). The combination of racial and national classification used can be criticised for reducing ethnicity to race (or the 'racialisation' of people) and compounding this problem

Table 1.1 Ethnic question in the 2001 census for England and Wales

---

What is your ethnic group?
Choose ONE section from A to E, then tick *the appropriate box to indicate your ethnic group.*

A White
☐British
☐Any Other White background, *please write in*

B Mixed
☐White and Black Caribbean
☐White and Black African
☐White and Asian
☐Any Other Mixed background, *please write in*

C Asian or Asian British
☐Indian
☐Pakistani
☐Bangladeshi
☐Any Other Asian background, *please write in*

D Black or Black British
☐Caribbean
☐African
☐Any Other Black background, *please write in*

E Chinese or other ethnic group
☐Chinese
☐Any Other, *please write in*

Source: Office for National Statistics (2003).

by encouraging people, for example from Eastern Europe or the Middle East, who do not categorise themselves as 'White' in their own societies (unless they belonged to far-right groups), to do so for statistical purposes in the United Kingdom under the 'Other White' category.

Census data for England and Wales show that the ethnic minority population increased from 6 per cent of the total population in 1991, to 9 per cent in 2001, and is made up of 4.21 million people. The biggest increase, at 240 per cent and accounting for 514,000 people, was from the African continent. The Census also showed the arrival of significant numbers of immigrants from Eastern Europe. This factor was not revealed fully in the 2001 Census and did not capture the large scale migration from the Accession 8 states which joined the European Union in 2004, particularly from Poland to the United Kingdom. One new factor revealed in the data collected for 2001 was that the inclusion for the first time of a 'Mixed' ethnic group category in the data gathered by the Census saw nearly one million people who defined themselves as belonging to this category (Office for National Statistics, 2004a).

Immigration is playing an important role in receiving countries, largely due to demographic trends in these countries towards an ageing population. Demographic trends in the United Kingdom show that there are more pensioners over the age of 65 than persons under the age of 16. The oldest age group, those aged 80 and over, is the fastest-growing group and accounts for 5 per cent of the total population. Between 1981 and 2007 this group increased by more than 1.2m persons (Taylor, 2008a). It is estimated that between 1995 and 2031 the number of elderly persons in England aged 65 and over will have risen by nearly 57 per cent. The numbers of very elderly (aged 85 and over) are projected to rise more rapidly, by around 79 per cent. Almost half the growth in overall numbers is expected to occur between 2020 and 2031 (PSSRU, 1998, p. 46). The dependency ratio – the ratio of dependents to working-age people in the United Kingdom – currently stands at 61 per cent and will rise to 74 per cent over the next 50 years. With zero net migration it would increase to 82 per cent (Smith, 2007). In southern European countries, in parallel with the growing number of elderly people, there is a significant reduction in the average size of the family, with people tending to marry later and to have fewer children. While many of the current elderly are those who had large families in the pre-war period, future generations will progressively have to draw on much smaller number of children as potential carers (Mesthenos and Triantafillou, 1993; Panayiotopoulos, 2005).

Migration is substantially a response to the demographic trends described above and in the case of Western Europe, which was experiencing below-replacement levels of fertility, immigration appeared as particularly significant (UNPF, 2006, p. 15). The growing demand for elderly care and the increase in the number of migrant domestic workers employed for this purpose is one globally recognisable labour market response to demographic trends towards an ageing population. The expansion of the employment of eastern European migrant workers in the care sector is one area which has seen the development of a significant labour diaspora (Elrick and Lewandowska, 2008).

Migration has re-shaped the ethnic composition of London more than any other major urban centre in the United Kingdom. London contains at least 50 different language groups with 10,000 or more speakers. At least a quarter of school children in London speak a language other than English at home, with the most common first language (other than

English) being Bengali, spoken by 5 per cent of all pupils. Another 7 per cent speak Punjabi, Gujarati or Hindi. London contained 12.2 per cent of the total population but nearly half (44.6 per cent) of the United Kingdom's ethnic minority population on the basis of country of birth data (Storkey and Lewis, 1997, p. 201). The inclusion for the first time of the ethnic group question in the 1991 Census allowed us to assess the relative size of the United Kingdom-born population of ethnic minority origin. This showed that 43 per cent of London's minority population was in fact born in the United Kingdom (Storkey, 1993, p. 205). The 2001 Census for England and Wales registered a 40 per cent increase in people enumerated as 'Black' and 'Asian' when compared to 1991. This stood in marked contrast to the 0.2 per cent growth in the population enumerated as 'White'. Half of the non-White population was born in the United Kingdom (Office for National Statistics, 2004a).

The London Census data showed that during 2001 more than one in three of London's population had ethnic minority origins. The decline in the 'White' population was most pronounced in London, where it fell by 7 per cent to 71.3 per cent of the population, with the non-White population at more than two million people, compared to 1.3 million in the 1991 Census. Another 795,000 people from 'Other White' groups (Irish, Cypriot, American and Continental European) were also enumerated. Those defined as 'White British' made up 60 per cent of the total. Christians made up 70 per cent of England's population but in London accounted for 58 per cent of the population, with people categorising themselves as Muslims accounting for 8.5 per cent of all Londoners (Office for National Statistics, 2004b). The Census revealed that 3.2 per cent of the London population was of 'Mixed' origins (Mackintosh, 2005, p. 17). There were nine boroughs in total which had an ethnic minority population (classified as all ethnic groups other than 'White British') greater than 50 per cent. Three of the boroughs (Newham, Tower Hamlets and Hackney) were situated in East London. The borough with the largest concentration of ethnic minorities was Brent, where 71 per cent were from ethnic minority groups. The boroughs with the lowest minority representation included the outer ring boroughs of Barking and Dagenham at 19.1 per cent, and Bexley at 12.1 per cent (Mackintosh, 2005, p. 20).

Significantly, the Census revealed that London accounted for 70 per cent of the United Kingdom's population growth between 1991–2001, even though it was home to only 12 per cent of the total population. It is in part due to immigration and higher birth rates amongst ethnic minority groups that London has seen the reversal of a long period of population decline. This decline lasted from the late 1930s, when the population of London stood at 8.6 million, until the mid-1980s, by which period it had fallen to 6.8m people, of whom only 2.5m lived in Inner London (made up of 13 out of 32 London Boroughs). During the 1990s, 400,000 people were added to London's population and another 700,000 people are projected to live in London by the year 2016 (Office for National Statistics, 2004b). These trends were not predicted by policy-makers. An important aspect of the demographic and economic regeneration of London has been the contribution made by ethnic minorities to London's enterprise structure. According to a study by the UK Cabinet Office (2003) there were 100,000 ethnic minority-owned enterprises in London, employing around 800,000 people (see also Kitching et al., 2009; London Skills Forecasting Unit, 2001). Many of them are found in the 'No Data' category (see Table 1.2).

Migration from the European Union Accession 8 states and in particular Poland has become a significant part of the demographic restructuring of the United Kingdom. Data from the Office for National Statistics indicate that until the mid-1990s natural population increase was the main factor in population growth in the United Kingdom but that since the 1990s, net international migration has become an increasingly key factor in population change, with immigration accounting for half the increase in Britain's population growth over the ten year period of 1995 to 2005 (Office for National Statistics, 2006; see also Kyambi, 2005). Between 2001 and 2008, the population of the United Kingdom increased by 2m to just below 61m. Net migration – the difference between new arrivals and those leaving the country – accounted for 52 per cent of population growth during the twelve months to mid-2007 and 55 per cent during the previous year. The United Kingdom immigrant population in 2008 – defined as individuals born abroad,

Table 1.2 Ethnicity of London entrepreneurs, 2007

Ethnic group	Total	Per cent
'White'	260,376	73.1
Asian	36,581	0.3
Black	12,483	3.5
Chinese/Other	4,459	1.3
Mixed	5,135	1.4
Multiple ownership	1,635	0.5
No data	35,300	9.9
Total	355,969	100.0

Source: Kitching et al. (2009), p. 691.

or the 'foreign-born' – was about 6.6 million, of whom 4.2 million are nationals of other countries, and another 2.4 million who are UK citizens because they have either been naturalised or are the children of British citizens living abroad. Foreign-born workers in 2008 made up 12.1 per cent of the United Kingdom's labour force, compared to 7.1 per cent in 1979. They made up 80 per cent of seasonal agricultural labour. Polish immigrants made up the second largest group of persons born outside the United Kingdom, representing 12 per cent of all foreign-born nationals (Somerville and Sumption, 2009, pp. 10–11).

Contentious data from the ONS (2009a, p. 4) show that the number of people born overseas who were resident in Britain increased between June 2007 and June 2008 by 290,000 people to 6.5 million, or 'one in nine' of the resident population. This number is roughly equal to the estimated 5.5 million British nationals living overseas. The figure includes 4.2 million foreign nationals, with Indian nationals accounting for the largest group (619,000 people), followed by Polish-born residents (461,000) in second position. The politicised nature of immigration policy in the United Kingdom is frequently reflected in statistical disputes. The 'one in nine' conclusions presented by the Office for National Statistics produced a conflict between the ONS and Cabinet Ministers responsible for immigration. Indeed Ministers accused the ONS of 'sinister' motives in the release of raw immigration figures which did not indicate, for example, that people born overseas and living in the United Kingdom included 370,000 undergraduate students and 300,000 people born to British armed forces personnel serving overseas (Eaglesham, 2009, p. 3).

What is beyond doubt is that foreign-born mothers are playing a significant role in population change and increased fertility in the United Kingdom. More than a quarter of babies born in Britain during 2005 had at least one parent born outside the United Kingdom, compared to one-fifth in 2000. The fertility rate in the United Kingdom in 2006 stood at 1.8 children per woman – the highest level since 1980. The estimated fertility rate for UK-born women increased to 1.7 from 1.5 in 2002 and for women born outside the United Kingdom, it increased to 2.5 from 2.3. The fertility rate is not, however, evenly distributed across the United Kingdom and reflects the tendency for most migrant groups to be concentrated in particular regions, cities and neighbourhoods in the United Kingdom. London is a case in point. In London 51 per cent of live births were to a mother who was born overseas, but in the north-east of the United Kingdom it was only 8 per cent (Office for National Statistics, 2007a). One significant impact of the migration of foreign-born mothers has been to mitigate trends towards an ageing population.

The significance of migration to population growth is reflected in the growing role of international migration to London. In 1991 the net impact of migration to London was a loss of 21,000 people, with 265,000 arrivals and 286,000 departures. By 2004 the net impact was a gain of 21,000 made up of an inflow of 373,000 and an outflow of 352,000. Virtually all the rise in inflow (102,000 out of 108,000), was due to international migration (Office for National Statistics, 2007b, p. 9). London acted as a major magnet with about 41 per cent of all migrants in Britain living in the capital where they make up a quarter of the population (Kyambi, 2005). Whilst the pattern of settlement by new Polish migrants suggests that employment is a key driver of a much wider spatial distribution, London also plays a key role in settlement. Since Poland entered the EU in 2004, the sharp increase in outward migration was not reflected in the 2001 UK Census. The 2001 Census enumerated only 58,107 persons born in Poland and resident in the United Kingdom, of whom only 22,224 lived in London (most of whom were part of an ageing exile community concentrated round Ealing, West London) (Mackintosh, 2005, pp. 70, 151). By 2008 one (optimistic) estimate by Caesar Olszewski, publisher of the UK mass-circulation Polish-language weekly *Goniec Polski*, was that 750,000 Polish nationals lived in London out of an estimated UK total of about 1.5 million (Warrel, 2009, p. 3).

Transnationalism and globalisation 'from below'

Studies of transnational communities frequently point to the role of ethnicity in the structuring of relations which cut across frontiers. Frequently this involves studies of gateway cities, such as London, which act as key nodes in the circulation of people. The cities of Los Angeles, San Francisco, New York, Miami and Chicago, for example, accounted during 2003 for approximately 14 million immigrants, or nearly 50 per cent of all immigrants in the United States (Clark, 2003, p. 39). Erdemir and Vasta (2007, p. 24) described transnationalism amongst among the diverse Turkish immigrant community in London as a phenomenon in which 'old compatriot transnational networks operate alongside emergent solidarity structures'. Hatziprokopiou (2004) pointed to the development of transnationalism among Albanian and Bulgarian migrants in Greece. Many studies focus on the role of transnational crime organisations (the Russian Mafia, the Chinese Triad) involved in the human trafficking of women for the purposes of forced prostitution, forced domestic work and commercial marriage, or in the trafficking of economic migrants from China, Afghanistan, Pakistan and elsewhere (Bilger et al., 2006; Chu and Song, 2008; Koser, 2008; Salt, 2000; Salt and Stein, 1997; UNFP, 2006).

Transnationalism and population movement have been linked to the development of regional economic and political formations such as the European Union and the North American Free Trade Area (NAFTA). In the case of EU enlargement this facilitated the development of 'temporary and circular migration trends' (Favell, 2008, p. 706) amongst labour migrants from Poland and the other eastern and central European states which joined the European Union in 2004. Polish labour migrants, for example, have been incorporated in general and specific labour markets, such as the domestic elderly care sector, construction and agricultural labour. Employment in these sectors, more than others, tends to be of short duration and is characterised by high labour turnover. This factor facilitated patterns of circular labour migration (Elrick and Lewandowska, 2008; Jordan, 2002). In these circumstances, Garapich (2008, pp. 736–737) noted that the 'migration industry' became a powerful vehicle in setting and reproducing a self-sustaining transnationalism. Agents used in the recruitment of labour became key actors in both easing the incorporation of migrants into the host society and helping migrants to maintain transnational links with the sending country.

Amongst Moroccan migrants primarily to France an 'intense circulation' has been identified, which involves an estimated two million people moving between Morocco and Europe during the summer months (Dumont, 2008, p. 793). Remittances send to Morocco account for the largest source of national income. In Morocco, and elsewhere, remittances involve important transnational and 'transgenerational' links between migrants and non-migrants (de Haas and Plug, 2006; UNFP, 2006). Transgenerational links are often features of families and migration with the implications of 'transnational families' where members of the same family live in different countries (Huang et al., 2008; Ryan et al., 2009). Transnational families were identified by the UNFP (2006, p. 33) as a 'new phenomenon'. This phenomenon, however, whilst apparently new, has been the status of many Hispanic and Asian women domestic workers employed in the United States, East Asia and Europe for many decades (Panayiotopoulos, 2005). Hondagneu-Sotelo and Avila (1997) used the term 'transnational mothers' to describe the role of many Latina domestic workers. In family migration, Ryan et al. (2009, p. 63) pointed to varied patterns of family migration and obligations in complex transnational strategies, an important dimension of which was the management of their own inter-generational caring responsibilities.

Research on transnational communities (Gokturk, 1999; Henry et al., 2000; Pecoud, 2001; Saxenian, 2006) purports to show that contemporary patterns of migration have resulted in the undermining of the nation-state, leading to the formation of diaspora, transnational networks and communities which feel equally at home in receiving and sending countries. Transnationalism has been identified as the basis for the formation of new hybrid identities (Cohen, 1994; Hall, 1996; Mohan, 2002; Robertson, 1998). Basch et al. (1994, p. 6) have used the term 'de-territorialized nation-states' to describe such networks and define transnationalism as 'the process by which immigrants form and sustain multi-stranded social relations that link together their societies of origin and settlement', and which cut across geographic, cultural and political borders. Portes writes that transnational communities are

> characterized by dense networks across space and by an increasing number of people who lead dual lives. Members are at least bilingual, move easily between different cultures, frequently maintain houses in two countries, and pursue economic, political and cultural interests that require a simultaneous presence in both. (Portes, 1997, p. 15)

The emergence of transnational communities with immigrant enterprise as its epicentre would indicate a distinct phenomenon at variance with traditional patterns of immigrant adaptation. Portes argues that whilst the process is set in motion by the interests and needs of capital in the advanced countries, it can nevertheless 'offer a broader field for autonomous popular initiatives' (Portes, 1997, p. 3). These can act (as the argument runs) as alternative ways to deal with world-roaming capital, to those associated with international trade union solidarity or attempts to impose labour standards in developing countries. In this discourse, the emergence of immigrant enterprise and transnational communities is presented as a response by working-class immigrants to the globalisation of capitalist production characterised by persistent global income inequality:

> what common people have done in response to the processes of globalization is to create communities that sit astride political borders and that, in a very real sense, are 'neither here nor there' but in both places simultaneously. The economic activities that sustain

these communities are grounded precisely on the differentials of advantage created by state boundaries. In this respect, they are no different from the large corporations, except that these enterprises emerge at the grassroots level and its activities are often informal. (Portes, 1997, p. 2)

Transnationalism and the globalisation from below thesis converged with the re-discovery of the 'informal sector' in the urban centres of Europe and North America during the 1980s recession (Gerry, 1987). Sassen (1988) in a study of unregistered activities in New York's economy in sectors such as construction, garments, footwear, furniture, retail activity and electronics, argued that important sources for the informalisation of various activities are to be found in characteristics of the larger city's economy. Among these are the demand for products and services that lend themselves to small-scale production, or are associated with rapid transformations brought about by commercial and residential gentrification, or are not satisfactorily provided by the formal sector. Sassen suggests 'that a good share of the informal sector is not the result of immigrant survival strategies, but rather an outcome of structural patterns or transformations in the larger economy of a city such as New York' (Sassen, 1988, p. 3).

Globalisation from below is a process which means that the restructuring of gateway cities in Europe and the United States has been shaped by immigrants and ethnic minorities themselves, acting as their own agents, in spite of official hostility and restrictions. It is a process, however, which has to negotiate immense structural constraints and opportunities. Ivan Light (2000), in a re-working of migration network theory ('chain migration'), challenges Sassen's view that informalisation and the expansion of low-wage jobs acts independently of immigration. Sassen's argument that globalisation involves structural relationships between immigration, localities and particular sectors, has been (mis) understood by Light as assigning no independent role for immigration in the formation of informal labour markets. Leaving aside whether this actually represents Sassen's argument – note, for example, the suggestion that 'immigrants, in so far as they form communities, may be in a favourable position to seize the opportunities presented by informalisation' (Sassen, 1996, p. 588) – migration network theory purports to show that migration creates self-sustaining labour flows, which in gathering momentum begin to act independently of factors which initiated migration in the first place. Light argues that the solidarity intrinsic in membership of an ethnic network sharing common migratory experiences also has strong cost-cutting capabilities linked to informal systems of production and in this sense, immigration 'co-causes' informalisation. Light writes:

> To a substantial extent, immigration has caused itself and also the economic informalisation that is a condition of its self-reproduction. This view explains immigration and informalisation by reference to the mature migrations network's capacity to lower the economic, social and emotional costs and hardships of immigration. This cost-cutting capacity increases the degrees of informalisation in and migration to developed countries by permitting the economic exploitation of unorganised and covert demand that would otherwise have remained inaccessible. (Light, 2000, p. 176)

Light proposes a reformulation of existing migration network analysis and introduces the concept of 'spill over immigration' to explain conditions in which mass migration becomes unresponsive to declining opportunities, resulting in an 'expanding supply of migrants and lowering their reservation cost' (Light, 2000, p. 177). This explanation points to the activities of immigrants themselves as the key agency in the structuring of immigration, settlement and labour market incorporation. Light et al. (1999), however, also offer criticism of migration network theory and the way it has been used to substantiate the view that 'waves' of immigrants are 'taking over' American jobs. They argue that existing network theory as a theory about labour transfer is limited. Crucially, it cannot sufficiently take into account the labour demand created by the development of immigrant and ethnic minority enterprise. In this respect, immigrants, far from taking jobs away from native workers, create employment, typically linked to the employment of other immigrants. Light et al. use the term 'immigrant economy' to explain this expansive labour market formation. They suggest that existing network theory exaggerates both the capacities of immigrant networks and differences between native-born and immigrant workers.

Castles (2004, pp. 222–223) similarly identified family reunions between Turkish guestworkers with their families as substantially responsible for the demise of the guestworker system, originally envisaged as a temporary mechanism for fine-tuning Germany's labour market. The conclusion by Castles is that migration policies fail and that 'the self-sustaining nature of migratory processes once they are started', began to act independently of sending and receiving country policies, turning 'post-1945 labour migration into unplanned processes of settlement and community formation'. What unites the analyses presented by Castles, Portes, Sassen and Light, and the wider transnational literature, is that they point in various ways to immigrant and ethnic minorities acting as their own agency in the shaping of contemporary patterns of immigration and labour market incorporation.

Economic restructuring, spill over migration and the formation of diasporic or transnational communities, however, say little about the role of the institutional framework, the role of the state and the consequences of its actions. Immigration controls and state regulation are (by most accounts) a critical factor in shaping the pattern of immigration and its selectivity (Harris, 2002). Asylum-seeking refugees, for example, who formed an increased component of European and North American migrants in the 1980s and 1990s, would be unresponsive to declining economic opportunities, yet are the most impacted by state regulation. Jenny Robinson argues that the idea of de-territoralisation, explicit in various theories of globalisation and transnationalism, appears at its weakest in relation to the international refugee regime:

> *the phenomenon of displacement does not diminish the significance of territories or places.* For both refugees and resettlers, it is usually the nation-state which not only causes displacement, but which also assumes responsibility for attempting to deal with the undesirable effects of its consequences. (Robinson, 2002, p. 3, italics in original)

Transnationalism, like multiculturalism, has been impacted by the post-9/11 environment and this has surfaced in discussion about multiple loyalties, or assumptions about them, which impacted particularly on Muslim communities in Europe and the United States in 'questioning Muslim transnational loyalties' (Grillo, 2007, p. 992). A more typical view is that of any ethnic and immigrant organisations as agents of 'meddling foreign governments' (Portes et al., 2008, p. 1058). In a study of US-based Hispanic first-generation immigrant organisations with a transnational character, Portes et al. (2008, p. 1056) found that almost without exception the leaders of these organisations saw 'no contradiction between home-country loyalties and activities and US citizenship'. Not only did they find that immigrant organisations did not retard or prevent political integration, but also considered the possibility that 'ethnic and transnational politics may not be incompatible' (Portes et al., 2008, p. 1059). The study, however, examined several aspects of bureaucratic transnational activism, such as the tendency for many of the organisations to see 'only a minority of members being regularly involved' and to be more likely to represent those who have been established in the United States for longer. Only 1.75 per cent of the sample membership, for example, have lived in the United States for less than five years (Portes et al., 2008, pp. 1073–1074). These types of organisations are quite different from genuine social mass movements, which may be of short duration and develop around specific demands, such as the protests of 1 May 2007 over stringent immigration controls proposed by the Bush administration (at the time targeting Hispanic migrants). The overarching conclusions drawn by Portes, both about transnational loyalties and transnational activism, is that they are quite fluid, but at the same time move in predictable directions:

> The level of commitment to transnational activism may [thus] be portrayed as a bell curve moving along with the passage of time: low at arrival; increasing with the consolidation of the first generation; and declining with the passage of that generation from the scene and the arrival of the second. (Portes, 2009, p. 11)

The ethnic media (newspapers, TV and radio stations) is relevant to the discussion of transnational loyalties, since it has the capacity to provide alternative explanations both about events in the home country and also the status of a migrant ethnic community. The ethnic media reinforces notions of identity among Turkish immigrants in Germany, Hispanic migrants in the United States and Indian migrants in the United Kingdom and elsewhere, helping them to keep the connection to their country of origin, language and culture and therefore to consolidate their ethnic identity in a foreign country (Sen, 2002). At the same time, such as amongst the Turkish community in Germany, the ethnic media works closely with diasporic organisations, which are sometimes politically sponsored by governments in the home country (Erdem and Schmidt, 2008; Pecoud, 1999).

Ethnicity and enterprise

The relationship between ethnicity and enterprise is often revealed in the histories of particular ethnic groups and in statistics which reveal significant variation in the pattern of employment. In the United Kingdom, those classified as belonging to Pakistani, Chinese and Irish ethnic groups have significantly higher rates of self-employment than other groups. One in five in the Pakistani group was classified as self-employed (21 per cent), as were one in six in the Chinese (16 per cent) and Irish (15 per cent) groups. Amongst the 'White British' group it was just over one in ten (12 per cent) and amongst those in the 'Mixed or 'Black' ethnic groups it was fewer than one in ten. In terms of distribution by industry, which gives us a broad idea of the tendency in ethnic enterprise to 'crowd around' particular sectors and sub-sectors, three-fifths of Bangladeshi men and just under half of Chinese men in employment worked in the distribution, hotel and restaurant industry, compared with one sixth of their White British counterparts. Pakistani men were the group most likely to work in the transport and communication industry: 23 per cent of them worked in this sector compared with 10 per cent of employed men overall. White Irish men were more likely than other men to work in the construction industry: 20 per cent compared with 13 per cent overall. Bangladeshi and Chinese women are also concentrated in the distribution, hotel and restaurant industry. Two in five Chinese women and one in three Bangladeshi women worked in this industry, compared with one in five of all women in employment. Half of Black Caribbean and Black African women (54 per cent and 52 per cent respectively) worked in the public administration, education or health sectors (Office for National Statistics, 2004c).

In an introductory discussion on ethnicity and enterprise there is the need to establish some broad definition of what is meant by the terms 'enterprise' and 'entrepreneur' and how they relate to ethnicity. It is the case, for example, that most ethnic minority enterprises are small, and this has important implications for how enterprises function and are managed. An enterprise can be understood as containing physical and social features, characteristics and functions (see below). Frequently, however, an enterprise is thought of as the concrete result of just one of the factors of production, namely 'entrepreneurship'. The fact that we often refer to the skills performed by entrepreneurs as 'enterprise' merely increases the potential confusion surrounding this term, or rather, its reduction to the activities and the personality of the owner. Clearly, in small enterprise involving face-to-face relations, the personality of the entrepreneur is a critical factor. Nowhere is this more apparent than amongst the self-employed. However, all enterprises involve relations with internal and external economic agents and institutional actors. Micro and small enterprises which employ other workers necessarily acquire new functions, at least those of the 'management' of labour.

Enterprise characteristics

Physical characteristics, a building, for example, in which various factors of production (such as raw materials, capital equipment, labour and entrepreneurship) are assembled and combined to produce goods or services.

Social features, comprising (a) the *internal* relations between those owning its productive assets and those supplying labour (including a specific division of labour and internal organisation) and (b) its *external* relations with the market and with other (government and non-governmental) institutions, which make up the environment in which goods and services are produced and traded.

Whilst ethnic minority enterprises, as we shall see, are differentiated – and it would be reductionist to generalise about an essential enterprise with its requisite essential characteristics – there are a number of features which appear to be common to many if not most enterprises (see below). Many of these characteristics, however, (such as the combination of ownership and management, and informal production systems) should not be seen as the property of immigrant enterprises. Many small-scale, family-owned and 'informal sector' enterprises have similar characteristics to those associated with ethnic minority enterprises. We need to caution against the danger of identifying certain characteristics as 'ethnic' when in reality they are often variants on a widespread small-enterprise culture. Given that most ethnic minority enterprises are small, measured in terms of assets, turnover and level of employment, issues to do with (small) size have disproportionate implications for the internal and external enterprise functions of ethnic enterprises, but at the same time, exist independently of the ethnicity of the owner.

Ethnic minority enterprise: Characteristics

1. The entrepreneur combines ownership and management functions.
2. No clear division of labour exists between management and direct production.
3. Levels of productivity are low.
4. Both production and administration are conducted along traditional, personalised and paternalistic lines.
5. Close personal relations exist both among those active in the enterprise and between the entrepreneur and other enterprises.

6. There is a strong dependence on family labour.
7. The enterprise finds it difficult to access formal financial and credit markets.
8. There is a strong dependence on informal systems of labour recruitment, management and production. Such enterprises frequently act as contractors and sub-contractors in extensive and difficult-to-monitor production networks.

   That ethnic minority and migrant groups can and do act as agents in their own economic development is frequently thought of as an 'ethnic economy'. Studies have pointed to ethnic economies amongst Turks and Arabs in the neighbourhood of Moabit West, Berlin, Chinese immigrants in Italy, as reception areas for illegal migrant workers, such as in the London economy, in the mobilisation of capital through Rotating and credit Associations amongst Korean entrepreneurs in the Nail Salon industry in New York–New Jersey and in the development of restaurant areas such as Manchester's 'curry mile' in the United Kingdom, to name a few (Ahmad, 2008; Barret and McEvoy, 2006; Oh, 2007; Uzar, 2007, p. 52; Wu and Zanin, 2007, p. 2). Favell (2008, p. 709) identified the Polish migrant communities in Germany as an 'instance of an emergent, spatially organised, transnational ethnic economy that has a clear influence from below'. Economic arrangements in Paris, articulated in the idiom of ethnicity, are described by Mung and Lacroix (2000) in terms of a 'Chinese' economic arrangement, or 'an ensemble of interconnected enterprises...moving toward relative autonomy'. The number of Chinese-owned enterprises in Paris increased from 1044 in 1985 to 1646 by 1992 (Yu-Sion, 1999, p. 316). Most of them show very high levels of intra-community employment, with one estimate that 'somewhere between half and three fourths of the active Chinese population in France works for a Chinese business' (Mung and Lacroix, 2000, p. 10).

   Commodity and sectoral studies offer insight. They allow us to consider the relationship between ethnicity, markets and corporate restructuring in sectors such as the women's fashion-wear industry, where the drive is to find shorter and cheaper supply lines is particularly significant. The Greek and Turkish Cypriot community in London, the Hispanic and Chinese communities in New York and Miami, Asian and Latino immigrants in Los Angeles are, as the literature indicates, strongly associated with the sector (Rath, 2002, ed.). The suggestion in many of these sectoral studies of immigration, ethnicity and enterprise, is that the restructuring of the garment industry and the fashion-wear sector may be a more significant factor in the incorporation of ethnic minority and immigrant groups than any cultural characteristics associated with any particular group (Panayiotopoulos and Dreef, 2002; Rutherford and Blackburn, 1999).

The relationship between ethnicity and enterprise is revealed in transnational networks. Krogstad (2004, p. 200) suggests that among Chinese migrant entrepreneurs 'globalisation consists of the establishment of a transnational community, which allies the former home country with the present through strong social relations and network migration'. Often this appears as a characteristic of particular commodity chains. Wigs are a case in point. The wig boom began in the early 1960s and continued until the early 1970s. During 1974, an estimated 38 per cent of American women over the age of 17 possessed at least one wig. Chin et al. (1996) pointed to the import–export of wigs as an early ethnic niche created by Korean entrepreneurs in Los Angeles. Entrepreneurs formed transnational links in a vertical integration developed between Korean wig manufacturers in South Korea and Korean importers, wholesalers, and retailers in the United States This relationship reflected on South Korea's early industrialisation in light and labour-intensive industries, demand for this product in the United States (the world's largest market for wigs) and the existence of an immigrant community in the United States who saw this as an initial business opportunity. During the period 1968–1977, wig retailing 'became the most prevalent business among Korean immigrants during that time' (Chin et al., 1996, p. 493). Bonacich et al. (1976) found that during 1975, over 90 per cent of all wig stores in the Los Angeles area were Korean-owned. By the mid-1970s changes in fashion saw the bubble burst in wig retailing, but nevertheless, this was a formative experience for Korean enterprise.

Another example is the development of Silicon Valley, which reflects the wider role of ethnic minority and immigrant enterprise in the United States. Saxenian's (1999) study showed that Silicon Valley's Asian immigrants are a key part of the high technology industry which drives employment growth in California and the United States generally. Almost 3000 of the region's high-tech companies (a quarter of the total) were run by Chinese and Indian Chief Executive Officers who employed 58,000 workers and generated annual sales of almost $17bn. They have established long-distance business networks, especially with Taiwan, India and increasingly China. During 1980–84, 12 per cent of the new start-ups in Silicon Valley were by Chinese and Indian nationals. During 1995–98 the figure was significantly higher, at 29 per cent.

Many raise capital in Asia, subcontract manufacturing or software development to India, and sell virtually all their products in Asian markets. Their activities illustrate processes of agglomeration and transnationalism. Silicon Valley acts as a key cluster of globalisation. Many successful Asian Silicon entrepreneurs are effectively 'trans-Pacific commuters', or have relocated to home countries. In the case of Hsinchu Science Park in Taipei, some 40 per cent of enterprises were established by returnees, who in many cases had gone to the United States in order to study (Parkes, 1999, p. 12).

Commodity chains can be found in other products and markets.

Attempts to explain the relationship between ethnicity and enterprise intensified partly as the result of the crisis experienced by mainstream assimilation thinking during the 1960s in the face of emergent ethnicities, and partly in the challenge posed by multiculturalism as an alternative model of integration for migrant and ethnic minority groups. This was reflected in a growing interest in the economic arrangements of ethnicity and the role of communal affiliations, self-help institutions and ethnic solidarity in the day-to-day activities of ethnic minority enterprises (Bonacich and Modell, 1980; Cummings, 1980; Light, 1972). Many of the early analyses made use of residual theories which pointed towards cultural endowment, that is, variables specific to the ethnic group itself and its collective institutions, such as their social capital, as causal explanation for the emergence of enterprise. Labour and trade diaspora continue to be analysed substantially as the result of cultural endowment associated with an ethnic group. Other approaches point to the historical circumstances facing an ethnic group and the social organisations they create as equally significant as explanations for the development of transnational commercial networks (Cohen, 1997; Mohan, 2002). Mohan and Kale (2007, p. 2) write in a study of the Chinese diaspora in Africa that 'Chinese entrepreneurialism is a product of networks not an innate cultural characteristic'.

One of the earliest and most widely used cultural explanations for the phenomenon of minority enterprise looked at Middleman Minorities (MMs) in the economies of both the developed and developing countries (Bonacich, 1972, 1973). MMs appear as a concentrated example of a 'trade diaspora' but are exceptions to most ethnic groups, in that most minorities are seen as peculiarly disadvantaged, 'within, or even beneath, the working class'. Here we find a group which is identified as wealthy and 'in between' classes. At the same time, the analysis proposed that

> Despite the fact that they are found in capitalist societies, middlemen minorities are not themselves modern capitalists in orientation.

Rather they are essentially petit bourgeois, failing to engage in the kind of activity that epitomises modern capitalism, namely the hiring of contracted wage labour from which profits are extracted. Instead they work as single units, in which the distinction between owner and employee is blurred. Their shops depend on the use of the ethnic and familiar ties, not on personal contacts. (Bonacich and Modell, 1980, pp. 31–32)

MMs are equally distinguished by their particular location in the stratification system and the occupational structure. As Edna Bonacich noted (1972, pp. 34–51), they are likely to occupy middle rank positions and to act as economic middlemen, in other words, as brokers in the movement of goods and services. Their economic role is thus presented as a function of intermediation (traders or agents, labour contractors, money lenders and brokers) in relation to spaces between production and consumption, employer and employee, owner and rentier, ultimately acting as a link between the 'elite' and the 'masses'. Often they become targets of popular discontent, such as in the experience of East African Asian traders in the Native Reserves during British colonial rule. This reinforces MM group solidarity and insecurity, creating a material basis for a 'sojourning' orientation (desire to return to perceived homeland). Bonacich (1973, p. 585) saw sojourning as a necessary condition for the development of MM roles. Other categorisations of this intermediary role have been 'middleman trading peoples' (Becker, 1956, pp. 225–237), 'marginal trading peoples' (Schermenhorn, 1970, pp. 74–76), and 'permanent minorities' (Stryker, 1959).

The term may originate in the terms 'pariah people' or 'pariah capitalism' used by Weber to describe the economics of the Jewish diaspora (Weber, 1958). The analysis of a 'pariah' capitalism used by Weber to describe the Jewish Diaspora, whether real or imagined (Rose, 2004), disguises the fact that Jewish merchants were at the centre of the economic life of the court, and in this lay both their power and their weakness. Leon (1998, p. 129) noted that during the first half of the Middle Ages Jewish merchants 'constituted the only economic link which survived between East and West'; their situation was extremely favourable and 'Jews were considered as being part of the upper classes'. In fourteenth-century Castile a decree stated that Jews 'belong to the king to whom they pay taxes'. Royal protection was decreed in Poland. Judicially, the Jews were '*Kammerknechte*', or 'slaves of the royal treasury'. The financial support provided to kings by Jewish merchants became critical in maintaining armies of mercenaries. The King of Aragon, for example, borrowed large sums of money to defeat the Arabs in Spain. However, it was in this relationship, that the weakness of Jewish capitalism lay. On the one hand the king protected 'his' Jews, but at the same time he had the greatest material interest of all in the persecution and expulsion of Jews, wiping out at a stroke money owed to them. In situations where usury took on a more popular form, such as in Germany, then persecutions including the 'burning' of Jews (*Judenbrand*), 'were first and foremost efforts to destroy the letters of credit' (Leon, 1998, p. 171).

Much of the discussion on MMs illustrates how vulgar cultural theorists provide explanations for the activities of these peoples in terms of particular cultural endowments, values and heritages, which paradoxically remain unmodified, despite (in some cases) new-found niches and diversification. One treats with scepticism the hypothesis that of immigrants who become Middlemen Minorities, 'almost all that do derive from Asia and the Near East' (Fallers, 1967), or that 'overseas Indians in general', or 'overseas Greeks in general' (Jiang, 1968) or 'overseas Chinese, Indians, Lebanese *and* Armenians in general' (Hamilton, 1978, emphasis added), have a greater propensity for such economic roles. Current applications of trade diaspora analyses include the ancient Phoenicians, Venetians, Lebanese, Chinese and others (Cohen, 1997; Mohan, 2002). Criticisms made of the application of both trade diaspora and Middleman Minority notions is that they appear as ahistorical in content and cut across social and economic formations, some of which pre-date the development of the nation-state. One conclusion is that the expansive application of diaspora and MM analyses results in the majority of humanity described as showing a cultural disposition towards enterprise, and as such, this may have limited analytical value.

A second body of thought applied in explaining the development of ethnic enterprise was in the form of marginality theories. These early theories pointed to enterprise as substantially a response to discrimination in the (segmented) labour market and as a collective survival mechanism in the face of ethnic disadvantage and lack of opportunity (Anthias, 1992; Bonacich, 1972, 1973; Ladbury, 1984). Race is an important signifier. Research from the Greater London Authority found that start-up capital was a key operational problem for many black and ethnic minority enterprises in London, but this was greater for African-Caribbean entrepreneurs than for South Asian, Pakistani and Turkish and Greek Cypriot entrepreneurs. Many respondents across the groups, claimed that they had been treated prejudicially by bank managers and other business advisers. Others, mainly African-Caribbean, complained of the "text-book" manner with which they were being treated, which for them showed that the support providers generally did not understand the ethnic community they were dealing with' (CEEDR, 2000, p. 18). This (pessimistic) view of minority enterprise is summed-up as one which 'simply allows a small minority to exchange the role of marginal worker for that of marginal proprietor' and, as such (they conclude), 'represents a truce with racial inequality rather than a victory over it' (Aldrich et al., 1984, p. 209). Mitter referred to a 'sideways shift from lumpen proletariat to lumpen bourgeoisie' (1986, p. 59). Contemporary marginalisation theories (Kloosterman and Rath, 2002; Rath, ed., 2000), in offering an explanation for the incorporation of most ethnic entrepreneurs on the 'fringes' of European and American economies, direct our attention to the critical role played by the political–institutional framework in the structuring of labour market segmentation and in the positioning of migrant and ethnic groups in the enterprise spectrum.

A third collection of theories with a basis in neo-liberal economics (i.e. analyses which look to markets for solutions to problems facing ethnic minorities) pointed to various 'trickle-up' theories to explain the incorporation of ethnic entrepreneurs. They pointed to the 'ethnic niche' as the typical and rational response by minority entrepreneurs to (limited) market opportunity (Boissevain et al., 1990, pp. 131–156; Jenkins, 1984, pp. 231–232; Waldinger, 1984; Waldinger et al., eds, 1990). One early attempt to explain the relationship between ethnicity and enterprise consisted of the optimising longitudinal theory of ecological succession (Aldrich and Reiss, 1981, pp. 846–866). This view suggested a gradual progression by an immigrant group into the lower rungs of enterprise from which they were displaced in an upward direction by the next immigrant group. Waldinger (1996a, 1996b) applied the concept of the ethnic 'labour queue' to explain how minorities face, negotiate and generally overcome structural constraints in US cities. This model makes use of ecological succession and niche theories to explain employment changes amongst immigrant groups, with one suggestion being that some groups may be 'predisposed towards certain types of work' (Waldinger, 1996a, p. 21). The concept of the 'queue' draws from a long tradition of succession theories applied in the United States to explain the relationship between ethnicity and enterprise, which share common assumptions in the familiar theme of the assimilationist prowess of American society. Rath (2001) referred to Waldinger's analyses of the labour 'queue' as analogous to a game of 'ethnic musical armchairs', in which somebody is always left without a chair.

A fourth and more substantial collection of theories about the economics of ethnicity has been presented in the re-emergence of economic sociology and its attempts to show and explain ways in which social relations such as ethnicity modify economic behaviour (Granovetter 1985, 1995; Portes, 1995a). The new economic sociology combines theories from world development, the sociology of immigration and ethnicity, and has added to both marginality and neo-liberal thinking. It points to the social institutions of ethnic minority entrepreneurs as extra-market cultural resources, which underpin, parallel, complement, and on occasions disguise, formal systems of production and transaction. Much of this analysis points to ethnic mobilisation and solidarity as providing causal explanation for how ethnic and migrant groups cope in the face of adversity and also as an explanation for the development and management of enterprises. Portes and Sensenbrenner (1993, pp. 1343–1344) suggest that situations where migrant ethnic groups have faced prolonged periods of exclusion and blocked upward mobility have often led to 'the emergence of collective solidarity based on opposition to these conditions and an accompanying explanation of the group's social and economic position'. One implication for enterprise, Portes (1995a, p. 29) argues, is that 'bounded solidarity and trust enables employers in ethnic economies to demand greater discipline and effort from their workers'. Waldinger (1995, p. 555) suggests that embeddedness in ethnic networks 'leads to cooperation, if not conformist, behaviour among ethnic economic actors'.

The application of culturally derived explanations for economic organisation and action see market transactions as systematically governed by reciprocity, which for practical purposes links ethnic minority enterprise formation to ethnic niches, ethnic enclaves and ethnic economies. Whilst there are distinct analyses associated with these approaches (Barret et al., 1996; Light et al., 1994), many share necessary assumptions about the centrality of ethnicity. This appears in theories which point to ethnicity as the revealed interface between enterprise and market transactions. It is frequently ethnicity which underpins the concerns of diaspora research and studies of the formation of transnational communities.

Portes and Jensen (1989, pp. 929–949) have pointed to the agglomeration of immigrant enterprise in an 'ethnic enclave' as the most concentrated form of social embeddedness. Drawing initially from studies of Cuban exiles in Miami (Wilson and Portes, 1980), they attempt an explanation of the repositioning of an ethnic group which remains critical of conventional theories of structural incorporation and assimilation. The ethnic enclave economy thesis – with entrepreneurs at its epicentre – proposes that immigrants in the ethnic-enclave labour market, far from being disadvantaged in separation and segregation, receive earnings/returns to human capital commensurate with earnings in the primary (general) labour market. Portes and Jensen were optimistic about enterprise as 'an effective vehicle for upward mobility among immigrant minorities' (1989, p. 930), and more specifically, as 'a vehicle for first-generation upward mobility' (1987, p. 769; see also Portes and Stepick, 1985) (see Chapter 4). The assertion in the ethnic enclave thesis is that a social mechanism based on reciprocity operates, in which ethnic bosses assist co-ethnic workers in their attempts at upward social and economic mobility. This approach has influenced research amongst other ethnic groups (Portes and Zhou, 1996). Zhou (1992) suggests that most members of the Chinese community in New York's Chinatown are employed in the ethnic enclave economy and enjoy greater returns on human capital than they would command in the wider labour market. In a previous work, however, Zhou and Logan (1989, p. 810) argued that in practice 'only a modest proportion of persons identified as within the enclave actually are employed in minority-owned firms'.

More recent material has challenged the idea of the ethnic enclave as providing a 'warm embrace' for migrants. A variety of studies, such as those drawing from current US data, have challenged the view that enclaves provide economic benefits to ethnic wage and salary earners similar those in the mainstream economy (Pedace and Rohn, 2008). Ahmad (2008, p. 866), in a study of the labour market consequences of irregular migration and 'human smuggling' in London's migrant economy, point to very harsh conditions, and suggest that 'within the service end of the ethnic enclave, a more despotic kind of regime is suffered by those who, without strong or weak ties, lacked enough social capital to insert themselves into the labour market'.

The ethnic enclave thesis has also been criticised by transnationalist thinking. In Wilson and Portes' (1980) original formulation of the ethnic economy thesis, it was presented as either a concentration of ethnic enterprise in physical space with a significant proportion of workers from the same ethnic group, or as ethnic residential agglomeration. Garapich (2008, pp. 377–378) located the multiple role of agents facilitating labour migration between Poland and the United Kingdom as operating in an 'ethnic enclave', but one which is more expansive and transnational in scope rather than the 'bounded closed entity' associated with more typical applications of the thesis. Similarly, in a study of ethnic minority enterprises in London, Kitching et al. (2009), found that transnational enterprises lend support to those such as Zhou (2004), who question the adequacy of existing models of ethnic minority entrepreneurship (such as the ethnic enclave thesis) in accounting for transnational activity, because they presuppose a local and national context within which the structure of opportunities and resources for ethnic entrepreneurship emerges.

Much of the discussion on ethnic minority entrepreneurs makes use of ethnicity as a description of a relatively homogenous (and compliant) unit of analysis. In this exercise, however, a significant difference appears between seeing ethnic identities as rooted in claims to common origins and those rooted in different experiences by members of the same ethnic group, despite any common origins they share or perceive that they share. Gender is a case in point. The intersection between ethnicity and socio-economic status influences general attitudes held by migrants and ethnic minorities about all aspects of life. For example, Chu and Song (2008, p. 625), in a study of Chinese working-class immigrant perceptions of the police in Toronto, Canada, noted that 'a combination of ethnicity and socio-economic status may generate specific neighbourhood cultures that can influence attitudes towards police'.

A common problem with the theories surveyed – residual, marginalisation, neo-liberal and the new economic sociology – is that they appear at their weakest in trying to explain processes of social and economic differentiation inside ethnic communities. Social differentiation can be understood at one level in the emergence of entrepreneurs themselves, typically from the ranks of manual workers and artisans. At a more general level it is about the reproduction of social categories rooted in class, gender, race, age and other ways by which social groups are shaped. Economic differentiation is a feature of variation between enterprises. One key dimension is in labour input. Some are small, family enterprises, dependent on family labour input, whilst others are large employers who recruit labour from a wide range of ethnic groups. Economic differentiation represents a move away from weak positions in production and distribution systems in which many ethnic entrepreneurs operate as contractors, franchisees, or are disadvantaged in some way or other by distortions to the price mechanism imposed by quasi-monopolistic suppliers. Since entrepreneurs operate in given sectors, they are differentiated in ways which reflect the structures of subcontracting in particular sectors. In the garment industry, emergent immigrant enterprises have typically taken on the functions associated with the role of the manufacturer or 'jobber'. Buyers who have found it more convenient to deal directly with some of their larger ethnic CMT units have encouraged the repositioning of the entrepreneurs (Panayiotopoulos, 2006; Panayiotopoulos and Dreef, 2002). This kind of thinking challenges the idea of an 'essential' ethnic enterprise, typically reliant on family labour.

Economic differentiation has also been described as 'breaking out' of the ethnic economy. Many examples show that a significant proportion of entrepreneurs have, or are trying to, break out of the confines of the ethnic economy and to enter the economic mainstream (Poutziouris, 1998, 1999; Ram and Jones, 1998; Rutherford and Blackburn, 2000). Most of this literature comes from the management sciences and parallels the kind of vulgar cultural theories applied to analyses of MMs. Altinay and Altinay (2008, p. 33) write that Turkish entrepreneurs in London had 'managed to break out of the ethnic enclave and move away from traditional Turkish culture with Islamic dominance', unlike 'traditional' Pakistani and Bangladeshi Muslim entrepreneurs, and that this accounts for their 'success'. Basu and Altinay (2002) earlier described a move away from 'traditional' Turkish management culture characterised by co-ethnic and family participation, with centralised control of the businesses by family members.

Conclusions: Structure and agency

The relationship between ethnicity, migration and enterprise can be seen as a concentrated example of the contradiction between economics and politics. On one hand the world has experienced unprecedented levels of economic interdependence in which international migration is a key dimension. This is reflected in the changing ethnic composition of Europe and the United States and the development of immigrant and ethnic minority-owned enterprises. On the other hand, identities grounded in nationalism and ethnicity remain dominant ideologies on a world scale. Nationalism and ethnicity, however, are very broad categories and there is the need to contextualise their development and assess their change over time, as well as to critically assess more fundamental assumptions made by ethnocultural approaches about homogeneous communities. By ethnocultural we mean the view that ethnicity defines culture, when in real life it is frequently the other way round. It is in the culture of everyday life and day to day learned experiences of the conventions and norms which govern sociability, that the ethnicity of 'being' is itself shaped and re-shaped, creating possibilities for a multiculturalism 'from below'. This is quite different from globalisation 'from below' and its assumptions about permeable borders.

Frequently class is an important proxy indicator that there are many competing claims to ethnicity, some shaped round common occupations, others round common political positions, others round legal status, which indicate different experiences among members of the same ethnic group. Parker and Song (2001, p. 10) argue that the (necessary) application of ethnocultural categories as the unit of analysis in discussion of multiculturalism, for example, tends 'to ignore horizontal affiliations of consent and focus instead on vertical relations of descent'. Similarly, ethnocultural approaches have problems in explaining the social-economic differentiation explicit in the development of ethnic minority and immigrant-owned enterprises.

Concepts such as transnationalism, ethnicity, ethnic solidarity, ethnic minority enterprise, the ethnic enclave economy, the immigrant enclave economy, ethnic social capital and multiculturalism 'from below' (see Glossary of key terms and concepts) all point in some way to the role of ethnic minorities acting as their own agency in cultural and economic development. As significant as the role of agency are the structures within which ethnic minority entrepreneurs have to operate: the structure of government and the institutional behaviour towards ethnic minority groups, the role of immigration and naturalisation policies, the structure of local economies and the restructuring of particular sectors and sub-sectors in which ethnic minority entrepreneurs are most concentrated, point to important structural variables in the development of minority enterprise. Perhaps a more appropriate approach is to look at the relationship between structure and agency. This is often revealed in studies of particular industries, urban centres and local economies, in the quality of ethnic mobilisation and in the specifications adopted by the regulatory framework. An illustration of this is offered in the UK points-based immigration system (see Table 1.3).

The relationship between ethnicity, migration and enterprise is examined in more detail in subsequent chapters. It is important in this introductory discussion, however, to understand how this relationship, if there is one, has been influenced by wider debates in society about multiculturalism and the social 'integration' of minority groups, punctuated by rising xenophobia, sometimes directed at migrant workers, at other times at refugees and asylum seekers and, more typically, at the Muslim communities of Europe and the United States. Whilst xenophobia, like ethnicity, can be understood as an emergent and submergent phenomenon, the behaviour of the political–institutional framework,

Table 1.3 United Kingdom points-based system of immigration (75 points required)

Qualifications	Points	Previous earnings* £ (000)	Points	Age	Points
Bachelors	30	16–18	5	27 or under	20
or		18–20	10		
Masters	35	20–23	15	28 or 29	10
or		23–26	20		
PhD	50	26–29	25	30 or 31	5
		29–32	30		
		32–35	35	Over 31	0
		35–40	40		
		40+	45		

Note: *UK equivalent.

Source: Home Office (2006).

whether disabling or enabling, can have a more profound impact on outcomes for ethnic communities. This is examined further in the study of Polish labour migrants and how they were affected by recession in the United Kingdom. In this instance 'managed migration' (or immigration controls) worked in the interest of migrants from the recent Accession 8 states and facilitated their entry and incorporation in the UK labour market, as European citizens (see Chapter 5). This experience stands in marked contrast to the experience of ethnic groups with long histories of settlement in Europe, such as the Arab community in France or the Turkish community in Germany. The experience of a disabling relationship between the institutional framework and an ethnic group is presented in Chapter 2, which draws on the experience of Turkish ethnic minority entrepreneurs in the European Union.

The familiar proposition that self-employment is an avenue for economic improvement and social integration by members of an ethnic group, whilst at the same time many enterprises, whether by design or economic coercion, participate in 'informal economies', raises stubborn issues for integration. These are elaborated further in Chapter 3, in a study of Chinese-owned enterprises involved in the production and retailing of fake designer goods in Southern and Western Europe. As suggested in the earlier introduction on ethnicity and enterprise, ethnicity is a particularly messy concept, and nowhere more so than in the relationship between Hispanic ethnic identity and race in the United States. It is not simply that ethnicity and race are complex categories which need to be historically understood, but also that 'race' in the United States has acquired specific characteristics, which also need to be similarly historically understood. Chapter 4 examines this relationship between ethnicity, enterprise and race in a contrasting study of Hispanic American enterprise among Cuban and Mexican Americans. This example, like that of Turkish migration to Germany, directs our attention to the role of the institutional framework and the large number of Hispanic persons who are non-US citizens.

Whilst life is green, theory is grey, or rather shaded by uncertainties about future prospects for ethnic minorities in Europe and America. Only the foolhardy can predict with accuracy the trajectory of processes in formation. Two assertions that the book does make, however, are firstly, that the wider literature underestimates the extent to which ethnic and immigrant groups act as their own agency, or at least shape economic activity in ways that would not have existed otherwise. Secondly, that assumptions made about homogenous ethnic groups fail to explain processes of social and economic differentiation inside ethnic minorities. By 'social differentiation' we mean the reproduction of social stratification inside immigrant and ethnic communities, such as in the emergence of entrepreneurs from the ranks of wage-workers, or the development of social categories and social hierarchies rooted in class, gender, race, age and religious affiliation, and the intersections between them. By 'economic differentiation' we mean differences between ethnic minority-owned enterprises in terms of purpose, size and labour input: many are small, survival-orientated, family enterprises dependent on family labour, whilst others are large employers, who recruit labour from a range of ethnic groups, and in cases operate as micro-multinational companies engaging in international outward processing. Ethnicity under these circumstances can equally be understood as a struggle taking place inside ethnic communities and their social and cultural organisations and associations, over meaning and power between economic interest groups in formation.

2
Turkish Entrepreneurs in the European Union: A Political–Institutional Analysis

Introduction

People of Turkish origin constitute the single largest ethnic group in the European Union. Many Turkish entrepreneurs began as labour migrants during the post-war boom (mostly to West Germany) and were perceived as short-term *gastarbeiter* (guestworkers). Economic recession during the mid-1970s saw the dismantling of the guestworker system amidst high and persistent rates of unemployment in Europe. Under these circumstances, far from returning 'home', many ex-guestworkers and their children sought alternatives in self-employment and became a significant force in retail, fast-food and garment production. This chapter considers the relevance of the case study for wider debates about the relationship between the political–institutional framework and ethnic minority enterprise. Whilst most of the entrepreneurs have either worked in Europe for decades, or were born in Germany, the Netherlands or Britain, most lack citizenship, and this has important implications for the development of enterprise activities. It is also the case that whilst many small enterprises operate outside legal structures or in contravention to them, many of them are also subordinated to other larger companies operating on a formal basis. Transnationalism and the globalisation 'from below' thesis attach primacy to immigrants acting as their own agency in economic development. Marginality theories argue that whilst immigrant enterprises may act as an agency for capitalism from below, they also operate on the 'fringes' of economic and political systems. The chapter points to a growing economic differentiation between Turkish enterprises, which offers an alternative basis for analysis, and one which remains critical of both transnational and marginality theories.

Immigrant enterprise in the European Union

Analyses of ethnic minority and immigrant participation in local economies have progressively become more relevant to an enlarged European
Union. The growth of communities that are multi-ethnic, multi-racial
and multi-religious in Europe's gateway cities have seen, albeit unevenly,
both the quantitative and qualitative expansion of minority-owned
enterprises in Europe. This has been reflected in the expansion of a
new research focus on immigrant-owned enterprises (Kloosterman and
Rath, 2003; Panayiotopoulos, 2006; Rath, 2000). Studies of entrepreneurial behaviour often point to variables such as size, sector, ethnicity,
gender, black and ethnic minority status as important socio-economic
reference points for enterprise activity and decision-making (Altinay
and Altinay, 2008; Basu, 2004; Dobbs and Hamilton, 2007; Williams,
2007). Whilst analyses rooted in these variables have provided useful insights, they say relatively little about how the status of being an
immigrant influences the development of enterprise. Neither do they
consider fully the implications that for many immigrants the experience consists of lack of citizenship, lack of political rights and, in some
European Union member states, significant institutional barriers to
non-national entry into the (small) enterprise sector. Much of this literature directs our attention to the critical role played by the political–
institutional framework in the shaping of immigrant enterprise and in
the structuring of entrepreneurial behaviour.

The economic significance of territorially based political and legal
systems, whilst ignored by conventional transnational thinking, is evident in analyses of immigrant and ethnic minority enterprises which
point to the role of agglomeration in particular local economies and sub-
sectors and the impact of economic restructuring in particular urban
centres and gateway cities (Kabeer, 2000; Kitching et al., 2009; London
Skills Forecasting Unit, 2001; Panayiotopoulos, 2008; Panayiotopoulos
and Dreef, 2002; Rekers and van Kempen, 2000; Waldinger, 1986;
Watson et al., 2000). Territorially based political and legal systems
require legitimacy, usually constructed round notions of nationhood
and citizenship applied in the framing of immigration and naturalisation policies as well as in the regulation of enterprises and other areas of
life. Frequently, the quality of political mobilisation and representation
available to ethnic minority communities which began as communities

of immigrants is influenced by the nature of the local political economy and to what extent they are a significant force within it, and the attitudes taken by local, if not national, policy-making (Rath, 2000, 2002; Sassen, 1991).

A factor not fully elaborated in the broad sweep of transnational thinking is the real significance of the social characteristics of entrepreneurs themselves, how these are ranked by political systems in terms of naturalisation policies and the implications of this for defining the opportunity structure. Race, ethnicity, gender and age are factors which influence selectivity in both immigration policy and in the formation and extension of immigrant enterprises. One trend appears in second-generation resistance to entering first-generation immigrant 'niche' sectors if other opportunities are available. Selectivity appears in widely observed racial and gender disparities in the accessing of bank loans, both in Europe and the United States. Many African Caribbean and Black American entrepreneurs in the United Kingdom and United States have common tales of rejection by bank managers. A report, commissioned by the British Bankers' Association, found significant variation in the treatment of black entrepreneurs when accessing loans. Only 21 per cent of African Caribbean entrepreneurs secured start-up capital, compared to 34 per cent of those of white or Pakistani extraction and 49 per cent of those of Chinese extraction. This was despite the finding that 46 per cent of black entrepreneurs had formal management qualifications, more than whites or Asians (Ram et al., 2002, p. 4).

Explanations for the phenomenon of Turkish enterprise have frequently focussed on the formation of transnational communities and globalisation 'from below' (Gokturk, 1999; Henry et al., 2000; Pecoud, 2002; Portes, 1997; see also Castles, 2000). One suggestion from the globalisation from below thesis is that the gateway cities of Europe are being increasingly transformed by immigrant entrepreneurs themselves with limited assistance from government or the commercial banking sector. Indeed, that much of this is taking place in the face of governments and restrictive immigration policies is cited as confirmation of the thesis (Panayiotopoulos, 2001a). Alternatively, explanations provided by the marginalisation thesis points to the subordinate positioning of immigrant entrepreneurs as a function of their relations with the institutional framework (Rath, 2000). Rath (2002) and Kloosterman and Rath (2001, 2002), point to 'mixed embeddedness' and its absence as an important source for marginalisation. They suggest that embeddedness in ethnic immigrant communities is not a sufficient condition for the development of sustainable enterprises and that another and perhaps necessary condition is that entrepreneurs also need to be embedded in the dominant institutions of the host society, or at least have the ability to influence their behaviour as other people do. The 'mixed embeddedness' approach locates immigrant social relations and transactions within wider political and economic processes and stands in contrast to cultural analyses which attach primacy to ethnicity as the key variable in immigrant adaptation (see also Barrett et al., 2002).

The marginalisation thesis points to significant institutional variation in European policy towards ethnic minority and immigrant-owned enterprises and the association frequently made by policy between them and the informal economy. Estimates of the informal sector by the European Commission range from a third to a quarter of GDP in Greece and Italy, to less than 10 per cent in the Scandinavian countries. It is assumed that the EU's undeclared work amounts to 7 to 16 per cent of GDP, corresponding to 7 to 19 per cent of declared employment, some 28 million jobs (Panayiotopoulos, 2006, pp. 123–124). Some countries are more tolerant of the informal economy and there is a clear regional variation, with countries in Southern Europe characterised by the presence of large numbers of self-employed and micro-enterprises which makes them structurally more tolerant to the informal economy. The 'Third Italy', containing the dynamic sub-region of Emilia Romagna with Bologna as its centre, is a case in point. The small-scale manufacturing sector here goes hand-in-hand with the informal sector, and policy-makers have drawn the conclusion that there is a trade-off between some acceptance of informality and economic growth (Magatti and Quassoli, 2003; Quassoli, 1999).

The Northern European countries, by comparison, show less tolerance towards unregistered economic activity. Germany, for example, declared war on the *Schattenwirtschaft* (shadow economy) and in one initiative the government created the FKS, a 120-strong customs cell overseeing special customs, and a taxation force comprised of 7000 officers 'dressed in combat boots and green berets' (Benoit, 2004, p. 10). Similarly, the Netherlands during the mid-1990s applied the full wrath of the 'social' state in an unprecedented crackdown on immigrant entrepreneurs in the Amsterdam garment industry. The contrast between Germany and the Netherlands and Italy is drawn in a comparison between two studies. Quassoli (1999) identified the tolerance of the informal sector in Italy by the institutional framework as an explanation for a system of informal labour, estimated at 25 per cent of all labour in Southern Italy. Hillmann (2000, p. 7), argues that 'the opposite was true in Germany ... here the polarisation of the new migration movements in the labour market has produced a highly stigmatised sector'.

Kloosterman (1996, 2000) identified the far more restrictive policy environment for immigrant enterprises and the informal economy in the Northern European Union countries as a causal factor in the positioning of most enterprises on the 'fringes' of economic and political systems. Haberfellner (2003) similarly points to the example of Austria, as a country where strict regulations, high barriers to start-ups and a tendency towards concentration of the retail sector limit opportunities for immigrant entrepreneurs to less prosperous niches and create a 'disadvantaged' group of entrepreneurs. Hillmann (2000) describes immigrant enterprise in Germany as 'liminal', that is, occupying a position like no others, typically at the intersection of formal and informal labour markets, or alternatively, on the fringes of both the formal and the informal economy.

The above (pessimistic) interpretations may well be a more accurate description of some regions and cities within Europe when compared to others. At the same time, a general view of immigrant enterprise as essentially marginal is highly prejudicial. Pang (2003) suggests that the failure to recognise the diversity and socio-economic differentiation of immigrant enterprises and immigrant communities is in part the result of the 'victim-driven' nature of much of the research on ethnic minorities and their economic activities. It is also in part the result of a policy-orientated research agenda in the European Union aimed at bringing ethnic minority and immigrant-owned enterprises out of the 'fringes' and at proposing practical ideas for policy-makers to formalise and 'integrate' their activities.

Turkish immigrants in Europe

The 3.5 million Turkish-speaking people in Europe make up a quarter of all immigrants in Europe and form the single largest ethnic group in the European Union (EU). Erdem and Schmidt (2008, p. 212) put the number of Turkish and Turkish-originated persons in Germany at about 2.6 million with an estimated spending power of €16 billion. Many entrepreneurs began as labour migrants during the postwar boom (mostly to West Germany) and were perceived as short-term *Gastarbeiter* (guestworkers). Economic recession during the mid-1970s saw the dismantling of the guestworker system amidst high and persistent rates of unemployment in Europe. Under these circumstances, far from returning 'home', many ex-guestworkers and their children sought alternatives in self-employment and became a significant force in retail, fast-food and garment production. An estimated one-third of

Turkish speakers are under 18 years of age and more than 80 per cent of them have been educated in Europe. Germany accounts for nearly two-thirds of all immigration from Turkey in the EU and the old industrial state of North Rhineland–Westphalia alone accounts for nearly one-quarter of Europe's Turkish population (Bayar, 1996, p. 2; Manco, 2004, p. 4). Over half (50.5 per cent) of Turks are between the ages of 14 and 29, when compared to 25 per cent for native Germans (Sen, 2002, p. 30). Purely male migration was a feature from 1965 to 1973 and family reunions peaked between 1973 and 1985. For this reason, the Turkish population in Europe consists of families, with the male to female ratio moving nearer the average: in Germany 45.5 per cent (and in Belgium 49 per cent) of the Turkish population are women. Women form, typically though marriage, a significant and continuing source of new immigrants (Manco, 2004, p. 2).

Turkish-speaking immigrants are diverse. Many are Kurdish. Most are Sunni and a significant proportion of them are Alavi (Shiite). In London a large number are Turkish Cypriots. An increasing number are born in Europe and are not immigrants at all. Some migrated from one European country to another. The diversity of the Turkish-speaking community is illustrated by London. There are an estimated 90,000–120,000 Turkish-speakers in the United Kingdom of whom 80 per cent are concentrated in the Greater London area (Struder, 2003a, p. 12). The Turkish Foreign Ministry estimates that 97,000 Turkish citizens are residents in the United Kingdom with most (90 per cent) living in London (Struder, 2003b, p. 186). A growing number are immigrants from other EU countries. Enneli et al. (2005), in a study of Turkish-speaking young people in the North London Borough of Haringey, showed that they were disproportionately represented among the Government's NEET category (Not in Employment, Education or Training) but also identified significant variation between the established Turkish Cypriot community, who have been living in London in large numbers since the 1950s, and more recent immigrants from mainland Turkey, many of whom are Kurdish refugees (Abdullah, 2006; Ladbury, 1984). The study pointed to an increasing social and economic polarisation between these three groups in, for example, house ownership, and in the different sets of problems they faced.

The origin of Turkish migration to Europe was in pro-active policies by governments to facilitate labour migration – a common feature of the Western European economies during the post-war boom. This was managed in different ways by European countries: Britain, France and The Netherlands relied on their colonies and ex-colonies as labour reservoirs, whilst Germany, which lost its colonies during the First World War, drew initially from the large number of refugees from Eastern Europe and introduced the guestworker system in 1955, for labour migrants from the southern European countries, the former Yugoslavia and Turkey. The guestworker system became a key mechanism in the 'European labour market' during the post-war boom, and in retrospect a leading example of globalisation 'from above' (Bohning, 1972; Castles and Kosack, 1973; Kindleberger, 1967). West Germany signed agreements with Italy (1955 and 1965), Greece and Spain (1964), Morocco (1963), Portugal and Turkey (1964), Tunisia (1965), Yugoslavia (1968) and even Korea (1962). By 1973 migrant workers in France and Germany made up about 10 per cent of the labour force (Marfleet, 2005). In West Germany guestworkers were seen as a temporary recourse, with workers initially on two-year contracts. The 'rotation principle' was abandoned in 1964 as German employers argued, successfully, that having to replace reliable and fully trained guestworkers with fresh immigrants every two years added considerable cost and effort to their activities (Erdem and Schmidt, 2008, p. 213).

Despite European Union convergence the labour demands of national economies remain a key factor which drives immigration policy and this introduces significant national variation in policies. This is illustrated in a contrast between Germany and the United Kingdom and France. In the latter, migrants from the colonies had no choice but to travel with passports issued by their colonial masters and this made it more likely that they would gain access to citizenship and formal political rights. One significant consequence was the acceptance of family reunions. In Germany, in contrast, where immigrant labour was seen as a temporary measure, this was characterised by the absence of formal political rights and representation. Lack of rights fostered insecurity and this delayed family reunions. To a large extent, the intended non-incorporation of immigrants in Germany led to them being defined as 'foreigners', and this has continuing implications and raises wider questions not only about policy towards immigration and settlement, but also definitions of citizenship and political rights.

Immigration from Turkey to Germany amplifies the role of the political–institutional framework and the (unintended) consequence of labour transfer in the transition by a significant number from temporary guestworkers to entrepreneurs. The guestworker system was introduced during 1955 and the number peaked at 1.3 million in 1966. Whilst Turkish guestworkers were latter arrivals, when compared to Greek and Italian workers, they more than made up in numbers, increasing from 13 per cent of the foreign population in 1972 to one-third by 1980 (Geddes, 2003, p. 81).

Karen Schonwalder (2004) offers an explanation for why Germany's guestworkers were largely white European, and within that group, largely Turkish. In Germany, of 7.3 million immigrants admitted until 2000, 5.8 million were Europeans (including Turks). Schonwalder (2004, p. 248) argues that this was 'the result of a deliberate policy pursued by West German governments of the 1950s to 1970s' to exclude persons referred to as 'Afro-Asians'. Where recruitment treaties existed, with North African countries such as Morocco and Tunisia, they excluded provisions on the immigration of family members. Effectively, policy ranked potential guestworkers according to racial preference. In the case of Portugal and its significant African migrant population, it was decided to inform the Portuguese authorities that 'German employers were not interested in dark-skinned workers' (Schonwalder, 2004, p. 250) and left it to the local authorities to ensure none were. During 1960–61, West Germany concluded recruitment treaties with Greece, Spain and Turkey, to add to Italy and Portugal. In response to inquiries from countries such as India, Iran, the West Indies, Togo, and the Central African Federation, amongst others,

> it was decided not only to refrain from concluding recruitment treaties with non-European countries but actively to prevent employers from recruiting workers from Asian and African countries and to make sure that such individuals would not become settled in West Germany. (Schonwalder, 2004, p. 249)

Whilst the guestworker system was abandoned during the mid-1970s, an integral part of the legacy of German immigration policy remains, in that only a fraction of the estimated 7.3 million persons of immigrant origins have the right to vote and to take part in the limited democratic process. Of the estimated three million people of Turkish origins, only an estimated 370,000 are eligible to vote (Wassener, 2002, p. 8). Despite in many cases being born and educated in Germany, or having spent a lifetime on an Opal production line, only a minority (28 per cent) of Turks in Germany are naturalised and the rate of naturalisation is significantly lower when compared to other EU countries (see Table 2.1).

The incorporation of immigrants reflects the contrasting historical development of nation-states, firstly, in whether an already existing nation or people becomes the basis for claims to statehood (as in Germany), or secondly, in whether the idea of nation-state is used to

Table 2.1 Turkish population in the European Union: By legal status, in 000s

Countries	Turkish origin	Turkish nationals	Naturalised	
			Number	Per cent
Austria	200	120	80	40
Belgium	110	67	43	39
Denmark	53	39	14	26
France	370	196	174	47
Germany	2,642	1,912	730	28
Netherlands	270	96	174	64
Sweden	37	14	23	62
United Kingdom	70	37	33	47
Other EU	20	19	1	5
Total EU	3,772	2,500	1,272	34

Source: Tumbas (2003), p. 2.

meld together a culturally and linguistically diverse population (as in the United Kingdom and the United States). One area of convergence, as Turton (2002, p. 25) reminds us, is that 'the nation-state exists, by definition, to protect the rights only of its own citizens', and this has important implications for immigrants. This issued was highlighted by the question of the incorporation of guestworkers in Germany, given Germany's ethnocultural definition of national community. An ethnocultural definition does not see nationhood as a political construct. Rather, the 1913 Nationality Law defined the German nation as comprised of a community based on 'descent'. Bauder and Semmelroggen (2009, p. 3) suggest that this ethnocultural *Volk*-centred understanding of nationhood readily lends itself to the exclusion of immigrants 'from the imagined national community'. It certainly placed immense obstacles in the path of non-Germans becoming citizens and has been referred to by Czarina Wilpert (1993) as a form of 'institutional racism'. Progressively, this position became untenable. In 1990, over 70 per cent of the 'foreign' population had lived in Germany for more than ten years and Geddes (2003, p. 95) notes that around 1.5 million 'so-called foreigners had actually been born in Germany'. The 1990 Foreigners Law made some significant amendments: it gave immigrants statutory residence and family rights for the first time and allowed for naturalisation after 15 years' residence (eight in the case of second- and third-generation youth in the 16 to 25 age group).

The uptake of German citizenship (and hence, the right to vote) amongst Turkish nationals is low for various reasons. One factor is national pride. Many do not want to give up their nationality and emphasise their Turkish origins as a defensive social posture adopted by the community in the face of hostility. A major factor in this is a sense of insecurity, which the guestworker system was designed to produce, and which reinforces the unwillingness to give up Turkish for German nationality. Many see dual nationality as preferable, and as insurance. A dual nationality policy, which would have addressed these concerns, was rejected by both left and right in Germany.

Rights to citizenship have important implications both at central and local city levels, at the very least, in the capacity of so-called immigrants to politically integrate themselves and to influence society. This also has important implications for enterprise functions. Wilpert suggests that the later development of Turkish enterprise in Germany, when compared to other guestworker groups, may reflect on the 'differential treatment of former guestworkers' and 'exclusionary processes towards certain groups' (Wilpert, 2003, p. 233). These include the requirement of eight years legal residence and an assessment by the police and the Chamber of Industry and Commerce, which determines 'whether or not the proposed venture is considered harmful or not to the overall economy', and which approves, or not, the permit for self-employment (Wilpert, 2003, p. 237). Similarly, France has a vast array of institutional restrictions on the employment of immigrants. Many sectors that are open for nationals from other EU states are closed to other immigrants, who cannot practice as physicians, dentists, pharmacists, veterinarians, architects, surveyors, accountants, bailiffs or lawyers. It is hardly surprising, perhaps, that only about 1 per cent of the total number of licensed professionals in France are foreigners. In addition, immigrants cannot own a periodical, a television or broadcasting agency, or sell tobacco and alcoholic beverages (Mung and Lacroix, 2003, p. 175).

Turkish entrepreneurs in the gateway cities

The Turkish community in Europe is made up of a significantly younger population when compared to the EU population, and it is one that needs to work. Self-employment began as an alternative employment path for many first-generation redundant guestworkers but it also became a significant response by second-generation youth, often assisted by parents who had in mind securing the future livelihoods of their children. An increasing number of entrepreneurs come from the ranks of the second generation and the emerging literature on Turkish entrepreneurs points to rapid expansion across the generational spectrum. The overall proportion of Turks who are self-employed in the EU lies at 4.8 per cent, which is significantly below the EU average of 12.3 per cent. Nearly 70 per cent of all Turkish enterprises in the EU are in Germany, of which four-fifths are found in only three sectors: retail, restaurant and take-aways, and the service sector. Over one-third (39.7 per cent) of the entrepreneurs have been living in Germany for 11 to 30 years (Arastirmalar and Vakfi, 2003). Constant et al. (2003, p. 16) in one study of Turkish entrepreneurs in Germany found that only 15 per cent were German citizens and that 41 per cent, whilst born in Germany, had their parents' (Turkish) nationality.

Turkish entrepreneurs represent a significant and growing economic force in Europe. According to Manco (2004, pp. 6–7), during 1996 an estimated 58,000 enterprises employed a total of 186,000 workers throughout Europe. The vast bulk of the firms (42,000) were in Germany, with the Netherlands, France and Austria making up the remainder. Findings from the Turkish Research Centre (TRC) at the University of Essen estimate that during 2002 an estimated 82,300 firms employed 411,000 people. As the above indicates, during the five year period (1996 to 2002), nearly 25,000 more enterprises were added to the total, representing a 41.8 per cent increase. Employment during the same period increased by 225,000: an increase of 82.6 per cent (Arastirmalar and Vakfi, 2003) (see Table 2.2). According to Tumbas (2003, p. 5) something like 77 per cent of Turkish entrepreneurs in Germany have German suppliers and an increasing number rely on German consumers. About 17 per cent of employees in firms are Germans and 9 per cent from other nationalities. The estimated turnover of the firms was equivalent to one-fifth of

Table 2.2 Turkish enterprises in the European Union: Economic indicators, 1995–2002

Indicators	1996	1998	2000	2002
Number	56,500	67,400	80,600	82,300
Total number of employees	232,000	323,000	419,000	411,000
Average number of employees	4.1	4.8	5.2	5.0
Average investment by enterprise (€)	99,500	104,800	110,400	112,000
Total investment (billion €)	5.6	7.0	8.9	9.2
Total annual turnover (billion €)	21.8	28.7	34.8	36.0

Source: Tumbas (2003), p. 4.

Denmark's Gross Domestic Product (GDP). One conservative estimate of the total contribution made by Turkish immigrant entrepreneurs to the European economy is that it is equivalent to 51 per cent of Greece's GDP (TRC, 2000, p. 3) (see Table 2.2, prev. cit.).

The location of the enterprises is often a reflection of the pattern of contemporary Turkish immigration and community formation. A strong feature of this appears in the communities' concentration in Europe's gateway cities. Working-class neighbourhoods in Berlin, Hamburg, Amsterdam, Vienna, Rotterdam and London have seen the formation of communities which over the last four decades (some longer than others) have become centres for immigrant enterprise (see Table 2.3) (Abdullah, 2006; Ali, 2001; Avci, 2006; Basu and Altinay, 2003; Constant et al., 2003; Enneli et al., 2005; Jansen et al., 2003; Struder, 2003b). Areas of London such as Green Lanes, Tottenham, Stoke Newington and Hackney are significant centres of Turkish entrepreneurship, both in the old sectors such as garments, taxi-driving, groceries and restaurants, but also in new sectors, including a clustering in food and meat wholesaling. Problems identified by Turkish entrepreneurs in the garment and other industries included raising finance from the commercial banking sector and the need for appropriate training and support agencies (CEEDR, 2000, pp. 15–18; Evans and Smith, 2004). The downturn in the London garment industry gave a push towards self-employment in other sectors such as IT services (Struder, 2003a, pp. 21–23). In the cities of Brussels, Antwerp and Ghent, Turkish entrepreneurs form the largest group of immigrant entrepreneurs. Most started with little capital and

Table 2.3 Turkish population in European cities: Main concentrations

Host country	Population (000s)	Per cent	Main city	Per cent
Germany	2014	66.4	Berlin	7.0
France	261	8.6	Paris	25.0
Netherlands	260.1	8.6	Amsterdam	20.0
Austria	143.2	4.7	Vienna	32.0
Belgium	119.0	3.9	Brussels	33.0
Switzerland	79.4	2.6	Zurich	21.0
United Kingdom	58.2	1.9	London	80.0*
Sweden	35.7	1.2	Stockholm	50.0
Denmark	35.7	1.2	Copenhagen	50.0

Note: *Struder (2003a), p. 21.

Source: Manco (2004), pp. 4–5.

tend to crowd around similar sectors, such as food processing, retail and catering. Turkish entrepreneurs come into conflict with the regulatory regime in 'old' Europe, in novel ways. Pang writes that

> Since the Middle Ages, each street in Ghent is organised in a 'dekenij', a merchant association with the status of a non-profit making organisation. It has been very difficult to convince these traditional merchant associations to include immigrant business people in their associations as equal members. (Pang, 2000, p. 5)

Most first-generation entrepreneurs came from the ranks of shop-floor workers. A not unusual trajectory is that entrepreneurs began their working lives on the production line, moved to working as 'apprentices' for other immigrants as waiters, cooks, taxi-drivers, hairdressers, shop-assistants, pressers and cutters, before becoming owners of their own shops, salons, restaurants and small factories. It is for this reason that entrepreneurs can come under moral pressure to assist their workers if they want to establish independent enterprise activities, by, for example, advancing them loans (Wilpert, 2003). One complimentary factor is that workers are often family members. Basu and Altinay (2003) point to participation by the entrepreneurs' immediate and extended family, with wives often playing an important informal and invisible role, as critical in explaining enterprise functions.

Amongst second-generation entrepreneurs, other factors played a role. One survey of 100 Turkish firms in Brussels found that most of the entrepreneurs were young, below 35 years of age, and that one-fifth were university graduates. Only one-third of them had any training specific to their work. Nearly 45 per cent were in the retail sector (groceries) and had mainly Turkish customers. Over one-third of them used start-up capital of $15,000 or less, and only one in five used the commercial banking sector to do so. In terms of labour input they are described as 'small-scale family enterprises', yet of the total of 412 persons employed, only 23 per cent actually were family workers and 65 per cent were of Turkish origin. A significant proportion of employment generated, therefore (35 per cent), consisted of the employment of other immigrant groups (Bayar, 1996, pp. 3, 6–7).

Berlin and the 'Doner Revolution'

Berlin is the major centre of Turkish settlement in Europe and the development of enterprise has been influenced, in a positive as well as a negative way, by the prolonged recession of the German economy and high levels of unemployment during the 1990s. One powerful view is that the loss of employment or fear of unemployment was a significant 'push' factor for many ex-guestworkers and their children to look to alternatives. Bayar (1996) and Hillmann (2000) argue that due to lack of new technical or transferable skills, many redundant Turkish workers were forced into self-employment and the small enterprise sector. There is an increasing body of knowledge about Turkish entrepreneurs in Berlin (Gokturk, 1999; Hillmann, 1999, 2000; Pecoud, 2002). Hillmann (2000, pp. 13–14) found some 3600 firms listed in the Turkish Yellow Pages for 1998, and estimates that by the end of the 1990s, 6000 enterprises were owned by immigrants from Turkey. Most of these were small enterprises relying on family labour (four-fifths of employment) in the restaurant, services and retail sectors. The bulk of the enterprises were located in working-class neighbourhoods, such as Kreuzberg, Tiergarten, Wedding and Neukolm and impacted by economic recession translated to low spending power, leading to 'the collapse of many businesses'. The food sector, in the form of ethnic restaurants, take-aways, groceries and vegetable stalls, although initially set up to cater to ethnic groups, have become part of the neighbourhood shopping of many non-ethnic residents, and are the most significant areas of sectoral concentration by immigrant entrepreneurs. Bayar (1996, p. 2) estimates that about three-quarters of Turkish-owned enterprises in Germany are in retail and catering.

Czarina Wilpert (2003, p. 246) writes that the doner-kebab was 'invented in Berlin'. Leaving aside that a doner could have been had in Hackney, East London in 1972, what the 'Doner Revolution' represented was the commodification of 'traditional' ethnic food (Hillmann and Rudolph, 1997), another example being the 'Italian' pizza. Doner-kebab take-aways have been the single most significant source of enterprise formation for Turkish immigrants in Germany and throughout Europe. The 'doner revolution' can be seen as the selective adaptation of traditional and now commoditised Turkish cuisine. It monopolised and initially displaced other forms of Middle-Eastern take-away food, such as the shish-kebab, the preparation and cooking of which is more labour intensive, since instead of using one lump of meat (as with the doner), it involves cutting the meat into smaller pieces which are individually skewered. Commoditisation also represented an increase in the ratio of capital (equipment) to labour and many of the take-aways can literally consist of two or three men in a kiosk. When compared to other areas of take-away consumption, such as fish and chip shops and 'Chinese' take-aways, the doner take-away sector has significantly lowered the cost of entry.

The above would not have been possible in Germany (or elsewhere) without the economic differentiation of Turkish entrepreneurs. Wilpert (2003, pp. 252–253) notes that some 'have moved from retail to wholesale'. The movement to a wholesaler position was an early feature of Turkish groceries in Berlin, where in 1972 a system (akin to a cooperative) saw bulk-buying introduced in order to reduce the cost of goods imported from Turkey for consumption by the Turkish community. More significantly, we have seen the emergence of manufacturers and wholesalers of processed meat used in the doner-kebab trade. It is this, more than any other factor, which has made it possible for many entrepreneurs to start up. One Turkish Cypriot-owned company in London delivers to over 1000 outlets in the United Kingdom (Panayiotopoulos, 2006). The application of economies of scale in the industrial processing of meat has eliminated labour costs involved in the preparation of the doner by the individual take-away and also lowered prices for the meat paid by the retailers of ready-made doner to the wholesalers. The application of economies of scale has also led to the resurgence of the shish-kebab, as thousands of (mainly) immigrant workers are employed in factories cutting and skewering the meat, which is delivered to retailers according to demand.

One consequence of the doner take-away phenomenon is that Turkish entrepreneurs have developed a specialisation in meat processing, which points to significant supply side considerations. Turkish entrepreneurs have become important producers and suppliers to Turkish-owned groceries and also to some of the chain stores. They have also developed a speciality as bakers, particularly of pitta bread, but also other breads, sweets, dried nuts, cakes and confectionary. The development of meat and food processing points to qualitative differences between Turkish entrepreneurs: between on one hand the mass of doner-kebab take-aways and on the other the smaller number of suppliers of these products. The suppliers are involved in value-adding manufacturing processing, whilst take-aways (and the retail sector generally) rely primarily on the price mark-up and consumer naivety. The development of Turkish wholesalers and the emergence of a significant layer of large capitalist enterprises and commodity chains which operate across borders, points to significant variation amongst enterprises and provides evidence that many of the enterprises have significantly pushed out of the 'fringes'.

Amsterdam and the garment industry

Turkish immigrants in the Netherlands are widely distributed, a development that was shaped in part by the location of industries, services and workplaces which had recruited guestworkers in the past. That the location of Turkish entrepreneurs reflected the pattern of dispersal associated with the incorporation of ex-guestworkers is one reason why only 14 per cent of Turkish enterprises are located in Amsterdam (Rath and Kloosterman, 2003, p. 131). Another factor which explains the distribution of Turkish enterprises surfaces in the influence of sectoral and sub-sectoral variables and the traditions of particular urban centres. For example, as Rekers and van Kempen (2000) note, whilst industrial Rotterdam has a larger Turkish population than Amsterdam, there are five times more Turkish restaurants in Amsterdam. The concentration of amenities in Amsterdam is driven in part by urban traditions where 'going out' to eat or to be entertained is more popular, at least amongst the many tourists who visit the city, and reflected in the amount of money spent in restaurants and cafés, which in turn influences the number of establishments in this sector.

The development of Turkish-owned enterprises was initially linked to the provision of services to the community and subsequently services to the wider economy: butchers, bakers, shopkeepers, restaurant owners and market stall holders, provided entry routes into enterprise. Some of the earliest examples of immigrant enterprise were guestworkers' hostels, coffee-houses and *halal* butchers run by immigrants themselves. Turkish entrepreneurs became particularly significant as contractors in garment production and as producers and retailers of confectionary (Hartog and Zorlu, 1999; Raes et al., 2002). Self-employment amongst Turkish immigrants at 12.2 per cent for 1997 was significantly higher than the national average of 10.2 per cent. Indeed the growth in self-employment amongst Turkish immigrants in the Netherlands was such that it provided the single most significant source of net additions to employment in the Netherlands during the period 1986 to 1992 (Rath and Kloosterman, 2000, p. 659). Indeed, Jansen et al. (2003, p. 41), in a report partly funded by the Dutch Ministry of Economic Affairs, commented that 'the high rate of entrepreneurship amongst immigrants from Turkey indicates that this group does not need any additional policy measures' (when compared to Moroccan immigrants).

During the mid-1990s, nearly 60 per cent of all immigrant enterprises were in the retail, wholesale and restaurant sectors (RWR). During 2000, the figure stood at 57 per cent. Of the estimated 7478 enterprises owned by immigrants from Turkey, a smaller proportion (54 per cent) were concentrated in the three sectors, when compared to Turks in Germany and other ethnic groups in the Netherlands. Amongst Chinese and Hong Kong immigrant entrepreneurs, this rises to 93 and 89 per cent respectively. One of the reasons why Turkish entrepreneurs in the Netherlands were less concentrated in the RWR sectors than other immigrant groups, was their role as contractors in the Amsterdam garment industry. Most firms were owned by immigrants from Turkey and a small number were Dutch nationals (Raes et al., 2002, pp. 97–98) (see Table 2.4).

One of the earliest studies of Turkish enterprises in Amsterdam's garment industry was carried out during the mid-1980s by Roeland van Geuns and investigated the role of informal labour markets and Turkish 'sweatshops' in the women's fashion-wear industry. It presented an analysis of the restructuring in the garment industry and the incorporation of an immigrant group into production channels which operate outside the legal structures, but which are also, 'subordinate to other companies operating on a formal basis' (van Geuns, 1992, p. 126). The study pointed to a low degree of autonomy in economic action, with most entrepreneurs constrained by their position as relatively weak contractors and subcontractors. Van Geuns also pointed to restructuring in the women's fashion-wear industry as substantially driven by the sourcing preferences of principal buyers for rapidly changing styles

Table 2.4 Ethnic minority entrepreneurs in the Netherlands: Sectoral concentration

Ethnic group	No. of enterprises	Sectoral concentration (per cent)		
		First	Second	Third
Turkey	7,478	Catering 22	Retail 17	Wholesale 15
China	2,297	Catering 79	Wholesale 10	Retail 4
Hong Kong	1,113	Catering 75	Wholesale 8	Retail 6
Turkey	7,478	Catering 22	Retail 17	Wholesale 15
Surinam	5,690	Personal 14	Wholesale 14	Retail services 17
Morocco	2,883	Retail 26	Catering 23	Personal services 10

Source: Rath and Kloosterman (2003), pp. 131, 133.

requiring smaller 'batches' and shorter turn-around supply lines. This can require production on a week-to-week basis and lays the basis, in the case of Amsterdam, for a limited 'spot-market'.

For the large 'formal' companies, inward processing allows them the ability to respond to fashion changes which cannot be addressed by international outward processing. Orders in the Far East have to be 'placed six months or more in advance' (van Geuns, 1992, pp. 126–127) and are extremely difficult to change afterwards (to a different colour for example), with the principal and associated manufacturers left having to carry large stocks in their warehouses. Other comparative research (Rath, 2002) confirms that the search for shorter supply lines also looked for sourcing in-country which was cheaper, with contracting and subcontracting often used for this purpose. In Amsterdam it was the Turkish community which provided the raw material by setting up clothing workshops during the 1970s making 'almost exclusively women's clothing' (van Geuns, 1992, p. 128).

The Institute for Migration and Ethnic Studies (IMES) at the University of Amsterdam conducted a major research project on Turkish contractors in the Amsterdam garment industry during the 1990s. The research pointed towards a dramatic growth and equally dramatic decline in Turkish-owned garment enterprises in Amsterdam between 1987 and 1992. The small firms were located in the neighbourhoods of Pijp, the western part of Oost, the Jordaan and the southern part of Oud West. Most were contractors who produced lower- to medium-quality women's fashion-wear and in cases lacked the capacity to cut garments. At the same time an increasing number began to engage in wholesaling and import–export activities. The number of registered contractors increased from 275 in 1987 to 1000 by 1992. After 1993 the sector went into sharp decline and was reduced to an estimated 300 firms by 1995. Employment dramatically declined from an estimated 20,000 workers to several hundred (IMES, 1998, p. 21). By 1997, there were only 40 to 50 firms left (see Table 2.5).

According to the Chamber of Commerce, during the peak of 1992–93 the overwhelming majority of entrepreneurs (some 60 per cent) were first-generation immigrants from Turkey. Raes estimated this to be significantly higher (at 76 per cent) and during the early 1990s approximately 75 per cent of the workers were of Turkish origin (Raes, 2000, p. 77). Some of the entrepreneurs were naturalised and the average length of stay in the Netherlands by legal migrants was 14 to 17 years. Many of them had previously worked in the clothing industry for Dutch contractors, most of whom abandoned the sector. Raes et al. (2002, pp. 96, 98)

Table 2.5 Turkish clothing contractors in Amsterdam: Employment and average firm size

Period	Number of contractors	Number of workers	
		Workers	Per firm
Early 1980s	100	1,304	12
Mid-1980s	192	2,500	15
Early 1990s	550	20,000	20
1996–97	40–50	900	18

Source: Raes (2000), pp. 78, 82.

notes that during the 1980s most of the initial entrepreneurs were older men, many of whom were ex-guestworkers in the Netherlands and Germany. Their 'success' encouraged an increasing number of youngsters to follow, many of whom were without valid documents and 'shaky legal status', relative short duration of stay and lacked familiarity with Dutch society or language. Along with lower levels of formal education, this impacted negatively on their entrepreneurial opportunities. The firms initially produced medium-quality women's fashion-wear (blouses, skirts, dresses) but many of the large number of new entrants supplied the lower quality end of the market. Many firms had been in existence for a short period of time, often less than a year.

The rise and subsequent crisis faced by Turkish entrepreneurs in the Amsterdam garment industry was in part due to significant changes in sourcing policy which began to look to Eastern Europe as a low-cost production centre of cheap ready-to-wear women's garments. This cannot, however, fully explain the crisis, since other centres of immigrant garment production (London, Los Angeles, Birmingham and Paris) continue in the face of similar circumstances which have been negotiated more successfully. What was specific about the Amsterdam experience was the severity of repression launched by the Dutch state, consisting of a comprehensive offensive against the informal practices in the industry leading to numerous raids against workshops. As IMES (1998, p. 62) noted, 'when undocumented workers were found, or when the payment of taxes and social benefits were evaded, entrepreneurs were heavily fined, leading to bankruptcy of a lot of firms, and undocumented workers were expelled'.

Stricter law enforcement took the form of the extension of the Law on Chain Liability to 'make retailers formally responsible for their contractor's illegal practices'. Contractors had to open accounts where retailers or manufacturers, that is, the suppliers, 'had to deposit 35 per cent of the price of each order as a guarantee that this sum would be paid to the tax and social security services'. The creation of the Clothing Intervention Team (CIT) brought together for the first time the courts and other enforcement agencies (Labour Relations, Taxation, Aliens Police and Industrial Insurance) who 'launched numerous raids, targeting in particular violations of the Law on Work by Foreigners', (Raes et al., 2002, pp. 106–107). The Compulsory Identification Act introduced in June 1994 made it necessary for all employers to provide documentation on their employees. The issuing of social insurance numbers was changed in 1991 and made conditional on having a residence permit. Previously, being a registered resident of the city was sufficient. These measures had the effect, as Staring (2000, pp. 187–188) argues, of effectively closing 'formal' sector employment and driving immigrant workers further into unregistered and casual employment.

Conclusions

What happens to immigrant entrepreneurs is influenced by their membership of particular ethnic groups and the historical circumstances they find themselves in. It is also influenced by the location of enterprises in particular commodity chains. More than perhaps is realised, it is influenced by the political–institutional framework and restrictions placed on non-citizens, as well as the consequences of xenophobia, which impacts on all foreigners irrespective of their legal status. One key finding is that despite the political constraints facing many of the entrepreneurs there is a growing economic complexity amongst Turkish immigrant enterprises and this challenges the view that they are either the living embodiment of globalisation from below or on the fringes of economic systems. Turkish entrepreneurs in Germany, despite the immense difficulties they face (not least in the long hours they work), lack of political rights and a hostile institutional environment, have not been driven into the economic margins. Their numerical expansion, the emergence of wholesalers and suppliers, diversification into other areas (most notably food processing) with greater control over value adding parts of the commodity chain, indicates a vibrant economy, which as the doner-kebab take-away sector illustrates, has come into the mainstream.

The accumulated evidence reveals far greater diversity than the 'fringe' literature suggests. In part this is driven by higher levels of education amongst the second generation and resistance by them to entering first-generation 'niche' sectors. Many of the younger generation do not wish to take over the businesses which their fathers or mothers have established and choose something else, if alternatives are available. 'For example, rather than taking over the corner shop they choose to start up an IT service-based company because this relates better to the education they have received' (Arastirmalar and Vakfi, 2003, p. 5). Manco (2004, p. 6) points to the emergence amongst the Turkish community, 'of a class of businessmen [*sic*] in Europe which increases the complexity of the Turkish immigrant population's social stratification while giving it a new dynamism. Henceforward, a Turkish population plagued by socio-economic marginalisation co-exists with a small class of businessmen that has the wind in its sails'. Yassar Tumbas (President of the Turkish Business Group – Brussels), writes of significant quantitative and qualitative change over the past 15 years as 'the small "Imbiss" snack shop has developed into a high class restaurant, [and] the doner kebab seller has become the producer and thus the distributor' (Tumbas, 2003, p. 5). These developments underpin the formation of what Yurdakul (2006, p. 435) refers to as a 'Turkish immigrant elite' which is increasingly challenging for dominance in community associations.

The experience of Turkish entrepreneurs in the Amsterdam garment industry raises questions over the fragility of transnational assumptions about contemporary patterns of migration and the formation of transnational communities. It also reveals important insight into economic restructuring, the role of the state and debate over policy for the informal sector. We noted that the entrepreneurs were mainly comprised of subcontractors producing on order for Dutch chain stores. This relationship raises wider questions about the basis of informality. A definition of the informal sector begins from a legal definition, that is, economic activity which is not registered for the purposes of GDP and within which labour is not protected by social legislation and is, therefore, cheaper. The ambiguity of the concept of the informal sector, particularly in contractor firms, rests on a legal superficiality. It is that suppliers and contractors are separate legal entities which are not liable for each others' action. This is a standard legal defence used in every market economy by firms such as NIKE, Marks and Spencer and GAP in the face of corporate critics (Panayiotopoulos, 2001b). All economies, that is, except the Netherlands when it came to Turkish entrepreneurs in the Amsterdam garment industry. In this instance – at a stroke – this legal defence was dissolved by The Law on Chain Liability which made suppliers responsible for the actions of their contractors. In this one action, the Dutch state imperiously removed this synthetic construct which forms the basis for 'dualist' theory, that is, explanations for economic activity rooted in bipolarity, such as between formal and informal, or between fringe and mainstream economies.

One conclusion is that the informal sector, far from being imported by Turkish immigrants, could not exist *but* for the pivotal role played by established Dutch-owned retail chains in the informalisation of production and the setting in motion of difficult-to-monitor systems of subcontracting. We noted that the evolution of a fashion-wear 'spot-market' requiring weekly production allowed the buyers to respond to fashion changes, in ways they could not do by sourcing to the Far East. Subcontracting is more generally used as a strategy by larger firms in order to avoid regulation and certain costs: transaction costs through transfer pricing, costs in the recruitment and management of labour, the elimination of marginal costs in the form of heating and electricity, and the avoidance of institutional costs in the shape of Value Added Tax (VAT), income tax and other contributions. The incorporation of Turkish contractors in structures of informality can be seen as part of a wider process of informalisation substantially driven by corporate restructuring of the fashion-wear industry rather than practices associated with any particular immigrant or ethnic group. The argument, however, that 'immigrants play a pivotal role in these informal economic activities' (Kloosterman et al., 1999, p. 252) did legitimise the drive against the entrepreneurs.

The example of Amsterdam shows a gateway city in crisis, within which multiculturalism and 'good' globalisation faced an onslaught. Whilst there are continuities found in this with other urban centres, there are also specific variables in institutional behaviour and relationships with immigrant groups. The political–institutional framework in the Netherlands swung against immigrants. The experience of Turkish entrepreneurs in the garment industry is a case in point. It illustrates one of the most significant examples of state repression directed at immigrant enterprise in the European Union. In this, we see the significance of what Rath (2002), Kloosterman (2000) and Kloosterman and Rath (2001, 2002) mean by 'mixed embeddedness', and the implications of its absence for an immigrant ethnic community in formation.

The influence of the political–institutional framework underpins, yet rarely surfaces in most analyses of ethnic minority and immigrant enterprise. Rather, they concentrate on the role of ethnicity or the small scale of their activities. Rath, Kloosterman and the wider literature on 'mixed embeddedness' have made an important and explicit contribution in correcting this deficiency. At the same time, the 'fringe' literature represented by Kloosterman et al. needs to move beyond generalisations and to identify the political mechanisms which render a group of immigrant entrepreneurs particularly vulnerable to institutional repression, that is, 'lacking' in mixed embeddedness. In order to understand lack of embeddedness in the political–institutional framework, we need to consider processes of exclusion and inclusion in political systems and the implications this has for the positioning and repositioning of immigrant entrepreneurs. Above all, we need to explain the selectivity in institutional behaviour. Why the Turkish community? Why the garment industry? In part this derived from the continuing legacy of the guestworker system and the lack of citizenship amongst many ex-guestworker and new immigrant entrepreneurs. It is debatable whether much of the repression would have taken place if it had been directed at Dutch (or German) nationals instead of 'foreigners', irrespective of their legal status. In important ways, rights to citizenship were actually taken away in the Netherlands. The Nationality Law was changed in 1992 to permit dual nationality, but reversed in 1997. The 2001 Aliens Act included Turkey amongst the countries from which travellers would require visas for the first time (Geddes, 2003, pp. 106, 117).

The potential entry of Turkey into the EU holds important implications for Turks in Germany and other member states. At a stroke, Turkey's entry would remove the ambiguity of their status and lack of political rights, by granting them rights as good as those that exist in any of the member countries. The granting of automatic political rights implied in Turkish EU membership was an innovation too far. During the inaugural rounds of Turkey's negotiations for entry, Frits Bolkestein, Austrian Single Market Commissioner, launched into a diatribe that Europe would be 'Islamicised' and went on to add that 'the liberation of Vienna [from the Turks] in 1683 would have been in vain' (quoted from Dombey, 2004, p. 8). Southern Cyprus also threatens to veto every single one of the 22 accession treaties. Turkey may have to accept emergency curbs on the free movement of its nationals, including on Turkish nationals living in Germany, as a condition for joining the EU. In Berlin, the call to prayer remains banned, 'because it violates noise pollution rules' (Boyes, 2004, p. 17).

This chapter concludes that the positioning and repositioning of Turkish immigrant communities and entrepreneurs in the European Union is structured by the political–institutional framework, in the form of the immigration and naturalisation systems and periodic drives against the informal economy. It is also structured by the economic restructuring of particular sectors, sub-sector, local economies and neighbourhoods in the gateway cities. The transition of many immigrants from 'guestworker' to entrepreneur, and the economic differentiation of some of them from the mass ranks of the self-employed and subordinate contractors into large capitalist enterprises, are potent symbols of this process of economic restructuring (Panayiotopoulos, 2008). The experience could be understood as immigrant communities applying forms of social organisation to take opportunities offered from 'above' (as guestworkers) and from 'below' as emergent entrepreneurs. Whilst the economic circumstances facing Turkish immigrants and their children today are profoundly different to those faced by the *Gastarbeiter* during the 1960s, a significant continuity appears in their lack of effective political rights and the implications this has for the development of sustainable enterprises.

3
Chinese Entrepreneurs in Europe and the United States: Studies in Informal Economies

Introduction

This chapter presents a review of Chinese immigrant-owned enterprise in order to examine the potential of enterprise as an agency for social integration. A related purpose is to consider the implications of participation by many of the entrepreneurs in informal economies. Many workers are faced with political systems which make it virtually impossible for them to migrate legally. Many entrepreneurs operate in local economies, systems of subcontracting and commodity chains underpinned by informality which structures economic behaviour and their relations with the institutional framework. The chapter suggests that informality is subtly linked to the dynamics of particular sectors, local economies and patterns of subcontracting. The conclusions point to ethnic adaptation and integration in local markets and informal economies as the visible end product of a process of informalisation, driven substantially by economic restructuring rather than by attributes associated with any particular ethnic group.

The 'new geography' of migration and the informal economy

Self-employment is a recognisable route for immigrant and ethnic minority self-improvement. Despite the political constraints faced by many immigrants, a significant number have gravitated towards the small enterprise sector in order to make a living, also hoping that owning a stake in the system in the form of a business might give them more respect and acceptance in the host society, and that this will result in lowering barriers to social integration, if not for them, then their children. This is a familiar enough immigrant story. At the same time, the tendency for many of these enterprises to operate in informal economies and commodity chains in which they are often incorporated as relatively weak subcontractors makes it hard for business to act as an agency for the social integration for immigrant and ethnic minorities. This is also a recognisable immigrant history. Sometimes sympathetic local policy-makers, such as in the London garment industry, find that it is difficult to assist enterprises because many of them are operating illegally (Panayiotopoulos and Dreef, 2002).

Informal labour markets and irregular migration are important areas of research in the 'new geography of migration' which highlight significant differences between the experience of state-sponsored labour migration to north-western Europe during the 1950s to the early 1970s and the current pattern of migration. Russell King (1993, 2000, 2001) referred to the 'southern European' or 'Mediterranean' model of migration in order to explain the transformation of southern European countries (such as Spain, Greece, Italy, Portugal and Turkey) from labour exporters during the 1950s and 1960s to major importers of labour today. In this model,

> migration begins spontaneously: it is not directed by national or local authorities and is not framed by legislation. The industrial sector is not the main absorber of the immigrant labour force; the informal economy plays an important role in the employment of immigrants. Other characteristics [of the model] are the variety of countries of origin and the importance of the female presence corresponding to a growing demand in female jobs (mainly services to private persons). In the migratory flows towards southern European countries, women represent half of the total. (Campani, 2007, p. 70)

Berggren et al. (2007, p. 8) argue that 'irregular migration and the social and political issues linked to it, constitute the most critical questions related to migration and the development of labour markets across Europe'. As this chapter explores, much of the analysis of irregular migration and informal economic activity has focussed on the 'new wave' of mainland Chinese migration. It is worth noting in this respect the work of Laczko (2003) which questioned perceptions in Europe that China is a major source of irregular migration. An analysis of border apprehension data collected in 11 eastern European countries indicated that

Chinese persons accounted for only 3 per cent of those apprehended at the borders of European countries. Subsequent border apprehension data in Germany showed that the percentage of Chinese nationals apprehended for attempted illegal entry rose only slightly from 370 in 1992 to 718 in 2000, which is a low figure compared with other nationalities. As Laczko (2003, p. 6) noted, 'these figures suggest that either Chinese migrants are very skilful at avoiding detection, or relatively few attempt to cross European borders illegally'. At the same time, France, Italy and Spain have regularised more than 60,000 Chinese since 1990, suggesting 'that a significant part of the increase in Chinese migration to southern Europe over the last decade has been due to irregular migration, with many Chinese migrants arriving to work in the informal economy' (Laczko, 2003, p. 8).

Whilst the new geography of migration points to genuine changes taking place in the pattern of European migration, it is less convincing in offering an explanation for the implications of institutional variation within the European Union towards different kinds of migrants, and the nature of the relationship between informal labour markets and the formal economy. Migrants are made up of diverse groups who are institutionally dealt with in different ways. Frequently this is influenced by the gender and nationality of the migrant, their legal status and the role of particular sectors and sub-sectors in which they might be employed. Female domestic workers are a case in point since they are frequently presented as the living embodiment of the new geography of migration (e.g. Lazaridis, 2007; Lutz, 2007).

Most domestic workers in states that have recently joined the European Union have been affected by the significant new differences created between immigrants who are EU citizens and those defined as Third-Country Nationals (TCNs). This 'new hierarchy of foreign workers' (Thomson, 2006) sees few or no restrictions placed on the freedom of movement and employment of EU citizens whilst in contrast, non-EU nationals from the Philippines and Sri Lanka, where most domestic workers come from, continue to face draconian restrictions. Trimikliniotis and Fulias-Souroulla (2006) noted that in Cyprus, for example, the nationals of recently acceded countries (such as Bulgaria and Romania), unlike TCNs, have no maximum stay if they find employment and work legally, and they may change status from visitors to workers. Employers must have a permit from the Labour Office in order to employ them, but no bank guarantee needs to be submitted by the employer. They may also change employer without a release paper. The experience of foreign domestic workers is, perhaps, where the new geography of migration thesis appears at its weakest. Most domestic workers employed in the European Union are TCNs and in their case, migration is anything but 'spontaneous' and 'irregular' in nature. Much of the evidence from Europe and the wider experience indicates a highly structured and regulated labour regime involving governments, bilateral agreements, agents, employers and the immigration services, the purpose of which is primarily to ensure a transient migrant labour force (Anderson, 2003; Chin, 1998; Ehrenreich and Hochschild, 2003; Panayiotopoulos, 2005).

The new geography of migration also shows a lack of clarity on the relationship between irregular migration and informal labour markets within the formal economy. In part this lack of clarity derives from an unquestioning use of the informal sector concept. The informal sector purports to account for all economic activity not registered for the purpose of GDP and within which labour is unprotected by any social legislation and is, therefore, cheaper. As a concept the informal sector was 'discovered' by the International Labour Office (ILO) in a number of studies in the developing countries during the late 1960s and early 1970s as an attempt to explain how the urban poor in the cities of Latin America, Sub-Saharan Africa and the newly independent countries coped in the face of failure (for the most part) of the 'modern' industrial sector to generate sufficient employment to meet the needs of the many young rural-to-urban migrants (ILO, 1972; Santos, 1975).

The informal sector analysis described circumstances in which the urban poor were forced to generate their own employment, either through marginal income activities such as petty street-vending and shoe-shining or in more significant value-adding manufacturing clusters in sectors such as carpentry, engineering and garment production. A number of significant studies, both of a theoretical and practical nature, pointed to a marginal economy which generated unexpected employment growth, produced mass commodities for low income consumption and was an important source for the learning of artisanal skills and the mobilisation of capital (Schlyter, 2002, Xaba et al., 2002). Hart (1973) described the informal sector as the 'poor people's economy' but at the same time saw the numerous workshops as a potential source for an indigenous capital goods sector. Labour standards raised, and continue to raise, concern, particularly over the treatment of the many family workers and apprentices employed in the sector. The dilemma of employment growth in an unregulated labour market was accentuated when governments in the developing countries, the World Bank and the International Office began to see the informal sector as the main source of future employment growth in regions such as Sub-Saharan Africa during the 1990s (World Bank, 1989, 1994). Under these circumstances many emergent informal enterprises underwent a process of 'formalisation' and benefited from government support and donor aid. One consequence of this has been a growing differentiation in the informal sector between the emergent profit-oriented enterprises and the larger number of subsistence petty-commodity producers (Atema and Panayiotopoulos, 1995; Panayiotopoulos and Capps, 2001).

As we noted in Chapter 1, rising unemployment in the United States and Europe during the 1980s coincided with what Gerry (1987) called the 're-discovery' of the informal sector in the urban centres of Europe and North America, and this informed the work of Sassen (1991, 1996) on the incorporation of diverse immigrant groups in informal labour markets as a general feature of contemporary patterns of migration. As we noted, Sassen argued that it was not immigration which was causing informalisation, but rather a more complex interaction between migration and economic restructuring in the global economy and cities, neighbourhoods and particular sectors and sub-sectors. The informalisation of various activities, it was argued, was driven by demand for products and services that lend themselves to small-scale production, or which were not satisfactorily provided by the formal sector. Sassen concluded that the relationship between the informal sector and immigrant survival strategies needs to be understood as part of a wider process involving the transformation of the larger economy, such as the city of New York (Sassen, 1988).

A substantial explanation for participation in informal economies is that it is a response to marginalisation and discrimination in the (segmented) labour market, and a collective survival mechanism in the face of ethnic and racial disadvantage (Kabeer, 1994, 2000; Mitter, 1986; Portes, 1994). Portes et al. (1989) identified the informal economy as substantially a response by working-class immigrants to a marginalisation driven by economic restructuring and the effects of globalisation. Rath and Kloosterman (2003) point to 'mixed embeddedness' and its absence as an important source for marginalisation. They suggest that embeddedness in immigrant communities is not a sufficient condition for the development of sustainable enterprises and that another, perhaps necessary, condition is that entrepreneurs need to be embedded in the dominant institutions of the host society, or at least have the ability to influence their behaviour as other people do. The 'mixed embeddedness' approach locates immigrant social relations and informal transactions within wider political and economic processes and stands in contrast to cultural analyses which attach primacy to ethnicity as the key variable in immigrant adaptation. This approach directs our attention to the role of the political–institutional framework, such as in the impact of periodic drives against the informal sector and, more generally, in how it shapes immigration and naturalisation policies (see also Panayiotopoulos, 2008).

Another explanation for informalisation and irregular migration is that it is a response to over-regulation by the state. Studies of immigrant workers and entrepreneurs, such as in the London women's fashion-wear sector, describe informalisation as a process involving practices, some which are specific to the sub-sector and others applicable to all small enterprises. Institutions such as homeworking, 'clear-money', illegal selling activities ('cabbage sales'), 'design pinching' (of the latest fashion) as well as 'doing a liquidation', primarily in order to avoid paying Value Added Tax (VAT), structure the day-to-day activities of entrepreneurs (Panayiotopoulos, 1996). This could give support to the view that informalisation is substantially a response to over-regulation and in particular to the introduction and increase in the amount of VAT paid by small enterprises. Jones et al. (2006) point to the reproduction of informality in the avoidance of UK National Minimum Wage (NMW) legislation, as another example of attempts to avoid regulation.

The changing application of the informal sector concept from the analysis of artisans in Third World cities to immigrant and ethnic minority entrepreneurs in the metropolitan heartlands of Europe has offered useful insight. At the same time, as Gerry (1987) concluded on the highly contested informal sector debate during the 1970s, the concept lacked clarity and it was difficult to clearly identify what it was studying. Iit failed to show how the economic activity described was 'informal' and in what sense, given its growing diversity, it constituted a 'sector'. More importantly from the point of view of the discussion which follows, it failed to explain in a satisfactory manner the nature of relationships between the formal and informal sector. Subcontracting, for example, is a form of organisation which can bring together enterprises of varying form and this can pose problems for dualist informal sector analyses.

The relationship between ethnic minority enterprise and informality raises important questions for social integration which are neither lineal nor reducible to cultural misunderstandings. There are familiar and powerful elements of continuity, such as the long and anti-social hours many entrepreneurs have to work and the limited time and space available to them for forming meaningful social relationships within the host society. Change, however, appears in the growing economic diversity both in the informal economy and amongst minority-owned enterprises (Panayiotopoulos, 2006). This can create conceptual problems for analyses which make assumptions about homogenous immigrant or transnational communities and their economic activity. Diversity adds an important note of caution when generalising about ethnic minority enterprises, which is that in order to understand the extent to which enterprise acts as an agency for integration, or the extent to which the informal economy acts as a barrier to social integration, we need to be aware of processes of social and economic differentiation inside ethnic communities and amongst ethnic minority enterprises. This requires an understanding of the development of different kinds of enterprises in terms of size, purpose, employment scale, and the implications this may have for integration amongst different sections of the same immigrant or ethnic group.

The Fuzhounese exodus

Irregular migration and informal economic activity from the early 1980s onwards became strongly associated, in both policy-making and wider social perceptions, with mainland Chinese migration. Chinese communities are often seen by policy-makers as tightly knit, difficult to penetrate, resisting integration but nevertheless economically successful. A common argument is that 'Chinese entrepreneurship is a direct result of cultural factors like hard work, a trading ethic and reliance on family labour and ethnic community networks' (Altinay and Altinay, 2008, p. 25). Chinatown is frequently presented as confirmation of this proposition. This stereotypical view of the Chinese community has been affected by the desperation of economic immigrants, which has driven many of them into the arms of human traffickers who facilitate transit and, in some cases, employment. This was cruelly revealed in the United Kingdom, when 21 workers collecting cockles in Morecambe Bay, Lancashire, were drowned by the oncoming tide: of these, 18 were Chinese, and 13 were seeking refugee status. The tragedy in Morecambe Bay followed 58 deaths amongst undocumented Chinese migrants at the port of Dover four years previously, where they suffocated in the back of an air-tight container truck during the five-hour ferry crossing from Zeebrugge, Belgium. In both cases 'Triad' (mainland China) gangsters were mentioned and attention focused on recent trends in a labour diaspora linking the Province of Fujian in China with Europe.

An extensive undercover Special Report by a Fujian-speaking journalist working for the British *Guardian*, and subsequent Parliamentary Inquiries on the Morecambe deaths, revealed a world of intimidation, misery, shared and overcrowded apartments and fear of the authorities (Pai, 2004, 2008).

Other sources point to a wider relationship between gangmasters and European agriculture. In the United Kingdom, Reports from the UK Parliamentary Environment, Food and Rural Affairs Committee and the UK Agricultural and Allied Workers Union, estimated that there were 3000 agents providing the agricultural sector with casual labour needed by the fruit and vegetable sector at peak picking times. In the last ten or fifteen years this has become big business and some gangmasters employ up to 2000 people, looking primarily to Eastern and Southern Europe for sources of labour (Bell, 2002; Lawrence, 2005). The role of gangmasters and the provision of agricultural seasonal labour in unregulated and casualised labour markets focused on Eastern Europe as a source for labour, particularly from the newly acceded states to the European Union such as Poland. It is also a reflection on transnational enterprise formation. In the Dover tragedy, the destination of the group was restaurants in Newport Street in London's Chinatown. There they hoped to get £167 per week and pay off in two years or so the debts incurred for the journey. One factor driving this is that 'there is a great shortage of workers there since many second generation Chinese go to universities and work in the professions' (Harris, 2002, p. xvi). London has a substantial Chinese community which makes up 1.1 per cent of the total population and of which one-third have been born in the United Kingdom. Between the 1991 and 2001 Census the Chinese community increased by 37 per cent and was the fastest growing group in the London area (Mackintosh, 2005, pp. 22–23, 130).

The impact of irregular migration and human trafficking add important introductory contextual notes to contemporary Chinese immigration and community formation. Another introductory note is that, historically, most migrants originated from the Fujian and Guangdong Provinces on China's south-eastern shoreline, with the major destination being countries in South-East Asia. A further introductory note is in the complexity contained within the term 'Chinese' diaspora. Frequently it refers to people who are ethnically Chinese but may be citizens and nationals of other countries, such as Vietnam, Hong Kong, Indonesia, Taiwan, Cambodia, Singapore and Malaysia. During the 1980s the direction of migration from Fujian changed and many began to migrate in large numbers to the United States and Europe.

This was made possible by changes to US immigration policy during the 1960s which ended Chinese exclusion (Tichenor, 2002), and also by the sympathy initially shown by Western governments towards students fleeing the repression which followed the Tiananmen Square Massacre in 1989.

Students became a significant dimension of the formation and transformation of Chinese communities in the United States and increasingly in Europe, particularly the United Kingdom, where cash-strapped universities have put a lot of effort into recruiting mainland Chinese students. Another factor in the increase in Chinese students in the United Kingdom has been the impact of tighter US immigration policies, particularly since 2001. It is likely that the number of Chinese students in Europe may soon approach the figure in the United States, where they made up 60,000 students in 2000–2001; today the number is significantly higher. China is still the major country of origin of foreign students in the United States. What is evident in the United Kingdom and elsewhere is that 'a large proportion of the working age population born in China is made up of full-time students' (Khan, 2008a, p. 3). Many indicators also make clear that after the completion of their studies overseas, the majority of Chinese students do not return home, but rather take up employment in the destination country, continue studying, or move on to another country. According to the Organization for Economic Cooperation and Development (OECD), the return rate of Chinese students in the United States over the period 1978–1999 was only 14.1 per cent. In contrast, nearly half of the Chinese students in Europe returned home (Laczko, 2003, p. 5).

The above forms the context for the development of existing and new Chinese communities. Canada is a case in point. During recent years (between 1980 and 2000) 800,000 Chinese immigrants arrived in Canada. Most (about 40 per cent) have settled in Toronto, Ontario; in the city of Toronto, with a population of 2.5 million, the Chinese community makes up the largest immigrant group and 10.6 per cent of the city population (Chu and Song, 2008, p. 611). From the mid-1990s onwards the liberal immigration regime went into reverse, as the United States and Europe introduced a clamp-down and more restrictive regulations towards people from China. It was under these circumstances that human trafficking developed into a mass phenomenon and was transformed into a multi-billion dollar business (Carling, 2007; Chin, 1999).

Hood (1998) describes a Fuzhounese exodus. By 1994, many villages had half their population living in the United States. In one case, Houyu village in Changle County, as many as 80 per cent of the entire population found its way to New York and its adjoining areas.

> Never in the Chinese immigrant experience have so many from a single locale moved so far by clandestine means within such a short period of time. Between 1979 and 1995, 300,000 to 400,000 people found their way by some combination of air, land, and sea routes to the lower east side of Manhattan. (Hood, 1998, p. 33)

Peter Kwong (1997, 1998) has been studying the Chinese-American community in New York for 25 years, for much of this time as a social movement activist, and has conducted hundreds of personal interviews with Chinese undocumented workers, from south Manhattan's traditional Chinatown to the growing Chinese neighbourhoods in Queens and Brooklyn. His work provides insight into the role of ethnic paternalism in transnational communities linking ethnic enclaves to regions of the homeland. The focus of the research has been on illegal immigration from mainland China to New York's Chinatown and its links with the rural areas of the southern province of Fujian. The Fuzhounese were relatively new and marginal within the Chinese community and for them, more than others, the use of existing ethnic social networks and resources was even more imperative in immigration and settlement, given their lack of economic power (class resources).

The basic units of Fujian rural social structure were the clans and localised unofficial civic organisations which sprang up during the Q'ing dynasty. Early Chinese immigrants, who were mainly bachelors, tended to live communally, sharing apartments to save money. Until 1965, most US Chinatowns were largely bachelor societies. This arrangement evolved into a formal collective called a *'fong'*, which literally means a 'room'. Members of a *fong* developed close relationships and great loyalty to one another. Group savings and lending associations often sprang from these circumstances. *Fongs* made up of people from the same village often acted as the basis for village associations. Also, people with the same surname often formed family or surname associations. They would raise money for good causes, such as building schools and hospitals in their home village. These associations were originally established to defend their members against a hostile world and to provide order within the community, but they also developed internal hierarchies: shopkeepers and restaurant owners became the patrons and big-shots (*'kiu ling'*) that also controlled the associations. These associations became conduits of support for immigrant workers and underpinned the Chinese labour diaspora. Finding work through friends, co-villagers and patrons often forces newcomers into a system of social obligations. The patron performs a *'ren-qing'* (personal favour) by means of *'quanxi'* (connections) and then the newcomer owes *'ren-qing'* to the patron/employer for giving him/her a job (Kwong, 1997, p. 372).

Kwong points out that the number of Chinese illegal workers in the United States is relatively small: 200,000 people out of an estimated five million illegal immigrants in the United States during the late 1990s. Unlike other immigrant workers in other cities, such as Mexicans who work for Korean greengrocers in Los Angeles, the Ecuadorians who work for Cuban garment factories in Miami and Polish and Eastern European illegals who work for Irish construction companies in New York, 'few Chinese are employed in the open and competitive labour market' (Kwong, 1997, p. 368). The liberalisation of US immigration policy during the 1960s led to an increase in the number of immigrants and major changes in the social composition of the Chinese community. The 1970s and 1980s were characterised by the mushrooming of family reunions and the arrival of many women immigrants who provided the backbone for Chinese entry as contractors and subcontractors in the New York garment industry. This experience created the material basis for analyses of the Chinese ethnic enclave economy (Zhou, 1992; Zhou, 2002).

In the case of the Fuzhounese, who were a growing proportion of the new immigration, Kwong argued that

> They are unique. They are victims of a large-scale and sophisticated international human smuggling network. After arrival in the US, they are forced to work for years under what amounts to indentured servitude to pay off large transportation debts, with constant threats of torture, rape and kidnapping. (Kwong, 1997, p. 366)

Many live with the constant double fear 'of detection by immigration officials' and the 'threat of torture from fellow Chinese debt enforcers' (Kwong, 1997, pp. 367–368). The economic relationships in this labour diaspora involve migrants from Fujian, southern China, traffickers ('Snakeheads'), labour contractors ('gangmasters') and employers in the cities of the United States. Kwong (1998) estimated that Chinese traffickers charge migrants about US$1000 as down payment, and if the migrant is delivered successfully to the destination, he or she has to pay the full fee, which ranges from $ 10,000 to $50,000 and is deducted from future wages. Rates today vary, but estimates for 2005 suggest that fees can be as high as $70,000 for a single person being smuggled from mainland China to the United States (Koser, 2008, p. 4; Petros, 2005). The debt to finance the venture typically comes from family, friends and neighbours who come under legitimate moral pressure to repay. When a person cannot borrow a sufficient sum they turn to loan sharks affiliated with the Snakeheads. In its traditional form, bonded labour involves a person who is tied, dependent, and rendering services to another person, usually the person who has advanced the loan, in relationships which are direct and clear.

Restrictive immigration policies have contributed towards making the experience of the Fuzhounese into a phenomenon found in Chinatowns in the United States and Europe, since Kwong's early description of the impact of a unique debt–bondage relationship in the structuring of New York's Chinese community. Whilst the literature focused initially on North America, there is growing research in Europe on illegal Chinese migration and the 'invisible' phenomena within these communities (Pieke, 2002; Salt, 2000; Salt and Stein, 1997; Spaan, Hillman and Naerssen, 2005; Skeldon, 2000). This literature raises challenging questions about the meaning of transnational communities and the role of immigrant enterprise as an agency of globalisation 'from below'. It also challenges much of the literature which regards the Chinese community in the United States as having better educational outcomes, higher incomes and lower rates of incarceration than other comparable ethnic groups (Portes and Fernandez-Kelly, 2008, p. 17). Zhou et al. (2008) point to significant generational social mobility. Indeed Harris et al., in their modelling of educational success, place the Chinese community in a group of Asian migrants referred to as a 'model minority', to distinguish them from other 'disadvantaged' Asian respondents. They write that the 'Chinese and, to a lesser extent, Korean display exceptional achievement' (Harris et al., 2008, p. 96).

The International Labour Office (ILO), in a Report on Chinese migrants and forced labour in Europe, writes that 'global concern with human trafficking has risen quite dramatically in recent years'. Under the ILO's Convention No. 29, 'forced' or 'compulsory' labour is defined as 'all work or service which is extracted from any person under the menace of any penalty, and for which the said person has not offered himself [sic] voluntarily' (Yun, 2004, p. 3). One manifestation of this condition appears, as Kwong observed, in the contemporary adaptation of traditional debtor–creditor bondage. The ILO noted that the contemporary form of debtor–creditor relationship was more complicated and less direct, due to the involvement of traffickers. In this instance the 'labourer does not necessarily render services directly to the trafficker but rather works in the trafficker's interest. This is a form of covered or hidden debt bondage' (Yun, 2004, p. 14).

Chinese migration and enterprise in Europe

Much of the research on Chinese immigration highlights the role of key gateway cities and harbour towns in Europe and different groups of migrants who migrated at different times and faced different historical circumstances (Benton and Pieke, 1998; Pieke and Benton, 1998; Spaan, Naerssen and Tillaart, 2005; Yu-Sion, 1998; Yun, 2004). Pieke (1998) describes how Chinese immigrants established some of the oldest immigrant communities in Europe, initially in ports such as Cardiff, Rotterdam, Liverpool and Hamburg. Before the Second World War most migrants were temporary contract labourers and many were recruited by shipping companies, sometimes as a way of undermining the unions. After the Second World War, de-colonisation and refugees from the Dutch East Indies and Indochina brought nearly half a million additional immigrants from South-East Asia to continental Europe (France and the Netherlands). Students also became a growing source of new immigration. The first independent immigration was by small merchants who originated from the hinterland of the port city of Wenzhou and built links with labour migrants, often supplying them with provisions (Pieke, 1998, pp. 3–5).

In the United Kingdom, Luk (2009, p. 575) identified the 1980s as a major 'turning-point' in the history of Chinese migration to the United Kingdom 'marking a substantial increase in the number and diversity' of the Chinese community. Unlike the original migrants of Hong Kong origin, the 'new wave' of migrants had multiple origins. The current Chinese community in the United Kingdom is made up of nearly a quarter of a million people from diverse backgrounds (Kitching et al., 2009, p. 696). The community has an age pyramid which is different to other ethnic groups, in that it is heavily concentrated in the working age group. It has the lowest representation for the 0–15 year old cohort of any other ethnic group except the Irish and other White groups (Mackintosh, 2005, p. 62; Smith, 2002, p. 659). This has important implications for future labour market needs in the ethnic economy, which are unlikely to be met without migration. During 2005, 5 per cent of work permits issued in the United Kingdom were to Chinese nationals and, of the total work permits issued, 7.5 per cent were for the catering and related sectors (Salt and Millar, 2006, pp. 344–345).

According to the Greater London Authority (GLA, 2008) Chinese people made up 3.5 per cent of the population of London in 2006, with Chinese males registering the highest rate of self-employment (at 20.8 per cent) of any ethnic group (Kitching et al., 2009, p. 692). Police raids on establishments are a not infrequent experience by Chinese-owned take-away and restaurant entrepreneurs. Many restaurants were raided in Chinatown in the West End of London during mid-October 2007. Over 200 restaurant employees reportedly took part in a three-hour strike in Chinatown on 23 October in protest against the largest immigration raid in the capital that year. Forty-nine Chinese workers were arrested for 'illegal working' during the busy lunch hour period on 11 October when 100 immigration staff and police officers raided five Chinatown restaurants. The operation in Chinatown was part of the government's intensified crackdown on illegal working. The Home Office had announced its Illegal Working Action Plan earlier that year and had stepped up workplace raids. Each week there are 60 raids in London. Robert Lee, manager of the Golden Dragon, said 'Thirty officers stormed into my restaurant. Three of my waiters and seven kitchen workers were treated like terrorists, pushed around, interrogated and handcuffed. My staff speak little English, and were so frightened by the presence of so many officers that some of them couldn't answer questions'. The majority of those arrested were Malaysian Chinese workers (Pai, 2007, p. 16).

In France, the largest source of Chinese immigration was the 145,000 refugees from Indochina who arrived between 1975 and 1987, many whom were of Chinese origin. Other immigrant groups arrived from Hong Kong, mainland China and other European countries. Yu-Sion (1998, pp. 96, 102) estimated a Chinese community of 120,000. Mung and Lacroix (2000, pp. 7, 13) estimated the number of people of Chinese origin significantly higher, at 250,000 to 300,000, with immigrants from South-East Asia (Cambodia, Laos and Vietnam) making up the majority. The intersection between ethnicity and nationality meant that many of the refugees who arrived from Laos, Vietnam and Cambodia, whilst nationals of those countries, were also ethnically Chinese. For example, of the one million refugees who left Vietnam between 1978 and 1989, an estimated '60–70 per cent of them were Chinese' (Tana, 1998, p. 233). Many of these refugees settled in Paris's main 'Chinatown' in the *Triangle de Choisy* which became the major living and working centre for Chinese settlement in France (Mung and Lacroix, 2003, p. 174).

The ranks of the Indochinese community were joined by mainland groups of migrants from Fujian and Zhejiang from the 1980s onwards (Beja and Chunguang, 1999). Collectively they withstood attempts by developers to drive them out of the *Triangle de Choisy*, which has a revealing history. From the early 1970s a number of 30-storey blocks were build in the area, which were boycotted at the time by French Parisians because of their expense and reputed lack of taste. Refugees from South-East Asia moved into the flats which by the 1980s became over-populated. Similarly, the dilapidated buildings of the Belleville area in the XXth *arrondissement* were also restored. In both cases many bought apartments in the renovated neighbourhoods and settled there between 1980 and 1985 (Yu-Sion, 1998, p. 106).

The XIIIth *arrondissement* in Paris is the centre for Chinese immigrant entrepreneurship in France, with an estimated 20.5 per cent of all firms concentrated in this one area and another 23 per cent in the four adjoining *arrondissements* of North-East Paris (Yu-Sion, 1998, p. 107). Unlike in Amsterdam, where 'Chinatown' is effectively a tourist attraction, it is also a residential area which has (paradoxically) grown as the result of urban development. In the XIIIth *arrondissement* there are a variety of Chinese and other immigrant-owned enterprises: garment manufacturing, estate agents, jewellers, bakers, butchers, grocers and driving schools, as well as more traditional activities such as catering, the manufacture of leatherwear, and furniture making.

The most significant area of expansion has been in the catering industry. The increase, primarily of restaurants, fast-food establishments and other food-related activities, has seen over half (51.4 per cent) of all Chinese-owned enterprises in Paris in this sector (Yu-Sion, 1999, p. 316). Expansion, however, has also had a qualitative dimension, with diversification by Chinese and other entrepreneurs into fusion-food, which in part, has been made possible by the role of Paris as a global city and the culinary inter-exchange this implies for the development of amalgamation between quite diverse culinary traditions. Many Chinese entrepreneurs own establishments classified as Japanese cuisine, Spanish tapas bars, Greek restaurants and Kosher Chinese food, as well as other forms. In the restaurant sector, diversification by the Chinese community into 'nouvelle cuisine' has been a significant trend.

Similarly, diversification by Chinese entrepreneurs in the leather goods sector has seen the production and wholesaling of middle- to lower-end 'designer' goods, as well as the continuation of more traditional areas of activity such as furniture making and joinery (Yu-Sion, 1999, pp. 311–317). Chinese entrepreneurs are involved in leather and garment production in many European cities. Whilst these sectors are in relative decline amongst the Chinese community in Paris, Paris remains an important centre of leatherwear production, with a long history of participation by the Chinese community. Wenzhounese itinerant merchants abandoned their trade in fancy goods and moved from the XIIth to the IIIrd *arrondissement* (the old Jewish quarter) to establish leather workshops after the Second World War. These involve the production and wholesaling of middle- to lower-end leather goods such as wallets and women's handbags. Emmanuel Mung estimated that about 140 Chinese wholesalers distributed the merchandise produced in the small workshops. One development from the 1990s onwards is that they began to distribute more products manufactured in Chinese-owned workshops imported from Italy and also from Asia (Mung and Lacroix, 2000, p. 5). Some of the workshops simply attach 'designer' labels to goods produced in centres such as Florence, Prato and Treviso. Furniture is an even more significant example. Many immigrant Chinese joiners, craftsmen and dealers are concentrated in the Faubourg Saint-Antoine in the XIth and XIIth *arrondissement* and turned it into 'the most important furniture centre of Europe' during the period 1960–1980 (Yu-Sion, 1998, p. 105). The total number of Chinese-owned enterprises in Paris increased from 1044 in 1985 to 1646 by 1992 (Yu-Sion, 1999, p. 316). Most of them show very high levels of co-ethnic employment: according to one estimate, 'somewhere between half and three fourths of the active Chinese population in France works for a Chinese business' (Mung and Lacroix, 2000, p. 10).

Economic arrangements articulated in the idiom of ethnicity are described by Mung and Lacroix (2000, p. 5) in terms of a 'Chinese economic arrangement', or 'an ensemble of interconnected enterprises...moving toward relative autonomy'. The economic circuit is presented at one level as a two-sectoral model characterised by the *intra-community market* orientated towards the (limited) Chinese household market for consumption items such as food, clothing, beauty and cultural items, and also business support and other services, accountants, real estate agents, GPs, machinery suppliers and repairers; and the *extra-community market* orientated towards non-Chinese households, such as restaurants and take-aways, or in sectors such as the garment industry and leatherwear (Mung and Lacroix, 2000, p. 9). They identify a progressive autonomy from the Chinese ethnic economic arrangement, characterised by a movement from intra- to extra-orientation and illustrated by a growing diversification of Chinese-owned enterprises in France. The concept of the 'arrangement' is used in a wide ranging manner. They write that, 'the expression "arrangement" puts the fluid and circumstantial interactions and exchanges of the phenomenon under observation, rather than insisting on a structural constraint' (Mung and Lacroix, 2000, p. 8).

The Chinese community in Italy in 1986 consisted of around 1500 people. By 1992 it had increased to 23,000, primarily concentrated in the large cities of central and northern Italy: Milan, Bologna, Florence, Rome and Turin. An equal number were estimated to be illegals (*clandestini*). Today the Chinese community is over 100,000 strong, forming in some instances *i quartieri cinesi* (Chinese quarters) in working-class neighbourhoods. Rome has the largest concentration, followed by the Tuscany metropolitan area, which includes Florence, Prato and Campi Bisenzio. This area accounted for an estimated 25,000 Chinese *clandestini* during the mid-1990s and even more today. Wong (1999, pp. 320–321) estimates that in some of the communes around Florence, 'the Chinese and Italian population are virtually equal in number'. Chinese immigrants are an important source of labour and new entrepreneurs for the small workshops of the 'Third Italy'. Immigrant groups are also central to the labour demands of agricultural sector in the south. Quassoli (1999) and Magatti and Quassoli (2003) suggest that these sectors of the economy would not function but for illegal migrant labour and the toleration shown by the political-institutional framework.

The Netherlands was the first country in Europe forced to confront issues of integration and policy towards ethnic minorities after the Dutch East Indies became independent in 1949. Over the next few years a quarter of a million 'East Indies Netherlanders' were repatriated, in what was a complex part of Dutch history (Locher-Scholten, 2003). The immigrants were ex-colonial repatriates, many of them of Chinese ethnic origins. These immigrants from Indonesia became the first major source of post-war immigration to the Netherlands, and with approximately 405,000 people they still account for the single largest group of persons of immigrant origin in the Netherlands today. Given the early arrival of many of these 'immigrants', one consequence is that about 65 per cent were in fact born in the Netherlands and are not immigrants at all (Willems, 2003). Subsequent waves followed anti-Chinese pogroms in Indonesia during 1959 and 1964 when the Chinese community took the brunt of the CIA-sponsored military coup by General Suharto. During the 1970s and 1980s this existing Chinese community in Holland and elsewhere was transformed by the arrival of new groups of non-Dutch-speaking immigrants from mainland China and Hong Kong linked to various trade and labour diaspora. By 1990 these new groups made up 64 per cent of the Chinese community in Holland (Pieke, 1999, p. 324).

Penninx et al. (1993, p. 102) write that it was not until the 1980s that the Netherlands began to see settlement as permanent and to accept the idea that immigrants 'should have the right to develop their own cultural identity' accepted by policy-makers. One (necessary) part of the definition of 'minority group' in the Netherlands, which had important implications for the Chinese community, is that in order to qualify as a minority group the Chinese community had to demonstrate that collectively they constituted a group whose 'social position is homogeneously low' (Penninx et al., 1993, p. 195). During the 1980s the Chinese community in the Netherlands were subjected to the equivalent of an ecclesiastical court, the purpose of which was to adjudicate on the question of 'whether the Chinese community was an ethnic minority or not'. This followed the mid-1980s reappraisal by the Dutch government of its ethnic minority policies, when the question was raised as to whether any additional ethnic groups should be officially recognised as minorities under government minority policies and be given additional support.

> The question of whether or not the Chinese community were a minority like any other had never been posed before because of the image of the Chinese community held by Dutch people and the Chinese themselves. The Chinese seemed to be well off; they rarely made any claim on the authorities. (Pieke, 1999, p. 326)

The above anecdotal view reinforced the image of a community which was 'self-sufficient'. At the same time, indicators pointed towards an ethnic Chinese community increasingly made up of recent mainland labour migrants who were routinely excluded from wider society and many of its services. Leaders of Chinese community organisations pointed to the needs of diverse sections of the Chinese community, ranging from recently arrived mainland labour migrants to second generation youth, in terms of expectations, and indicators of disadvantage such as unemployment, language proficiency, limited social space and general lack of integration in the wider society. Many of these indicators would have qualified the Chinese community as an 'ethnic minority'. However, for this to apply the government of the Netherlands had to accept special responsibility for the many non-Dutch-speaking mainland Chinese immigrants. This it was not politically willing to do and appointed a commission to help it find a way out of this quandary. Partly as the result of the research report written by Frank Pieke (Pieke, 1999; Pieke and Benton, 1998), the government declined to grant minority status to the Chinese community in the Netherlands.

The report gave as its reasons that

> the Chinese were not sufficiently underprivileged in terms of income, employment, education and housing [and] that minority status may have the unintended affect of stigmatizing an ethnic group, whose enjoyment of minority benefits could all too easily be seen as free-loading by the majority population. (Pieke, 1999, p. 327)

Clearly, the image of the successful restaurateur allowed anecdotal evidence to obscure the social and economic differentiation of the Chinese community in terms of immigration status, language proficiency and other intra-indicators of need amongst quite diverse members of the Chinese community. For operational purposes, the many recent migrants from mainland China who provide the labour for restaurants are assumed to have the same needs and socio-economic positioning as the established owners of the restaurants. The debate in the Netherlands may have raised more questions than it gave answers. One conclusion drawn by many in the Chinese community was that to 'be visible' opens you up to attention, scrutiny and makes you a potential target in a perverse game of musical chairs. Pieke observes (1999, p. 327) that the 'discussions left permanent scars on the Chinese community'.

Chinese-Indonesian restaurants in the Netherlands

The re-composition of the Chinese community in the Netherlands was substantially driven by the labour demands of the Chinese-Indonesian restaurant trade which was the first major concentration of ethnic minority entrepreneurship in post-war Europe (Spaan et al., 2005). A characteristic feature of the post-war boom, along with package holidays and the increased use of domestic appliances, was that more people in Western Europe were eating in restaurants and take-aways. Rising (and falling) living standards are sensitively linked to the catering industry. 'Eating-out', is often the first item to be given up when there is a retrenchment in personal budgets. The prolonged post-war boom created the material basis for the increase in the number of restaurants, but it would probably not have taken the course it did without the contribution of various Chinese immigrant flows which link Amsterdam and Rotterdam with villages in Fujian and elsewhere, in a barely understood trade and labour diaspora. The emergence of the catering sector as an early 'ethnic niche' amongst the Chinese community took the form of an adaptation of 'Chinese-Indonesian' cuisine which was initially aimed at colonial repatriates from the East Indies.

Pieke (1999, p. 323) suggests that one factor in the expansion of Chinese-Indonesian restaurants was the lack of a culinary 'tradition' of affordable restaurants for ordinary people in the Netherlands at the time (when compared to Italy or France), and that this was a pioneering experience for society as a whole. Initially the sector was monopolised by the small group of early immigrants in the cities of Amsterdam, Rotterdam and The Hague. Their success and subsequent expansion prompted chain-migration to meet the labour demand created by the rapid growth in restaurants and the exhaustion of available supplies of labour. One factor in this was second-generation resistance by young people educated in the Netherlands to entering the ethnic 'niche' of the catering trade.

By the 1980s an estimated 60 per cent of the Chinese community were employed in catering, indicating the highest rates of protracted employment concentration by any ethnic group in the Netherlands (Pieke, 1999, p. 324). Amongst entrepreneurs the rate of concentration was even higher, with 79 per cent of immigrant entrepreneurs from mainland China and 75 per cent from Hong Kong found in the catering sector (Rath and Kloosterman, 2003, p. 133; see Table 2.4, prev. cit.). The boom in Chinese-Indonesian restaurants during the 1970s also attracted other flows of immigrants. Indeed its expansion was dependent on these new arrivals. One early group consisted of workers and entrepreneurs from Hong Kong, many of whom had previously lived and worked in Britain. By the late 1970s they became the dominant entrepreneurial group. Another group were immigrants from Singapore and Malaysia. During the 1980s immigrants from Fujian became the main source of labour and a labour pool for new entrepreneurs. Today, immigrants from mainland China and Hong Kong make up the majority of the Netherlands Chinese population.

The number of restaurants increased from 225 in 1960 to 618 by 1970. Further massive expansion took place during the 1970s, and by 1982 the number had increased to 1916. Despite the impact of recession during the early 1980s, Chinese-Indonesian restaurants coped remarkably well in the face of high rates of unemployment and reduction in personal expenditure. Indeed, by 1991, the number of Chinese restaurants registered a modest increase to 1988 establishments (see Table 3.1). This can be deceptive, however. Whilst the number of enterprises remained constant, they were in many cases owned by different entrepreneurs. Most

Table 3.1 Chinese-Indonesian restaurants in the Netherlands

Year	Number	Average number	Yearly change (per cent)
1960	225	–	–
1970	618	+393	+17
1982	1,916	+1298	+17
1987	1,842	–84	–1
1991	1,988	+146	+2

Source: Pieke (1998), p. 145.

analyses points to the scissors effect of very high firm turnover rates and constant flows of new entrants willing to enter the vacated space. This illustrates one tension about the 'ethnic niche' which surfaces in the wider experience. In offering an explanation for the observed saturation in the number of restaurants, Pieke (1998, p. 145) argues that since 'new entrepreneurs learned their skills by serving as apprentices in sponsor's restaurants, new ideas could hardly penetrate the community because of its essential isolation from Dutch society'. As such, those in this pool of 'reserve' entrepreneurs appear as prisoners of the niche, in the sense that they lack not only information but also transferable skills that would allow them to enter other sectors. One dimension of the crisis and concerns over saturated markets and new arrivals 'killing the trade', were attempts at self-regulation. Some of the more economically powerful entrepreneurs, who have time to attend meetings, have formed professional and employers' associations. The largest was the Chinese section of the Dutch Catering Union with 600 members (Pieke, 1998, p. 150).

The response to the 1980s economic recession by the entrepreneurs revealed an emergent and more complex pattern. One assumption is that enterprises such as restaurants and take-aways dependent on family labour, often living on the premises, can be understood as Family Units of Production (FUPs). FUPs reveal challenging theoretical questions about enterprise functions and market incorporation. One question is over the hiring and firing of labour. A defining characteristic of FUPs, unlike clearly delineated capitalist enterprises, is that labour is a fixed rather than variable cost, and this has important implications for enterprise functions. For example it is difficult to exercise discipline over family members, or to fire one's own son, wife, mother or daughter. Nevertheless, the average number of employees of these firms did decline from 4.6 in 1982 to 2.7 by 1987 (Pieke, 1998, pp. 145–146). Other responses to the crisis were to convert restaurants to take-aways and remove the labour cost of employing waiters, and/or to move to cheaper premises in more outlying working-class neighbourhoods. Some employed cheaper illegal labour. One general response was to work longer hours. At the same time, as Pieke also notes, the restructuring of the catering sector saw the emergence of more clearly defined and market-functional enterprises relying more on hired labour, which adopted another strategy:

> The new type of Chinese restaurant that emerged in the Netherlands in the 1980s was no longer first and foremost a family enterprise but a calculated business venture aimed at profit maximisation. Location, decoration, size, menu and personnel were carefully chosen with the objective of catering for, or even creating, specific new markets, such as business lunches and dinners, exclusive parties and receptions. (Pieke, 1998, p. 147)

Trends towards profit-orientated firms responding to market opportunities outside the traditional catering sector were also identified by Leung (2002) in Germany, Mung and Lacroix (2000) in France and Krogstad (2004) in Norway. These studies observed diversification into new niche and geographical markets, as a response to market change, by new and sometimes second-generation profit-orientated enterprises. One observation from the above is that socio-economic differentiation between FUPs and more clearly delineated capitalist firms accelerated under the impact of economic crisis. This was also reflected in the development of a layer of wholesalers who act as distributors of ethnic foodstuffs for the many restaurateurs. As the Dutch economy came out of the 1980s recession, talk of the collapse of Chinese-Indonesian restaurants subsided.

The 'Third Italy': A network of informality

The production and distribution of fake designer goods is by no means the property of any given ethnic group. Nevertheless, Chinese entrepreneurs offer an example of a significant specialisation or trade diaspora in this sector. The sectoral focus, if there is one, involves clothing, leather goods (particularly, women's handbags), fashion-wear items and accessories. The most visible dimension is the hundreds of street-sellers, most of whom are not Chinese, trying to sell copies of

Cartier watches, Dolci and Gabbana sunglasses, Prada scarves, Gucci handbags and an assortment of other counterfeit designer fashion goods. These goods, which blend with legal products, are specifically targeted at tourists, both in the holiday resorts of southern Spain and also the major European city destinations, such as Venice, Paris, Florence, Madrid, Barcelona and Rome. Frequently they are sold in holiday shops owned by native workers. In Venice the army of mainly young male street-sellers negotiates amongst themselves for the best spots: those with more tourists, or wealthier tourists, or at bus and ferry stop-over points, or the best time of the day or night. There are few overheads or barriers to entry. Typically, selling involves the display of hand-held goods, or goods placed on a blanket on the ground which can be gathered up for a quick get-away from the police, depending on their attitude. Street-selling, such as that in the seaside holiday resorts is a seasonal activity, but in the perennial tourist cities such as Venice there is more scope for all-year activity (Panayiotopoulos, 2000; see also Quassoli, 1999, pp. 221–222).

The attitude of the law to street-sellers is lenient in Italy and Spain, but less tolerant in Paris and even less so in other north-western European cities. Street-selling is more tolerated in Italy than most other countries. Many of the sellers are from Senegal, but others come from China, Sri Lanka and elsewhere. In one observation made of Barcelona's seafront, which was developed to accommodate the Olympic Games of 1992, around one hundred sellers had laid down their goods on the ground on top of blankets. The street-sellers were of different colours, gender and world distribution, but all were young. Amongst a group of nine Chinese street-sellers, eight were students, three were female, and for five of them this was their only source of income to cover daily expenses (Panayiotopoulos, 2003).

The many street-sellers are the retail end-point of a production process which links tourists from all over the world to the small workshops in the 'Third Italy' and the cities of Florence, Milan, Treviso, Prato, Naples and Paris. Chinese entrepreneurs have integrated themselves into this production and distribution cycle, partly by utilising the network of existing merchants and enterprises in the cities of Europe. Yun (2004) and Yu-Sion (1998, p. 213) identified a number of labour and trade diaspora in this respect. One diaspora built on the existing community from Zhejiang and the southern regions of Wenzhou and Qingtian, in the *Arts-et-Métiers* area in Paris, where many specialise as dealers in leatherwear goods. Many of these Zhejiangnese immigrant entrepreneurs, bring with them (or so one argument runs) regional production systems from the Wenzhou area, in which each workshop specialises in the production of one part of the product, which is then assembled locally. Yun (2004, p. 6) suggests that in the Chinese trade diaspora in France and Italy involved in the production of leather goods and clothing, 'we recognise an extension of the overseas "Wenzhou Economic Model"'. Tomba (1999) pointed to the role of a Wenzhou network in Florence, specialising in the manufacture of leather handbags. It is of note that unlike most other labour migrant groups, Chinese immigrants in Italy have formed a significant number of enterprises, initially employing family members and co-ethnics, but subsequently also other immigrant groups, in sectors such as handicrafts production, restaurants, street-selling activities and the import and distribution of goods from Europe and China.

According to Ceccagno (2003), Chinese immigrants account for the largest number of small business owned by non-European Union (EU) immigrants in Italy (see also Cologna, 2005). In Milan there are an estimated 200 Chinese restaurants, and 600 leather firms which serve as an important centre for the industry. Similarly, in Rome, these two sectors dominate the pattern of enterprise and employment. In the Tuscany metropolitan region – the centre of the Italian clothing industry – many entrepreneurs have entered this sector (see Table 3.2). In Prato, 'most of the Chinese businesses became sub-contractors... to the ready-to-wear manufacturers of that city' (Wong, 1999, p. 321).

Magatti and Quassoli (2003, p. 169) write that Chinese business communities have been formed or 'exported' to other areas of Italy, both in traditional and new industrial districts. Areas such as Treviso, Prato and the hinterland of Naples have become new centres for the recent expansion in Chinese entrepreneurship. An 'industrial district' is a concept which derives from urban geography and is applied by

Table 3.2   Distribution of Chinese enterprises: Florence–Prato area

Sector	Florence	Prato	Campi Bisenzio
Leather	124	2	–
Clothing	14	261	81
Total manufacturing	*138*	*265*	*81*
Commercial	2	3	51
Restaurants	27	–	–
Other commercial activities	8	2	–
Total commercial activities	*37*	*5*	*51*
Grand total	175	270	132

Source: Tomba (1999), p. 225.

economists to an agglomeration of flexible producers, designers, contractors and subcontractors in a robust local economy (e.g. the Parisian women's fashion-wear industry). In the production and distribution of fake designer goods the 'district' is more expansive and connects cities across Europe in an ethnically informed network, linking producers in the 'Third Italy' and elsewhere with distributors such as street sellers in the major tourist cities of Europe.

Treviso in the North-East region of Veneto is historically the heart of right-wing politics in Italy and an area where there is strong support for the anti-immigrant Northern League. It is probably the nearest one gets to an Italian US-type 'Deep South'. The Mayor (Mr Giancarlo Gentilini), a leading member of the Northern League (a partner in the national coalition government), operates a policy of not tolerating mosques. In a recent interview he said 'there were never any mosques in Treviso. They tried to pray in public places but got sent away. You can't pray in a car park'. He observed further that Muslims can pray at home, 'like we do before going to bed' (Dinmore, 2009, p. 9). In a previous incident, the Mayor referred to all Africans as 'monkeys'. On the face of it, an unlikely place, institutionally, for the emergence of immigrant enterprise. It is, however, situated near Venice, which has more visitors than any other European tourist city (including Paris). During 2000 Treviso became the epicentre of a moral panic amplified by the national media about the 'phenomenon' of immigrants owning their own businesses. Researchers 'discovered' a total of 290 immigrant-owned enterprises, of which 230 had been established during a three year period (1997 to 1999). The largest grouping was 123 enterprises owned by men from the ex-Yugoslavian countries, with over 80 per cent of them in construction. The second largest group were Chinese women who accounted for 49 firms, with over 87 per cent in the clothing industry (Magatti and Quassoli, 2000, p. 16). In many cities, the emergence of a couple of hundred immigrant enterprises would not warrant this response. In Italy the 'phenomenon' of Treviso became a national issue mainly because the xenophobes, perversely, tried to use this example of immigrant innovation in the polarised debate about immigration. During this period Treviso became headline news in the Italian media.

The experience of Treviso was in fact, a concentrated example of trends in the wider Veneto region. Veneto, of which Treviso is part, is the fourth largest manufacturing region in Italy, with textiles, garments and leather products as the most significant sectors. For this reason it became an important area for Chinese labour migrants. By 2004 an estimated 12.6 per cent of all Chinese immigrants in Italy were resident in the Veneto region (Wu and Zanin, 2007, p. 9). Wu and Zanin (2007, pp. 10–11) identified a total of 2903 Chinese entrepreneurs in the region in 2005, including owners but also managers, partners and shareholders. Most of them began their activities later than in other regions and were more likely to enter manufacturing. During the decade of the 1970s only six entrepreneurs were recorded. During the 1980s this increased to 35 and during the 1990s to 312. The vast bulk of entrepreneurs, therefore, have been in operation since 2000, with manufacturing accounting for the biggest sectoral representation, followed by trade and retail (see Table 3.3).

The 'export' of a 'Wenzhou Economic Model' embedded in co-ethnic informal arrangements as an explanation for the Treviso or wider Veneto phenomenon and Chinese immigrant clustering, is, however, a limited explanation, which ignores the role of other than ethnic variables. Magatti and Quassoli (2003, p. 167) noted that Chinese enterprises in the leather goods and clothing sector 'are located in regions and cities [such as in Veneto and the metropolitan Tuscany] characterized by a traditional diffusion of informal arrangements'. They point to the only particular characteristic of Chinese-owned workshops as 'the employment of undocumented workers deeply indebted to their employers', and add that

> [Chinese] self-employment in small workshops and firms has not yet introduced any relevant innovation into the social organisation of these economic activities. On the contrary, there are exactly the same forms of organisation as in the small firms and workshops managed by Italian entrepreneurs. (Magatti and Quassoli, 2003, p. 168)

Table 3.3 Development of Chinese enterprise* in the Veneto Region by sector

Sector	1970–79	1980–89	1990–99	2000–05
Pubs/restaurants	6	30	132	609
Trade/retail	0	3	61	934
Manufactories	0	1	104	1,299
Other activities	0	1	15	61
Total	6	35	312	2,903

Note: *Owners, managers, partners, shareholders.

Source: Wu and Zanin (2007), p. 11.

In the above, Chinese entrepreneurs can be understood as an ethnic adaptation to an existing informal sector. Other explanations point to the labour content of the diaspora and in the skills held by immigrants, which might be relevant to the garment and leather-craft industries. Many of the Wenzhou immigrant entrepreneurs were tailors and leather-workers in China. One study in Paris found that none of the Zhejian business owners had ever worked for local French companies, or claimed unemployment benefit, before forming their own enterprises and in this sense, 'they form something of an exception' (Yun, 2004, p. 8). Another factor is the effect of proximity. All enterprises in the fashion-wear and accessories sector in cities in Italy and France benefit from the reputation of 'Made in Italy' leather products and 'Made in France' clothing. More significant is the impact of economic restructuring in Prato, Florence and the Tuscany metropolitan region, which saw the growth of subcontracting and which created the space for Chinese entrepreneurs to enter the lower end of garment production (such as assembling). There are indications that this was a process actively promoted by manufacturers and other intermediaries in other sectors such as leather goods, furniture and construction (Magatti and Quassoli, 2003, p. 170).

Conclusions

The conclusions return to the theoretical and practical questions raised about the capacity of enterprise to act as an agency for social integration. Much of the evidence on the entrepreneurs in the informal sector workshops of Paris and the 'Third Italy' point to a relationship between the considerable ingenuity shown by the entrepreneurs and the wider restructuring of particular sectors, sub-sectors and neighbourhoods in the cities of Europe. It is in trying to understand this relationship that the limited value of the informal sector/economy concept becomes apparent. We noted that the informal sector represents economic activity not registered for the purposes of GDP and within which labour is not protected by relevant social legislation. Whist this is a useful observation, it says little about the nature of the relationships between formal and informal enterprises. The formal–informal two-sector model rests on a legal superficiality: that suppliers and contractors are legally separate entities which are not liable for each others' action. Whilst, as we saw, this is a standard defence used by corporations in the face of corporate critics, this does not always apply (see Chapter 2).

In trying to understand immigrant and ethnic minority adaptation, perhaps a more useful working typology than that offered by the dualist thinking of a formal–informal dichotomy can be proposed: do informal enterprises emerge, and are they controlled, from 'above' or from 'below'. Partly this is an attempt to identify the degree of market autonomy enjoyed by entrepreneurs, that is, their relative capacity for independent economic action. This is a complex issue and is influenced by the economic arrangements and the nature of subcontracting in particular sectors and sub-sectors. However, 'independence' and market autonomy are ostensibly defining criteria for entrepreneurship itself, and this raises substantive questions about relationships in the informal economy. Enterprise formation from 'below' includes relatively autonomous enterprises which emerge in relation to the organic community experience, such as in response to specific demand for community goods and services or through the internal mobilisation of co-ethnic capital and labour to enter sectors and sub-sectors in which many of the entrepreneurs were previously employed as wage-workers. Enterprise formation from 'above' is often induced, synthetic, artificial and supported by native entrepreneurs 'who in cases are actually active in the establishment of ethnic business' (Magatti and Quassoli, 2000, p. 17).

Many Chinese enterprises in Florence and Prato involved in the production of leather goods were assisted in their entry by the sourcing preferences of native intermediaries. Native entrepreneurs understand the benefits of having many competing contractors and subcontractors. Subcontracting is generally used as a strategy by larger firms in order to avoid regulation and certain costs: transaction costs through transfer pricing, costs in the recruitment and management of labour, the expulsion of marginal costs in the form of heating and electricity and, more problematically, the avoidance of institutional costs in the shape of Value Added Tax (VAT), income tax and other contributions (Munck, 2007; Schierup, 2007). Subcontractors often bear the brunt of institutional and popular hostility about the 'return of sweatshops', rather than the established Italian and French firms. The expansion of contracting has been a particularly strong feature of economic restructuring in the 'Third Italy' in sectors such as garments, leatherwear and accessories. One dimension of this process has been the proliferation of small enterprises which operate outside the legal structures but are also subordinate to other companies operating on a formal basis. This has been a significant factor in placing Italy on the front line of toleration for the informal economy and innovative 'go with the grain' policies towards it (Samers, 2004). Many policy-makers see trade-offs between economic growth and the informal economy (Panayiotopoulos, 2006).

One conclusion is that the 'informal sector' was not imported, especially in the 'Third Italy' and the Veneto, by Chinese immigrants, but rather that it developed in a more complex and contingent relationship involving emergent ethnic enterprises and established native-owned enterprises underpinned by toleration shown by the state and regulatory framework. The incorporation of many entrepreneurs as subordinate contractors in structures of informality can be seen as part of a wider process of informalisation substantially driven by corporate restructuring of the fashion-wear and other sectors rather than practices associated with any particular immigrant or ethnic group. This does, however, raise major question marks for enterprise as an agency for integration and highlights the dilemma facing many entrepreneurs. It also identifies one potential direction for the new geography of migration as the need to further examine processes of informalisation, including the relationship between informal and formal economies, however defined.

In commenting on the many Chinatowns in the United States and South-East Asia, Pieke (1998, p. 13) reminds us that they 'were as much a product of racial segregation...as they were the natural outcome of Chinese cultural characteristics'. He points to differences between and within Chinese communities in Europe as partly the result of the historical 'timing' of various flows and the specific circumstances which faced them. Another factor is in the impact of 'growing social stratification within the Chinese population' (Pieke, 1998, pp. 8, 14). The relationship between the different historical circumstances faced by immigrants and the accumulated impact of social and economic stratification amongst diverse Chinese communities in Europe offers a useful avenue for future research which is equally relevant in the United States. The example of Chinese immigrant entrepreneurs in the Dutch catering industry offers insight into a Chinese community which has had a mass presence in Europe for over sixty years. The sectoral experience revealed significant variation in its responses to economic recession and restructuring. The example also shows the limits of the 'ethnic niche', when its often positively described multiplier effect went into (temporary) reverse during the 1980s recession. More significantly, given the long presence of the Chinese community in the Netherlands, the experience of the entrepreneurs also points to the limits of 'integration'.

> Specialisation in the restaurant sector, and regional dispersal, do not – contrary to some expectations and predictions – lead to integration, at least not for the first generation. (Pieke, 1998, p. 143)

If 'forced' integration means anything, it sums up the necessary experience of Chinese entrepreneurs in the restaurant and take-away trade. Substantially this comes from the nature of the 'niche' itself: catering. The industry is characterised by dispersal and isolation. Only 6 per cent of Chinese-owned enterprises, for example, are located in Amsterdam, with 81 per cent found outside the major cities (Rath and Kloosterman, 2003, p. 131). Unlike other immigrant employment concentrations, the nature of the restaurant trade did not in this instance lend itself to the physical formation of communities and neighbourhoods, such as in garment, leather and other production centres, which concentrate labour to a much greater extent in adjacent neighbouring urban districts and conurbations. This is revealed in the fact that whilst Amsterdam has a district known as Chinatown (*Chinese buurt*), it is a commercial and leisure centre, but unlike most of its counterparts in the United States or Paris, it is not a residential area.

Watson (1977, p. 181) in a pioneering study of Chinese entrepreneurs in the UK catering industry described 'a unique pattern of settlement that sets the Chinese apart from most other immigrants groups in Britain'. Whilst different from other groups, the same sectoral dynamics operating in the Netherlands were equally apparent in Britain where the restaurants, and in particular take-away enterprises, owned by the Chinese Hong Kong community were similarly widely dispersed. The impact of this on distribution was that they had 'not stayed together, and, hence, [did] not present a very significant "problem" for local authorities...they did not form ghettos'. This pattern of settlement was substantially driven by participation in the catering industry, which saw the number of enterprises peak in 1970 at 4000 businesses. One response by entrepreneurs in the United Kingdom to the 1970s recession was that many actually 'reemigrated to Holland, Belgium, Germany' (Watson, 1977, p. 183). As with the experience in the Netherlands, in the United Kingdom, the social geography of Chinese people indicates that they are 'the most diffused ethnic group in the country, with the least visible residential concentration' (Luk, 2009, p. 595).

The idea that the Chinese community in the Netherlands and Britain is more dispersed, and if this is an indicator of 'integration', more 'assimilated' than any other ethnic group, is not the image projected by politicians or researchers who see a discrete, 'achieving' minority unwilling to integrate and affected by human trafficking and the activities of criminal gangs. Many Chinese entrepreneurs are economically 'integrated', whilst at the same time excluded from most functioning parts of civil society. The nature of the work itself precludes much scope for social contact and the nature of their contact with society in work time is limited to superficial and subservient relationships. Long hours of work mean that few social spaces are available when the restaurants close. At that time in the morning, gambling places and casinos are some of the few places which are still open, and this is one major reason why many workers and entrepreneurs meet in these places to socialise.

In conclusion, it is worth reflecting for another reason on the Dover tragedy in the United Kingdom, during which nearly sixty illegal Chinese immigrants died. The local Kent Police refused to let relatives identify their loved ones until they first volunteered information about those who trade in refugees. Relatives, even though they had legal status in Britain, were too scared to claim the bodies (Lam, 2000). Ethnic stereotypes perpetuated about the Chinese community in Europe and the United States frequently focus on the Chinese community as an 'impenetrable' community, with illegal workers 'living in clandestinity and without legal rights of residence' (Yun, 2004, pp. iii, 8). It is hardly surprising that illegal workers want to remain invisible and very likely that this kind of institutional behaviour would drive people even further into the margins. Unlike other tragedies, there were no public announcements of sympathy or condolences from politicians or religious figures over Dover. One week after the deaths a demonstration to defend refugees made its way through London's Chinatown led by a group of Chinese restaurant workers (who in a rare show of militancy were trying to unionise their workplace) carrying a banner saying '58 Dead – Nothing Said'.

The demonisation of human traffickers and the informal economy distracts attention from the role of the regulatory framework and the extent to which traffickers and informal economies are a response to immigration policies which make it almost impossible for many Third Country National economic migrants to enter and work in a European Union country legally. In these circumstances the capacity of enterprise to act as an agency for integration is being severely tested. Whilst this impacts differently on different sections of the community, the wide-spread panic about Chinese immigration to Europe raises questions about the extent to which the current generation of mainland migrants will be able, as did many members of previous migrant groups, to make the transition from worker to entrepreneur.

4
Hispanic American Entrepreneurs in the United States

Introduction

The term 'Hispanic' is used to describe a wide range of Spanish-speaking immigrants and ethnic minorities from South and Central America and the Caribbean countries. It is interchangeable in US Census material with the term 'Latino'. The economic 'success' of the Cuban Hispanic community in Miami has seen the term Hispanic used to describe an 'achieving' minority. The Cuban community is a spatially concentrated community of political exiles and entrepreneurs who have transformed Miami into a global city and hub of the Americas. When the term 'Hispanic' is used in analyses of the Mexican, and Central American Hispanic presence, however, it often used to refer to social indicators which are considerably lower than those for Black Americans, and the concept of a reserve army of labour is widely used to describe the positioning of Mexican migrants in urban centres such as Los Angeles. More Black Americans than Hispanics in Los Angeles are college graduates, and fewer of them are found amongst the low paid. Many Hispanics also have to live with the fear of deportation. This chapter examines this contradictory representation of ethnicity and identifies factors which influence the positioning of different Hispanic groups and entrepreneurs in the United States. One factor appears in the role of the political–institutional framework and processes of racialisation in the incorporation of immigrant groups and ethnic minorities. Frequently this involves exclusion from US citizenship. Another appears in the intersection between ethnicity and race and ethnicity and class. The chapter concludes that the interplay between these factors may be more relevant to analyses of ethnic adaptation and segmented assimilation by Hispanic communities in the United States than attributes associated with national origins and variations of Hispanic identity.

Hispanic North America

The US Census conducted during 2000 enumerated 35 million people of Hispanic origins resident in the United States, compared to 22m in 1990. They made up 12.5 per cent of the population and had overtaken Black Americans as the largest minority in the United States (Camarota and McArdle, 2003). In 2002 it was estimated that there were 37.4 million people of Hispanic or Latino origin in the United States: more than one in eight people. The vast bulk was made up of people of Mexican origins (66.9%) while Cubans constitute a small section of the Hispanic community (at 3.7%) which is considerably smaller, not only in relation to the much larger Mexican Hispanic group but also to those with origins from 'old', Puerto Rican (at 8.6%), and 'new' Central and South American (14.3%) groups. Nearly seven out of ten people of Hispanic origins lived in the South and West of the United States, with the West making up 44.4 per cent of all Hispanic-origin people resident in the United States. Cubans were highly concentrated in the South (at 75.1%). Hispanics were also far more likely (at 45.6%) to live in inner cities or metropolitan areas when compared with Whites (at 21.1%) (Ramirez and de la Cruz, 2003, pp. 1–2).

According to US Census Bureau projections for 2050, persons categorised as Hispanic Americans are expected to increase to one in four of the US population. Asian Americans are expected to increase to nearly one in ten, and Black Americans are expected to register a smaller increase, from 12 to 14 per cent. Those described as 'Non-Hispanic White' are expected to decline to 53 per cent of the population. US government projections for 2050 pointed out that by 2010 the Hispanic-origin population were already the second largest race/ethnic group and that after 2020 it would add more people to the United States than all other race/ethnic groups combined. From 2030 to 2050 it is expected that the non-Hispanic White group 'would contribute nothing to population growth' (US Census Bureau, 2004).

One indicator of the Hispanic economic presence in North America is the estimate from The Inter-American Development Bank (2006a) that before the current economic crisis, Latin American immigrants in the United States had a total estimated income of more than $500 billion. A corollary of this has been the growth in advertising spending on Spanish language television by leading companies. This echoes the observations made by Sassen (1988) about economic restructuring in New York's construction industry during the 1980s and 1990s. As the industry experienced severe labour shortages, particularly in foundation excavations and trenching, as well as in highly specialised craftwork, such as stone cutting, masonry and plastering, it began to employ skilled Hispanic workers. Some of them became subcontractors, as Sassen noted, 'in an industry where Hispanics were excluded not long ago' (see also Hernandez, 2002).

That Miami has been transformed, substantially by Cuban Hispanic entrepreneurs, into a global city which serves as an important continental intermediary between Latin and North America, is axiomatic in the literature. During the 1990s accounts held by Latin American citizens in Miami were reputedly the equivalent to the total debt owed by Latin American countries to private creditors and the World Bank. The view of the Cuban community in Miami as an 'achieving minority' is widely held. Frequently, studies write of the 'remarkable success' of the Cuban exiles or the 'unique character' of the Cuban experience. Portes and Bach (1985, p. 268) in comparing Cuban and Mexican Hispanic groups, conclude that due to the absence of spatial clustering by co-ethnic owned firms which generated large numbers of jobs, Mexicans and, in particular, recent immigrants from Mexico are incorporated into 'low wage labor in the open economy', whilst Cubans benefited from a setting dominated by co-ethnic business networks and entered the ethnic economy. Waldinger (2001, p. 318) pointed to Miami as part of a peripheral region of the world economy and not particularly fertile ground for social mobility amongst immigrant groups. It has a limited manufacturing sector, a small representation of professional and advanced services and lacks opportunities when compared to other US cities. All the more remarkable then, as Waldinger writes, that it is 'still possible to conclude that the Cuban story is one of success'. Clark (2003, pp. 213–214) in a study of immigration and the remaking of the American middle class, points to Cubans as an 'achieving' minority and writes that 'the children of Mexican immigrant meat packers in Omaha, Nebraska, do not have the same advantages as children of Cuban businessmen in suburban Dade County, Florida (Miami)'.

Portes and Jensen (1987) pointed to the role of the 'ethnic enclave economy' in Miami as causal explanation for the positioning and repositioning of the Cuban Hispanic community formed by different waves of immigrants and exiles. As we noted in Chapter 1, they argue that the enclave, with ethnic enterprise as its epicentre, acts as 'an effective vehicle for upward mobility among immigrant minorities' (Portes and Jensen, 1989, p. 930) or as 'a vehicle for first-generation upward mobility' (Portes and Jensen, 1987, p. 769). They propose, contrary to most notions of conventional sociology about integration, that, immigrants in the enclave-labour market, far from being disadvantaged in separation, receive earnings/returns to human capital commensurate with the earnings/returns of immigrants in the primary labour market.

In Los Angeles and the wider state of California, opposite conclusions are offered. California is the world's eighth largest economy and creates immense labour demand, particularly for Hispanic immigrants. Mexican immigrants have always provided the labour force for the (seasonal) agricultural economy of California. Tichenor (2002) pointed to the two-tiered regulatory regime operating during the 1930s and 1940s, which denied admission to Jewish refugees fleeing for their lives but allowed the legal and illicit importation of Mexican labour for California's rural economy. Martin (1994) noted that agriculture has been the major side door and back door through which unskilled immigrants have entered the United States for the past half century, nowhere more so than the State of California. Immigration patterns during the 1980s–1990s showed that up to one-quarter of the working-aged immigrants who arrived during the period had their initial US employment in fruit and vegetable agriculture.

Hispanic immigrants provide most of the labour in the service sector (as cleaners, janitors, porters and domestics), in the construction and garment industries and other areas of mainly manual employment. Los Angeles has the largest concentration of garment production in the United States and has (after Chicago) the second largest concentration of manufacturing employment in the United States. The industry would find it difficult to exist in its present form but for Mexican women workers and entrepreneurs. Similarly, by the 1980s the New York City garment industry became dominated on the production side by the Chinese and Hispanic (Dominican) immigrant communities. By the end of the 1990s the garment industry in New York City was still the major manufacturing employer with 133,000 workers producing more than one in four dresses made in the United States, despite relocation by leading manufacturers out of the city. Of those employed, an estimated 33 per cent were Hispanic and 27 per cent Asian immigrants (Zhou, 2002, pp. 115–120).

An important characteristic of the Hispanic community in the Los Angeles region was the growing significance of the foreign-born as a proportion of all Hispanics. During a 20-year period (1970–90) the number of foreign-born Hispanics increased from 400,000 in 1970 to 2.359 million in 1990. In 1970 they made up over a quarter of all Hispanics and by 1990 over half. The Hispanic experience in Los Angeles became even more linked to a migrant experience. Another dimension appeared in a growing role of 'new wave' Hispanic migration, drawing mainly from Central and South America, which by 1990 made up over one-quarter of all foreign-born Hispanics (see Table 4.1). The experience for many of these migrants and particularly the undocumented workers amongst them was that the migrant experience was also a precarious experience. In the United States, 'illegals' account for 24 per cent of all farm workers, 17 per cent of cleaning workers, 14 per cent of construction workers and 12 per cent of those in food preparation. These sort of figures demonstrate that irregular migration is part of the fabric of US capitalism, that it is structural in character and 'deeply embedded' in the economy and in social relations (Shelley, 2007).

The Hispanic presence in North America was reflected not only in increasing numbers and entry into new sectors but also in a new and significant development in the form of increased regional and geographic dispersion across the United States, in response partly to better

Table 4.1 Population of ethnic groups by nativity, Los Angeles Region (CMSA*), 1970–90

Ethnic Group/Nativity	1970	1980	1990
Hispanic	1,399,600	2,862,120	4,697,509(a)
Native-born	1,001,400	1,665,980	2,338,369
Foreign-born	398,200	1,196,140	2,359,140
Asian	256,200	596,080	1,326,559
Native-born	147,600	222,640	414,427
Foreign-born	108,600	373,440	912,132
African-American			
Native-born	778,700	1,026,800	1,114,269
Foreign-born	2,300	17,000	31,415
White			
Native-born	6,577,500	6,425,560	6,494,372
Foreign-born	506,000	450,980	398,884
All Other	88,600	243,640	432,419(b)
Native-born	55,200	144,360	214,596
Foreign-born	33,400	99,200	217,832
Total native-born	8,868,600	9,485,340	10,576,033
Total foreign-born	1,090,300	2,136,840	3,919,394

Notes: *Consolidated Metropolitan Statistical Area: includes Orange, Riverside, San Bernadino, Ventura and Los Angeles Counties; (a) Of these, 3,718,383 are Mexicans of whom 2m were native born; (b) Of these, 300,546 are 'Middle Easterners' (including Iranians) and 62,533 American Indians.

Source: Sabagh and Bozorgmehr (1996), pp. 3, 95–96.

employment opportunities and partly the high cost of housing and overcrowding in centres such as Los Angeles (Light and Johnston, 2009). McConnell (2008, p. 767), in a study of the destinations of Mexican immigrants in the United States, pointed to the combined effect of human capital and social networks, and the previous occupational and residential experience of the migrant. The study found that the 'legal status of migrants clearly differentiates between destinations with unauthorised workers choosing small traditional areas rather than the larger urban destinations' (McConnell, 2008, p. 790). The above trends suggested a loosening of ethnic channelling in the incorporation of Hispanic labour. One indication of the changing Hispanic presence is the pattern of remittances sent back home by migrants. The Inter-American Development Bank estimated that Latin American and Caribbean workers living in the United States sent some $53.6bn in remittances back to their homelands in 2005. The volume has grown dramatically during the past decade and remittances are higher than foreign direct investment and overseas aid in most countries in the region. Mexico is the top recipient and its migrants sent home around $20bn, up from around $16.6bn in 2004 (Inter-American Development Bank, 2006a). As can be expected, states with long-established Hispanic communities (California, Texas, New York and Florida) are still the biggest sources of remittances. New data from the Inter-American Development Bank (2006b), however, indicated that some of the largest increases in the volume of remittances took place in Georgia, Virginia, Maryland, Pennsylvania, Tennessee, Indiana, Wisconsin, South Carolina, Arkansas, Kansas, Kentucky, Nebraska and Iowa, which have all seen increases of more than 80 per cent over the past two years. This indicates the increasing geographical dispersion of Hispanic labour in North America.

Much of this went into reverse as the crisis which began in the US housing and financial markets and led to a full blown recession, typified by housing repossessions and rising unemployment, impacted severely on Hispanic working-class America. Claims made by researchers working for the US Bureau of Census, even as late as January 2009, that 'a Mexican immigrant (perhaps with the exception of new arrivals) does not rely on a network to find a job. There are many, many jobs available in Los Angeles' (Hellerstein et al., 2009, p. 19), were sounding increasingly hollow. The unemployment rate in the United States pushed through the 10 per cent barrier by November 2009. According to the Pew Hispanic Center, among Hispanic immigrants the unemployment rate was higher, at 11.5 per cent. Construction, in which many undocumented workers are employed, and for whom there is no government safety net, had reduced the numbers employed by one-fifth since the recession began. 'Undocumented', 'unauthorised' and 'illegal' immigrants constitute over one-tenth of US labour (Ilias et al., 2008; Pew Hispanic Center, 2006). It was widely reported across the US labour market that the supply of willing workers had overwhelmed demand and as a result wages were falling. This was reflected in remittances, which the Inter-American Development Bank expected to drop 11 per centby the end of 2009. Only a quarter of Hispanic immigrants who lost their jobs managed to keep sending remittances and many were living on their savings. There were cases reported of 'reverse remittances' as families in Mexico 'wire money north of the border' (O'Connor, 2009, p. 10). The above indicates that whilst the Hispanic economic presence is an entrenched factor in the United States, it is also subject to cyclical fluctuation and affected by economic upturn and downturn.

The social, economic and political adaptation of people of Hispanic origin in Los Angeles is particularly complex. It is the most diverse metropolis in the United States. It is a Black, white, Asian but, above all, a Hispanic city. Waldinger presents a vision of an enduring pluralist society: 'ethnic Los Angeles is here to stay' (Waldinger, 1996a, p. 470). But at the same time, it is a city characterised by structural inequality and underpinned, as Davis (1992) points out, by growing social polarisation and gated development. It is the US city with the greatest gulf between rich and poor and has an estimated 30 per cent of its population living below the poverty line (Gumble, 2002, p. 12). Hispanics in Los Angeles show social indicators lower than those for Black Americans. Whilst nearly four out of ten Black Americans are college graduates, amongst Hispanics the proportion is nearer one in seven. More Hispanics are found amongst the low paid than amongst Black Americans (see Table 4.2). High school drop-out rates amongst Hispanic youth range from two

Table 4.2 Population of Los Angeles and key social indicators in the State of California by ethnic group (per cent)

	Per cent of Los Angeles population		Indicators State of California*	
Ethnic group	1970	1990	Income less than $20,000	College graduates (per cent)
White	71	47	8	46
Hispanic	14	32	26	15
Black	8	8	15	36
Asian	2.5	9	7	64

Note: *Indicators refer to State of California for 2000.

Source: Parkes (2002), p. 11.

to four times the rate amongst whites. California is home to about half the children in the United States deemed 'disadvantaged' by Limited English Proficiency (LEP). There are 1.4 million LEP children in the state – accounting for a quarter of California's school population – with half of them living in the LA metropolitan region (Parkes, 1998, p. 12).

In this context, Portes and MacLeod (1996) commented on the adoption by second-generation Hispanic children in Los Angeles of the general label 'Hispanic' as opposed to hyphenated American terms (such as Cuban-American):

> Contrary to the commonly-held assumption that the label 'Hispanic' denotes greater assimilation into the mainstream of US society, our findings indicate that children who adopt the Hispanic label are the least well assimilated: they report poorer English skills, lower self-esteem and higher rates of poverty than their counterparts who identify themselves as Americans or as hyphenated Americans. (Portes and MacLeod, 1996, p. 523)

An expanding literature on second-generation Hispanic youth has provided important insights into the contradictory positioning of members of the same ethnic group, which goes some way towards answering the pessimistic conclusions drawn by social conservatives such as Huntington (2004a,b) about a 'Hispanic challenge' driven by second-generation decline (Perlmann and Waldinger, 1997; Portes and Zhou, 1993; Waldinger and Feliciano, 2004). Much of this literature refers to segmented assimilation to describe the diverse possible outcomes of the process of adaptation. Portes and Zhou (1993) argue that outcomes amongst the growing new second generation in the United States present a new set of questions which cannot be predicted from the experience of their parents or indeed from the experiences of previous migrant flows to the United States. Portes's model of the Cuban enclave as a form of incorporation into American society assigns a key role to outcomes amongst second-generation youth. In examining the incorporation of Haitian youth in Miami, Portes (1995) described pressures and processes of racialisation leading to 'downward assimilation and mobility' amongst the 'foreign' residents of 'Little Haiti', adjacent to Cuban Liberty City, where second-generation Haitian children are sometimes made fun of for their Haitian accents. This group find themselves torn between conflicting ideas and values: 'to remain "Haitian" they would have to face social ostracism and continuing attacks in school; to become "American" (Black American in this case), they would forgo their parents' dreams of making it in America' (Portes, 1995b, p. 249).

In the case of Cuban second-generation youth, Portes points to the benefits (and costs) of a strong and authoritarian community. He suggests that in the Cuban enclave, ethnic solidarity was grounded in exceptionally dense relations revolving round a strong common cultural memory based on exile, which attempted to replicate home country institutions. This, so the argument runs, allows for a greater intensity of social networks, which make even more social capital available, and which can also be applied as an agency of parental 'social control'. Portes argues that this lowers 'the probability of downward assimilation', but at the same time reminds us, in commenting on what are effectively ideas rooted in ethnic competition, that 'there is at present no data set for any immigrant group that allows a rigorous test of the hypotheses' (Portes, 1995b, p. 262).

Analyses of segmented assimilation are considerably weaker in explaining the role of the political–institutional framework in shaping the terms of adaptation. A key factor in explaining the structuring of Hispanic incorporation in the United States and elsewhere has been the effect of institutional behaviour towards different groups of Hispanics. The Cuban anti-communist exiles were defined as a favoured client group of US immigration policy, until the *Marielitos* arrived en masse in 1980, whilst Mexican immigrants were, and are, seen purely in instrumental terms as an economic recourse.

Immigration policy is often structured by the racialisation of populations through immigration controls and nationality regulations which valorise groups of people, often by using notions of race difference (Carter et al., 1996). Racialisation is a particularly strong feature in the incorporation of Dominican, Cuban and other recently arrived immigrants from the Caribbean. Denton and Massey (1989) pointed to the particular racial traditions of the United States as ones which reduce racial taxonomy to a Black–White bipolarity. This subsumes the diverse racial codification common to the Hispanic and French Caribbean. C. L. R. James (1980), for example, described in *The Black Jacobins* the legal system of the French colony of Haiti as one which recognised 147 different shades of colour between black and white. Denton and Massey (1989, p. 790), in a breakdown of the 1970 and 1980 US Census data relevant to Hispanic identity and race, showed that in residential terms, 'people of mixed racial ancestry are accepted by white Hispanics on the basis of shared ethnicity but are rejected by

Anglos on the basis of race'. Further, that 'Anglos will view people of mixed race as black no matter how they see themselves' (Denton and Massey, 1989, p. 802).

Similarly, Rosenbaum's (1996, p. 217) research on the influence of race in Hispanic housing choices in New York City, indicated that racial status determined Hispanic residential choice and that 'white Hispanics are more successful than black Hispanics and other-race Hispanics in gaining access to predominantly Anglo sub areas, apparently by virtue of their non-black status'. This line of inquiry reveals the persistence of a particular model of race in the structuring of American society. More significantly, perhaps, it reflects on the incorporation of immigrant groups: the most recently arrived entrants into 'Americanisation'. In the case of immigrants from the Caribbean, people who have never thought of themselves as 'black' in their own countries have been forced to do so in the United States. Practically, this means that Hispanics of different colours are defined as 'black' independently of how they see themselves, and come under intense pressure in the United States to live in similar (racially segregated) neighbourhoods as those of other Black Americans, whilst many white, middle-class Hispanics have the option – and many exercise that option – of moving out of the neighbourhood and defining themselves by their racial rather than ethnic characteristics. The relationship between race, ethnicity, class, gender and other intersections is an important, re-occurring and growing theme in Hispanic adaptation in the United States. Black Hispanics make up approximately 3.7 per cent of the Black population. About 65 per cent of foreign-born Blacks living in the United States are born in Latin America and they form the material basis for the new social hybridity around the term 'Black Hispanic' (McKinnon, 2003, p. 1; US Census Bureau, 2007, p. 15).

An even more significant indicator in the positioning of Hispanic groups appears in the political ranking and the legal status of foreign-born persons by the institutional framework, and in whether foreign-born persons are citizens or not. According to The American Community Survey 3-Year Estimates, 1157 million people in Miami and 3482 m in Los Angeles were classified as foreign born. Those described as 'foreign-born not a US citizen' made up just over half of the total in Miami and 56 per cent in Los Angeles. Among those who described themselves as Hispanic or Latino, 72 per cent in Los Angeles and 82 per cent in Miami were non-citizens. The largest group were those aged 25 to 44 who made up nearly half of all foreign-born non-citizens in Los Angeles and 41.9 per cent in Miami. In both Los Angeles and Miami, wage-workers made up the vast bulk of the employment category (see Table 4.3; US Census Bureau, 2008a,b).

In terms of sectoral employment there are some differences between the two urban conurbations which are shaped by the make-up of the local economy, with manufacturing playing a more significant role in Los Angeles and retail and office employment more significant in

Table 4.3   Selected characteristics of the native- and foreign-born populations in Los Angeles and Miami–Dade County

	Native-born		Foreign-born naturalised		Foreign-born non-citizen	
	Los Angeles	Miami	Los Angeles	Miami	Los Angeles	Miami
Total	6.340	1.187	1.529	0.586	1.962	0.611
Male	49.7	49.6	46.3	43.6	51.4	50.9
Female	50.3	50.4	53.7	56.4	48.6	49.1
Age 25–44	22.7	21.8	32.4	23.4	49.7	41.9
Race and ethnicity						
White (alone)	37.3	29.9	21.1	6.9	8.3	5.3
Black American	12.8	27.3	1.8	10.8	1.4	12.6
Hispanic + Latino	40.9	41.9	42.4	80.6	72.0	82.1
Asian	6.3	0.7	33.9	2.5	17.9	2.1
Education						
Less than High School	10.7	14.5	28.1	24.9	50.0	31.3
With college degree	32.4	27.2	21.8	23.7	12.6	16.0
Language at home						
English only	66.2	54.5	10.2	8.8	5.3	6.3
Other language	33.8	45.5	89.8	91.2	94.7	93.7
Employment						
Self-employed	8.1	4.8	10.9	7.9	11.2	12.7
Wage-workers	75.9	76.6	76.4	79.3	84.4	83.5
Occupation						
Service	13.3	16.0	17.7	16.5	25.8	26.0
Production	8.0	6.8	14.9	10.1	24.7	14.9
Management	41.9	37.7	34.7	33.6	15.4	17.2
Retail + office jobs	30.7	33.3	25.4	31.8	18.4	22.9
Construction	6.0	6.2	7.2	7.9	15.3	18.3
Earnings						
Median male	53,282	44,757	43,358	41,000	25,023	26,052
Median female	43,032	36,325	37,009	31,776	20,495	19,802
Between $15–24,000	12.0	15.7	16.0	19.4	34.7	32.7
$75,000 or more	26.6	19.6	19.2	15.3	6.1	5.2
Poverty rate						
> 100% poverty line	14.2	15.5	9.3	12.8	22.2	20.5
Families in poverty	7.8	10.9	8.5	9.0	24.7	19.4

Continued

Table 4.3   Continued

	Native-born		Foreign-born naturalised		Foreign-born non-citizen	
	Los Angeles	Miami	Los Angeles	Miami	Los Angeles	Miami
Housing						
Per cent owners	53.7	63.5	57.8	72.1	25.8	39.0
Rent as % of income						
Less than 30%	50.2	44.9	46.4	40.1	39.8	32.2
30% or more	49.8	55.1	53.6	59.9	60.2	67.8
Owner cost 30% +	40.7	43.8	50.1	59.5	64.5	67.8
1.1+ occupants per rm	4.3	3.1	12.2	3.9	32.1	9.1

Note: Black American includes Black and African Americans; White alone excludes Hispanic; Wage and salary workers in private sector; Management, professional, and related occupations; > Below 100 per cent of poverty line; Occupants per room.

Source: US Census Bureau (2008a,b).

Miami. Earnings show that the largest group in both areas was made up of those earning $15–24,000, with a slightly higher representation in Miami for those earning over $75,000. The rate of self-employment amongst foreign-born non-citizens in Los Angeles was 11.2 per cent, compared with 8.1 per cent for the native born. In Miami 12.7 per cent of foreign-born non-citizens were self-employed, compared to 4.8 per cent of the native born. In both cases the self-employment rate was marginally higher than that for foreign-born persons who had acquired US citizenship. (see Table 4.3, prev. cit).

In separate statistics using language spoken at home as the unit of analysis, 15.4 per cent of Spanish and Creole speakers in Miami–Dade County were described as 'living below the poverty line' with 26 per cent having less than high school level education. At the same time 24.8 per cent have a Bachelors degree or Higher. Over one-third (34%) of foreign-born Spanish speakers are citizens in Miami. In Los Angeles County, the proportion in the Hispanic group living below the poverty line stands at 20 per cent, and a much larger number have less than a high school education (49%), with only 9.1 per cent having a Bachelors degree or higher. The number of foreign-born Spanish speakers who are citizens is also significantly lower at 17.5 per cent (US Census Bureau, 2008c,d).

Much of the above points to indicators of difference which cannot be fully understood, if at all, by comparing Hispanic Americans in Miami with those in Los Angeles, or Hispanics with another ethnic group. Whilst these kind of approaches provide useful insight into what is happening to members of an ethnic group, when compared to another group (Harris et al., 2008; Portes and Fernandez-Kelly, 2008; Zhou et al., 2008) they cannot reveal how an ethnic group is socially, economically and politically differentiated internally, or that different, and often predictable, outcomes are possible for members of the same ethnic group. The collapse of social groups into aggregate ethnic categories not only disregards anything we know from conventional sociology about social stratification but also disguises and excludes this possibility. A review of social and economic indicators, such as earnings, housing costs, educational attainment and poverty, shows that more significant differences appear between Hispanics who are native born or foreign born but naturalised, and those who are foreign born but not citizens, than can be explained by factors which can be attributed to the nature of the local economy or variations of Hispanic ethnicity in Los Angeles and Miami. At the same time, there are indicators which point to harsher circumstances in the human condition in Los Angeles when compared to Miami. For example, foreign-born non-citizens in Miami are more likely (at 39.8%) to own their home or to be paying a mortgage, when compared to those in Los Angeles (at 25.8%). In both cases, however, home ownership is much lower than amongst the native-born and also foreign-born persons who have acquired US citizenship. One revealing indicator is that only 9.1 per cent of the foreign-born non-citizens in Miami are likely to live in over-crowded conditions, involving cohabitation of more than one occupant per room, whilst in Los Angeles the rate is much higher, at 32.1 per cent. Amongst the native born in Los Angeles the rate is 4.3 per cent (see Table 4.3, prev. cit.).

Hispanic enterprise

A substantial account of Hispanic enterprise was presented in the 2002 Survey of Business Owners (SBO), released in 2006, which provided separate reports on ethnic minority enterprises and was part of the Economic Census for the same year. This combined survey data from a sample of more than 2.4 million businesses with administrative data. The Survey indicated that the number of Hispanic-owned firms increased by 31 per cent between 1997 and 2002, or three times the national average for all businesses, to nearly 1.6 million enterprises which generated nearly $222 billion in revenue, up 19 per cent from 1997. Hispanic-owned enterprises were defined as firms in which Hispanics own 51 per cent or more of the stock or equity of the business. The Survey indicated that Los Angeles County, with 188,472, and Miami–Dade County, with

163,188 enterprises, accounted for the most significant concentrations. The highlights for Hispanic-owned enterprises, showed that

- Nearly three in ten Hispanic-owned firms operated in construction and other services, such as personal services, and repair and maintenance,
- Firms owned by people of Mexican origin accounted for more than 44 per cent of all Hispanic-owned firms,
- Retail and wholesale trade accounted for 36 per cent of Hispanic-owned business revenue,
- There were 29,184 Hispanic-owned firms with receipts of $1m or more,
- There were 1510 Hispanic-owned firms with 100 employees or more, generating more than $42bn in gross receipts,
- States with the fastest rates of growth for Hispanic-owned firms between 1997 and 2002 included New York (57%), Rhode Island and Georgia (56% each), Nevada and South Carolina (48% each),
- Counties with the highest number of Hispanic-owned firms were Los Angeles County, California (188,472); Miami–Dade County, Florida (163,188); Harris County, Texas (61,934); and Bronx County, NY (38,325). (Source: US Census Bureau, 2006a,b)

The vast bulk of the 1.5 million Hispanic enterprises consist of the self-employed, with only 200,000 (12.6%) of the firms employing more than their owner. These firms were responsible for employing a total of 1536 million workers. Amongst Mexican-owned enterprises, 12.7 per cent employed at least one other person; amongst Cuban-owned enterprises the figure was higher, at 18.3 per cent. The average employment size in

Table 4.4 Hispanic-owned enterprises by ethnic sub-group and number of employees

| | | Firms with employees | |
| | | --- | --- |
Hispanic or Latino-owned enterprises	**All firms**	**No. of firms**	**Employment (000s)**
Total Hispanic or Latino	1,573,464	199,542	1,536,795
Mexican/Mexican American/ Chicano	701,078	89,285	720,288
Cuban	151,688	27,863	206,032
Puerto Rican	109,475	11,830	77,266
Other Spanish/Hispanic/Latino	596,000	67,326	503,620

Source: US Census Bureau (2006a), table 1.

Cuban-owned firms was 13 workers, and in Mexican-owned enterprises it was 12 (US Census Bureau, 2006a, see table 1) (see Table 4.4).

A comparison of Cuban- and Mexican-owned enterprises in Los Angeles and Miami shows that whilst, as one might expect, there are more Mexican than Cuban-owned firms, a similar number were found in the category of firms which employ other workers with, in Los Angeles, 15,805 Mexican-owned firms and in Miami, 16,860 Cuban-owned firms, employing other workers. More detailed analysis of the level of employment and annual payroll shows that in Miami nearly one in five of Cuban-owned enterprises employed more than their owner and had an average rate of employment of 17 workers per firm. Among the larger number of Mexican-owned firms in Los Angeles a significantly smaller number, fewer than one in ten, employed more than their owner and had an average employment size which was also lower, at 10.6 persons per firm. However, in terms of the annual payroll, Cuban-owned firms in Miami had a lower payroll at $2.792bn when compared to Mexican-owned firms in Los Angeles, which had an annual payroll of $3.417bn (see Table 4.5). This suggests that workers are more squeezed in Miami.

Table 4.5 Hispanic-owned enterprises in Miami and Los Angeles by employment and annual payroll

		Firms with employees		
	All firms	**No. of firms**	**Employment (000s)**	**Annual payroll ($1,000)**
Miami				
Total Hispanic or Latino	206,047	30,069	161,351	4,294,448
Cuban	94,960	16,860	100,540	2,792,634
Mexican/Mexican American/ Chicano	8,024	880	5,490	82,555
Puerto Rican	12,796	1,127	8,085	170,091
Other Spanish/Hispanic/Latino	86,771	10,336	42,623	1,106,786
Los Angeles				
Total Hispanic or Latino	277,858	25,703	239,492	5,634,645
Mexican/Mexican American/ Chicano	174,292	15,805	148,032	3,417,387
Cuban	6,809	866	11,528	277,002
Puerto Rican	NA	NA	NA	NA
Other Spanish/Hispanic/Latino	88,537	7,906	71,000	1,705,289

Note: Miami–Fort Lauderdale–Miami Beach, Fl Metropolitan Division; Los Angeles–Long Beach–Riverside, CA Combined Statistical Area.

Source: US Census Bureau, (2006a), table 5.

Mexican Hispanic enterprise in Los Angeles

A significant factor in the positioning of Hispanic workers in the Los Angeles economy is in whether they are immigrants or native-born. This was revealed in a study by Ellis and Wright (1999) who examined the role of 'ethnic channelling' in structuring the pattern of employment amongst recent immigrants and native-born workers in the metropolitan Los Angeles area between 1970 and 1990. During this period Los Angeles received about 400,000 foreign-born and 575,000 native-born workers. The greatest employment concentration was amongst Mexican immigrants in agriculture, in which they were twice more likely to be employed than Mexicans born in the United States. Other immigrant concentrations were in manufacturing, where Hispanic women accounted for 33.0 per cent of all employment, and in the garment industry, where they made up of 33.7 per cent of the labour force. Hispanic and Asian women are often seen as close labour market substitutes by employers, both in the garment industry and also the personal service sector (Scott, 1996, pp. 222–223; also see Hondagneu-Sotelo, 2001; Ehrenreich and Hochschild, 2003).

Ellis and Wright pointed to greater employment concentration by more recent immigrant groups as confirming the influence of ethnic networks in the channelling of recent immigrants and internal migrants into sectors where co-ethnics and co-nationals were concentrated. At the same time they noted that industrial distribution is also a function of individual human capital and skills and this leads to gravitation towards sectors where their skills are in greatest demand, rather than any ethnic channelling. For example, 'unskilled workers are more likely to find work in the ethnic niches than the skilled' (Ellis and Wright, 1999, p. 31). They suggest that 'job placement of recent arrivals will depend on some combination of skills and network connection' but hypothesise 'that ethnicity will be a more important determinant of sectoral employment than skill for recent immigrants' (Ellis and Wright, 1999, pp. 29–30).

An important sectoral manifestation of ethnic and gender channelling appears in the garment industry: an industry which coped remarkably well with imports which devastated the garment industry in other places. During 1982–1992 US garment manufacturers shed one in ten jobs; in New York the rate was even higher, at over one in three jobs (35 per cent). By contrast, sectoral employment in Los Angeles increased during the same period by one-third, with the estimated number of garment workshops in Los Angeles County up from 2332 in 1970 to 6364 in 1996 (Nutter, 1997, p. 200). Light and Ojeda (2002, p. 151) argue this was 'mainly as a result of its superior access to immigrant labour'. Whilst this is debatable, what is not in dispute is that in Los Angeles, as in New York, the sector acted as a key point of entry for Hispanic entrepreneurs and workers and that Los Angeles today is the centre of the largest concentration of garment production in North America. In California the sector employs an estimated 120–140,000 workers in over 5000 factories and countless homes (Light and Ojeda, 2002, p. 152; Nutter, 1999, p. 201).

Most of the sewing machinists in the garment industry are women, and official statistics exclude the employment of homeworkers, who are almost all women and typically not registered. An estimated 30 to 50 per cent of value generated by Los Angeles garment contractors was produced by homeworkers and unregulated workshops. Over 90 per cent of home-workers came from minority backgrounds with most of them recent immigrants (Portes, 1994, p. 435; see also Fernandez-Kelly and Garcia, 1989). Bonacich and Appelbaum (2000, p. 150) estimated homeworking amongst Korean-owned but Mexican-employing firms at 40 per cent of the total labour force. Nutter (1999, p. 207) notes that the labour force in the garment industry consists primarily, in ethnic terms, of Hispanic women. Mexican women make up three-quarters of the labour force, and other Central American Hispanic groups make up an additional 10 per cent. Asian workers, primarily from China and Vietnam, make up another 15 per cent. The majority have arrived in United States during the last 15 years and 'most are undocumented'. Sources of labour and the ethnicity of employers are listed (see Table 4.6).

Table 4.6   Ethnic groups in the Los Angeles garment industry

Entrepreneur by ethnic group	Per cent	Workers/labour supply by ethnic group
Hispanic/ Mexican	36	Mostly Hispanic (mainly Mexican, also Central American)
Korean	19	Mostly Hispanic and also Asian (Chinese, Vietnamese, Korean)
Vietnamese	13	Mostly Southeast Asian (Cambodia, Laos) and also Hispanic
Chinese	9	Only Chinese
Other Asian	10	Mostly Hispanic and also Asian
Other, Anglo, Armenian, etc.	13	Mostly Hispanic

Source: Nutter (1997), p. 205.

Relations in the Los Angeles garment industry are not substantially different from the standard structure of subcontracting involving retailers, manufacturers and Cut Make and Trim (CMT) units, which is applied in many situations. Bonacich (1994, p. 140) points to one variation which is indicative of the weak position of contractors in Los Angeles. Rather than the standard CMT pattern, many contractors were MT units: they received already processed work from the manufacturer in the form of bundles of cut fabric, which they simply sew and trim. The workshop has less capacity for value-adding or 'informal' appropriation of the manufacturer's fabric. At the same time, this further reduces the cost of entry by disposing some of the most expensive workers (cutters) and equipment, such as cutting tables. In Bonacich's (1994) study of Asian entrepreneurs, the most common configuration was one of Korean employers and Hispanic women workers. Light and Ojeda (2002, p. 155) estimated that 87 per cent of the employees of Korean-owned garment enterprises were Hispanic. Bonacich argues that the (Korean) contractor is the 'immediate' but not 'main' exploiter of the (women Hispanic) workers, but also adds that Korean contractors became the 'direct recipients' of the (justified) wrath of the workers (Bonacich, 1994, p. 152). In this, Bonacich notes parallel discussion on the buffer role of 'middleman minorities'. Since the research conducted by Bonacich, there has been an expansion in the number of Hispanic-owned enterprises and Hispanic entrepreneurs are highly represented in this sector, making up 38 per cent of all entrepreneurs (see Table 4.4, prev. cit.).

Bailey-Todd et al. (2008), in a study of apparel industry business patterns in Los Angeles, point to an industry which over the last 30 years has been making a long transition, repositioning itself as increasingly design and marketing intensive, while outsourcing many low-value added activities to offshore contractors Despite these trends, Los Angeles County continues as 'the only remaining area of the United States that boasts a strong onshore apparel manufacturers' (Bailey-Todd et al., 2008, pp. 260–262). Half of all firms employed fewer than nine workers.

At the same time, the garment industry and Hispanic immigrants in California have been on the front line of the return of an aggressive American nativism demanding tough controls against 'waves' of illegal immigrants. One aspect of this has been the idea that the 'sweatshop' is making a comeback in the US economy and that it is underpinned by undocumented Mexican labour in sectors such as garment production. Roger Waldinger (1996a, p. 445) writes that in Los Angeles 'with good times gone, the region's hospitality to outsiders disappeared'. Light and Ojeda (2002, p. 155) write that as the 'supply-driven' influx of Mexican workers increased, 'immigrant wages generally declined in Los Angeles, as did social conditions', particularly in the garment industry. As the media and politicians publicised negative conditions in immigrant workshops, it was the workers themselves who were targeted.

One proposition advanced by Ong and Valenzuela (1996, pp. 167–168) is that immigrants from Mexico and Central America are taking jobs from African Americans through a 'substitution effect'. They argue that whilst this is influenced by whether workers have similar skills, and even more so by their lack of them, it commonly occurs where 'a profit-maximising firm replaces workers from one group with workers from another group'. Scott (1996, pp. 236–237) writes that African American workers in Los Angeles have 'been ousted from manufacturing labour markets by immigrants' and that as Mexican and other Hispanics have moved into expanding industrial sectors in the region, *'their presence* [italics added] has come to constitute a set of barriers that have impeded African Americans'. Waldinger (1996c, p. 1078) wonders pessimistically 'how America's post-industrial cities can integrate the latest wave of newcomers just when the opportunities for native minorities seem to be at lowest ebb'. In the analyses above, Hispanic immigrants are presented as labour market substitutes for lower-level jobs in hotels and restaurants, domestic work, janitors and sewing machine operators, 'which African Americans formerly held' (Waldinger, 1996a, pp. 452–453).

Light et al. (1999) challenge the idea that Hispanic immigrants are 'taking over' jobs from African American or other native-born workers. They suggest that existing migration network theory, applied by authors such as Scott, Ong, Valenzuela and Waldinger, 'exaggerates the extent to which hyper-efficient immigrant networks deprive native workers of jobs, thus exaggerating the conflict of economic interest between native and immigrant workers' (p. 8).

Migration network theory applied to explain Hispanic migration purports to show how migration networks create self-sustaining labour flows, which in gathering momentum begin to act independently of factors which initiated migration in the first place. Light et al. (1999) point to the limited use of migration network theory and argue that, as a theory of labour transfer, it does not take into account the labour demand created by the expansion of immigrant-owned enterprises typically involving the employment of other immigrants in an expansive immigrant enclave economy. In the garment industry this led to a situation where 'immigrant-owned [Korean] firms were pulling non-co ethnic [Latina] immigrant workers into Los Angeles' (p. 16). Light et al. make the observation that labour demand outstripped available supplies of co-ethnic (Korean) labour and entrepreneurs began to recruit from any available immigrant labour source. They argue that far from immigrants 'taking jobs' away from native workers, they create employment, typically linked to the employment of other immigrants, and this is a significant factor in the continuity of, for example, the garment sector in urban centres such as Los Angeles, New York, London, Amsterdam and elsewhere (Panayiotopoulos and Dreef, 2002; Rath, ed., 2002). One estimate on the labour force composition of the Los Angeles garment industry indicates that only 6 per cent of the labour force consists of native-born Americans who are employed by native-born American entrepreneurs (Light and Ojeda, 2002, p. 156).

Light et al. (1999) used the term 'immigrant enclave economy' purposefully to describe the Los Angeles garment industry as an expansive labour market formation underpinned by high levels of ethnic interspersion in ownership and in the composition of the labour force. This approach raises questions for analyses rooted in ethnic competition, which point to ethnic economies in general or their adaptation into specific ethnic enclave economies as commonly characterised by the hiring of co-ethnic workers.

Cuban Hispanic immigrants in Miami: An 'achieving' minority

Mexican immigration to the State of California accounts for most movement by Hispanic immigrants to the United States, but nowhere is the presence of Hispanic enterprise more apparent than Miami. Whilst Cubans are a small proportion of Hispanic immigrants in the United States they are highly concentrated in Dade County, Florida (which includes Miami). The number of Hispanic residents in Miami increased from tens of thousands in 1960 to one million by 1990 and substantially drove the quadrupling of Miami's population from half a million to two million people. Over half of all Cuban immigrants in the United States arrived before 1980 (Clark, 2003, p. 36; Portes and Stepick, 1993, p. 210). Portes and Jensen (1989) have pointed to the Cuban community in Miami as an 'enclave economy' in which, far from disadvantaged by separation, Cuban workers receive earnings/returns similar to immigrants employed in the open labour market. The ethnic enclave economy appears as a concentrated example of the ethnic economy. It characterised by exceptionally high spatial concentration, with 65 per cent of all Cubans in the United States living in the Miami Metropolitan Area alone. This makes them 'far more concentrated in one place than any other group' (Waldinger and Lee, 2001, p. 48). Because it is an enclave made up of people who have acquired US citizenship, it has also, over time, assumed the role of a political enclave.

The Cuban Hispanic presence in Miami originated in the political exiles who fled Cuba after the Revolution, with approximately 135,000 people arriving between 1959 and April 1961. This experience of a community of exiles underpins analyses which point to the 'exceptional' nature of Cuban Miami: a picture 'unlikely to have been encountered elsewhere' (Waldinger, 2001a, p. 315), or as an 'economically undetermined' development of 'a city more the product of chance and individual wills than of geographic or commercial imperative' (Portes and Stepick, 1993, p. 204). Whilst the Cuban community began as a collection of anti-communist exiles, which gave it particular characteristics, it has also been transformed by the historical circumstances which faced it.

A key point in the transformation of the Cuban community in Miami was the experience of the *Marielitos*. They fled a collapsing Cuban economy characterised, at the time, by a shortage of basic foodstuffs and medicines. By 1980 the economic situation was so dire that even black Cubans – the bedrock of the Cuban Revolution – had had enough and were leaving in droves. Sieges of foreign embassies to obtain exit permits and organised flotillas from Miami funded by relatives to ferry the *Marielitos* initially characterised the events. Hundreds of boats picked up over 125,000 people from the Port of Mariel or on the high sea, with most of them landing in Dade County. This gave way to mass and disorganised waves of 'boat people' heading towards Florida on anything that floated, with Miami and family reunion in many cases as the goal (Portes and Stepick, 1985). At the same time, thousands of Haitian refugees were also similarly escaping poverty and political crisis and also headed for Miami and New York. During mid-May something like fifty thousand people were camped in emergency accommodation in the Orange Bowl and in public land.

The arrival of many working class and black *Marielitos* was a shocking experience for the established white Cuban community in Miami. One white Cuban-American official commented that 'the *Marielitos* are mostly Black and mulattoes of a color that I never saw or believed existed in Cuba' (quoted in Portes and Stepick, 1993, pp. 21, 47). *Mariel* refugees were subjected to exceptional hostility, with newspaper stories of 'undesirables' and 'Castro emptying his jails' fuelling hostility. They were

stigmatised by US officials, the Cuban government and by the existing Cuban community in Miami. In *A Statement by the Revolutionary
Government of Cuba*, published in *Granma*, the official organ of the
Central Committee of the Communist Party of Cuba, Cuba's position
on the *Marielitos* was made perfectly clear. They were referred to as
'common criminals and lumpen elements', or 'criminals, lumpen and
anti-social elements and parasites'. *Granma* further commented that
'to judge from their dress, manners and language, seldom has such a
"select" group gathered anywhere' and went on to say that

> Even though in our country homosexuals are not persecuted or har-
> assed, there are quite of few of them in the Peruvian embassy, aside
> from all those involved in gambling and drugs who find it difficult
> to satisfy their vices here ... Good riddance to the parasites! Good rid-
> dance to the antisocial elements! Good riddance to the lumpen! Good
> riddance to the scum! ('Cuba's Position', *Granma*, 7 April 1980)

The White House also took a hard line on mass asylum for the Cuban
and Haitian boat people commonly fleeing poverty. It decided that if
intercepted at sea they would not be allowed to enter the United States.
This, as Tichenor (2002, pp. 278–279) noted, 'marked a significant break
from three decades of treating all Cuban escapees as refugees' and contrasted with the 300,000 admissions of Indochinese refugees between
1975 and 1979 alone, all admitted under executive paroles (Portes and
Rumbaut, 2001, p. 275). The widely held belief that Cuba was emptying its jails and dumping undesirables on the shores of Florida legitimised changes in US immigration policy. This view was confirmed in
one study, which indicated that 42 per cent of all those who left Cuba
through the Port of Mariel had previous convictions. The single largest category of migrants came from Cuba's poor, as is indicated in the
40 per cent of all those with previous convictions involving crimes
against property (primarily theft). The second largest group of convictions (10.8 per cent) were for 'crimes against the normal development
of sexual relations', charges used routinely to criminalise Cuba's gay
community (Portes and Stepick, 1993, p. 21). Far from being 'lumpen',
the *Marielitos* probably represented a far more accurate reflection of the
breadth of Cuban society than the white, middle-class and ruling-class
exiles which fled Cuba in 1959. One reflection on the class composition
of the *Marielitos* was in their principal occupations in Cuba, which show
that over one in four (26.8 per cent) were craft workers and another
44.0 per cent were operatives, including transport operatives or labourers

(Fernandez, 2007, p. 605). For some of the refugees their first introduction to America was Ku Klux Klan members burning crosses on beaches and shouting 'Spics Go Home'.

This atmosphere was compounded by the Anglo-dominated Citizens of Dade County, who placed on the ballot box for referendum during the same time a proposition that would have prohibited expenditure of any county funds for the purpose of using any language other than English or any culture other than that of the United States. The 'English Only' campaign, directed primarily against Cubans but also other Hispanics, 'galvanised the refugee community into creating its first self defence organisations' (Portes, 1984, p. 395). The defeat of the anti-bilingual proposal gave the community a new-found confidence. In a manner similar to the experience of Irish immigrants in mid to late nineteenth century New York, the 1980s saw the consolidation of Cuban control of local political institutions. With the capture of City Hall the Cuban political patrons 'started to remake the city in its political own image' and to impose its 'monolithic outlook on the city, often with little regard for the concerns and interests of other sections of the population' (Portes and Stepick, 1993, p. 138).

One (of many) examples, which summed up the intolerance of the Cuban political elite in Miami, involved Nelson Mandela. During summer 1990 the recently released Mandela was to arrive in Miami. The black community were exuberant about the visit from a leading figure of black liberation. When Nelson Mandela said that he considered Fidel Castro as a friend, who had helped in the struggle against apartheid (an opinion that was public knowledge),

> Over the strenuous objections of Black community leaders, the Cuban-American mayors 'uninvited' Mandela. Although [he] came for a brief speech at a union convention and never accepted any local invitation, the mayors' action profoundly hurt Miami's Black community. (Portes and Stepick, 1993, p. 141)

The 'success' of the Cuban community in Miami has been substantially explained by Portes, Wilson, Stepick and Jensen as the function of the ethnic enclave economy. The thesis purports to show that the Cuban ethnic enclave laid the basis of its own development in large part through its internal redistributory capacities and functions. The conventional argument points to the 'bounded solidarity' and the social capital of political exiles as the essential mechanisms in their transformation from political exiles into ethnic entrepreneurs. For example, employers can come under pressure to assist co-ethnic workers who are often family members in their own entry into entrepreneurship and self-employment. This was facilitated by shared language and culture combined with closely knit social networks and practices, such as patronising other Cuban-owned businesses and preferring other co-nationals as business associates. Portes and Jensen argue that they are not advancing a 'separate but equal' proposition. As they write,

> enclave workers and businessmen are neither 'separate' (because their activities are closely intertwined with the broader economy), nor necessarily 'equal' (because new arrivals are often much worse off in terms of occupational status and income). (Portes and Jensen, 1987, p. 769)

The ethnic enclave economy thesis originated in Wilson and Portes' (1980) analyses of the Cuban enclave-labour market in Miami. To Wilson and Portes, the enclave was made up of the large bulk of men employed in Cuban-owned firms. They began with concerns about the labour market because they were trying to understand the experience of the majority of the Cuban community who, like other communities, are wage-workers. In doing so, Wilson and Portes conceptualised the immigrant refugees and political exiles as a peculiar example of labour transfer. Whilst the thesis was subsequently developed to include the self-employed, wage-workers and employers, one weakness remains in the non-disagregation of these quite distinct employment categories and income groups.

Wilson and Portes (1980) argued that in Miami, protracted intra-Cuban economic relations differed in intensity from those typically associated with other Hispanic ethnic economies and that substantial clustering and 'dense' co-ethnic linkages gave the Cuban ethnic economy a particularly strong 'enclave' character. Few Cuban businesses existed in Miami before 1962 and in this period the CIA was 'one of Miami's largest employers' (Portes and Stepick, 1993, p. 126). Portes and Stepick summarise the early experience of the Cuban enclave as a response to constraint and opportunity. Opportunity appeared in the substantial ethnic Cuban market, which generated the basis for many small firms and the self-employed, and in privileged access to a pool of cheap co-ethnic labour enjoyed by the entrepreneurs. Constraint appeared mainly in barriers to accessing the commercial banking sector. By 1987, nearly 35,000 Cuban-owned enterprises existed in Dade County and Miami Metropolitan Area. The vast bulk consisted of the self-employed, but a significant proportion (one in six) employed other workers (Portes and Stepick, 1993, p. 182).

Entry into enterprise followed a predictable sectoral trajectory: gas stations, grocery shops and restaurants were amongst the first areas in which businesses were established. Many used their skills as carpenters, plumbers and bricklayers to enter construction. They 'created their own home repair businesses by buying a truck and going door-to-door seeking work' and, by 1979, approximately 50 per cent of major construction companies in Dade County were Cuban-owned (Portes and Stepick, 1993, p. 133). From this followed entry into real estate. Many who entered low capital sectors, restaurants or construction, either as self-employed, or as owners of small enterprises, generated employment for other Cubans. These sectors are amongst the easiest to enter and as such generate immense competition. Ethnic solidarity networks in the enclave were used to generate 'character loans', as a means of circumventing restricted access to the commercial banking sector. Many mainstream banks, however, quickly realised the economic potential of the Cuban enclave and responded through the employment of Cuban staff and venture lending in which character acted *as* collateral. This implied more than the standard commercial knowledge, complicated by ever-changing credit managers. Portes and Stepick summarise the experience of one Cuban entrepreneur's experience of differing banking styles as follows:

> The American banker looks only at the balance sheet of the company. If he [sic] doesn't like it, he doesn't give you the loan. The Cuban banker has a different technique: he looks for signs of your character. If he knows you, knows that you will meet your obligations, he lends you without looking at the balance sheet ... they often even knew their families in Cuba. (Portes and Stepick, 1993, p. 133)

Perhaps the most favourable conclusions which can be drawn about the Cuban ethnic enclave are presented by Light and Gold (2000, pp. 97–98) in analyses of the post-*Mariel* environment. In comparing Cuban and Haitian refugees, they point to the existence of a vibrant Cuban immigrant economy in Miami, which was responsible for absorbing nearly half (46.1%) of the *Marielitos*. Amongst Haitian refugees employment in the immigrant economy stood at less than 1 per cent (0.7%). Among Cuban refugees those in self-employment made up 15.2 per cent of the total and a larger proportion (30.9%) were working in co-ethnic owned enterprises. A larger proportion still was employed in the general

Table 4.7   Cuban and Haitian refugees: Employment in Miami, 1980 (per cent)

Type of economy	Cuban *Mariel* refugees	Haitian refugees
Immigrant economy		
Self-employed	15.2	0.5
Working in co-ethnic firm	30.9	0.2
General labour market		
Unemployed	26.8	58.5
Employees	27.1	40.8
Total	100.0	100.0

Source: Stepick (1989), cited from Light and Gold (2000), p. 44.

labour market (37.1%) or was unemployed (26.8%). Amongst Haitian refugees 40.8 per cent were employed in the general labour market and the unemployed made up over half (58.8%) of the total (see Table 4.7).

Conclusions

The chapter concludes that Hispanic adaptation either as workers or entrepreneurs is influenced by their membership of an ethnic group. It is also influenced, however, by intersections with legal status, class, gender, race and other ways in which members of an ethnic group are socially differentiated. Yet attempts at explaining segmented assimilation and inter-generational mobility among diverse migrant groups in Los Angeles (Zhou et al., 2008) and much of the wider literature do not factor into their analysis the influence of social differentiation and citizenship in explaining divergent pathways to mobility among members of a second-generation group. Studies of 'integration', acculturation and adaptation usually tend to assess human capital by focussing on measurable indicators such as English language proficiency. Carter-Pokras et al. (2008, p. 484) argue that these proxies 'do not fully capture aspects of the US-born or immigrant experience'. Rather they focus on health disparities, using health as a proxy indicator for acculturation. They found that 'US-born Mexican-Americans have a higher morbidity and mortality compared to Mexico-born immigrants'. One crude deduction is that the longer Mexicans live in the United States the sicker they become. Whilst the reasons for this are debatable, this kind of thinking directs our attention towards the use of more meaningful indicators of adaptation which recognise both the 'heterogeneity' between the Mexican-origin group and, per-haps, the effects of institutional behaviour (Carter-Pokras et al., 2008, p. 475).

One salient lesson in the emergence of racial and ethnic identities in the United States is that many Hispanic immigrants discovered that they were 'black' in the United States. Processes of racialisation mean that whilst Hispanic adaptation is frequently presented as the reconstitution of an ethnic group, black Hispanics also find themselves impacted by US racial bipolarity and this exposes them to racial segre-gation in housing. Frequently the outcome is that they either become a segment living side-by-side with black America or for institutional purposes an anonymous section of Black America. The social differen-tiation of Hispanic communities in this and other ways raises questions about the basis of segmented assimilation, future outcomes and also who benefits from the ethnic or immigrant enclave economy.

Golash-Boza and Darity (2008, p. 900) criticise conclusions about the projected increase of the Hispanic population in the United States for assuming that 'current patterns of racial and ethnic identifications can be used to predict future identification patterns without taking into account the possibility that Hispanics' racial and ethnic identification can and do change'. They point to the failure to account fully for the relationship between race and ethnicity in Hispanic identity as a major fault-line in predicting outcomes for future generations of Hispanics in the United States. They point to 'volatility' in the formation of social hybridity but at the same time argue that 'skin color and experiences of discrimination affect whether people from Latin America and their descendants who live in the United States will choose to identify racially as black, white or Latina/o'. They conclude that 'some Hispanics will become white, others black, and not all are likely continue to identify as Hispanic' (Golash-Boza and Darity, 2008, pp. 899, 930). In terms of future trajectories for those who 'become' black, official statistics show that over one-fifth of all Black Americans have less than high school education and about a quarter lived below the poverty line before the onset of the current recession (US Census Bureau, 2007, p. 4). The impli-cations of Golash-Boza and Darity's argument, whilst useful, can be criticised for being over-structurally determined and for making similar assumptions to those it is critical of, in drawing from what we know about US racial classification to extrapolate future projections. This attaches little value to agency and excludes the possibility that US racial categorisation based in bipolarity, itself, may change under the impact of a growing Black Hispanic and mixed race presence.

Nevertheless, Fernandez (2007, pp. 612–614), in a study of the consequences of *Marielito* stigmatisation 20 years later, noted that the proportion of non-White *Marielitos* is greater than for all other groups (of Cubans), with about 18 per cent being non-White. Most, like other Cubans, continue to live in Florida. The *Marielitos'* economic incorporation, however, was found to be different and lagging behind in terms of unemployment, earnings and the proportion living below the poverty line when compared with other Cuban groups.

The ethnic enclave economy thesis as an explanation for immigrant incorporation and social mobility amongst members of the Cuban Hispanic community in Miami, but not Los Angeles, raises particularly challenging questions. One telling criticism is the argument presented by Sanders and Nee which constitutes a theoretical defence of the key lesson learned from conventional sociology; namely, that exclusion, and in particular the persistence of racial exclusion, in the United States has generally not been in the interest of most members of the excluded group. They point out that the central plank of the Civil Rights Movement in the Southern States was for faster integration. They argue that the enclave economy hypothesis 'contradicts the classical assimilation view that segregation retards the economic achievement of minorities' (Sanders and Nee, 1987, p. 745). In counter-defence, Portes et al. argue that the enclave economy thesis can be seen as an alternative model of integration which remains critical of conventional models of incorporation within which 'Americanisation' rather than the acceptance of cultural diversity was, and remains in large part, the end product. They invite studies on the social and economic development of second-generation immigrant workers and entrepreneurs, and the extent to which the ethnic enclave has acted in the long term (and by tortuous detours) as an agency for economic and social integration.

Sanders and Nee (1987, p. 745) point to the need to reformulate the enclave economy hypothesis so that it is 'sensitive to important differences between immigrant workers and immigrant bosses'. They question the methodology applied by Portes et al. for failing to make a distinction between self-employment and the employment of others and for ignoring previous findings (Portes and Bach, 1985, pp. 205–216), which 'report significant [income] differences between workers and bosses in the Cuban enclave', when estimating returns to human capital (Sanders and Nee, 1987, pp. 747–748). Similarly, an investigation which factored in the legal status of the many self-employed and ethnic employers who are foreign-born might, other things being equal, reveal significant differences between entrepreneurs who are foreign-born but natural-ised and those who are foreign-born but non-citizens.

Frequently 'success' depends on what we are measuring. If we are measuring average returns to labour in the immigrant or ethnic economy when compared to the general labour market, as is the case with the ethnic enclave thesis, then this would disguise the possibility that entrepreneurship might produce a small but significant number of high income earners and a large mass of low-paid hired workers. If we were to measure the redistributory impact of immigrant enterprise in income terms by class, gender, age and race, we might see differing trends and outcomes for different sections of the Cuban enclave. We note, for example, that in Miami, character loans are effectively class loans. Professionals and white-collar workers and 'those who brought money and contacts from Cuba...were more likely to access character loans' than workers or the *Marielitos* (Portes and Stepick, 1993, p. 128).

The Cuban Hispanic community in Miami is socially stratified and the growing complexity of the enclave is reflected in generational dif-ferences. At one level there are differences between 'first' and 'second' generation immigrants. At another level, there are qualitative social differences between different waves of refugees. The elite exiles that fled Cuba in 1959 and the *Marielitos* exodus in 1980 represented differ-ent sections of Cuban society. The working-class and black *Marielitos* faced far more difficult circumstances than the exiles from 1959, who found an early niche as political entrepreneurs in the anti-commu-nism industry. The elitist attitudes shown by the original group of exiles towards the *Marielitos* and other groups, such as Haitian and Nicaraguan refugees, have alienated popular sections in society and this has provoked a growing (class) polarisation inside the Cuban com-munity. In one survey of perceptions and experiences of discrimina-tion by *Mariel* refugees carried out in 1983 (three years after *Mariel*), 75 per cent of a random sample of 520 believed that 'Mariel Cubans are discriminated against by older-established Cubans' and that 52 per cent had 'personally experienced [such] discrimination' (Portes and Stepick, 1993, p. 33).

Pedace and Rohn (2008, pp. 22–24) found that 'enclaves do not provide net economic benefits to wage and salary earners' and that the overall impact of the ethnic enclave economy for both males and females is characterised by 'significant negative wage effects'. 'Although', they add, 'the foreign-born may benefit from social and cultural activities' and that 'enclaves may provide the desired social benefits for temporary workers'. In conclusion it is, perhaps, worth noting that the original formulation of the ethnic enclave economy by Wilson and Portes did not differ greatly from the conclusions presented for the US Bureau of Census by Pedace and Rohn. Neither did it make claims to universality. Rather, it pointed to the incorporation of Cuban refugees in a dense ethnic economy as substantially a first-generation survival mechanism. The development from this empirical observation to the ethnic enclave economy thesis as a theoretical explanation and alternative model for migrant integration into mainstream American society, as well as its subsequent adaptation to explain labour market incorporation among a multitude of ethnic groups, is something which came later.

One conclusion about the ethnic enclave thesis is that the case cannot be proven. In order to show that the enclave economy has redistributory functions which result in social mobility for all or most members of an immigrant or ethnic group, we need to move beyond a trickle-down theory of income distribution and returns to human capital. We need to know more about the social, political and economic structure of the enclave and how this impacts on the lives of different section of Cuban society in Miami over time. In important ways the benefits of the Cuban Hispanic enclave economy do not appear potent enough to alter the disadvantages faced by immigrants. Cuban-Americans have fewer professionals than other immigrant groups. Cuban, like Mexican immigrants, are 'more likely to be managers' than owners (Clark, 2003, p. 112); similarly, in levels of home ownership – a key indicator used by Clark as constituting 'middle class' status – 'a large number of Cuban households never managed to become owners, and those who did were not able to sustain the ownership rate' (Clark, 2003, p. 134). Roger Waldinger, comparing the relationship between education and employment amongst Cuban (and other immigrant groups) with the native-born, comments on claims made by the ethnic enclave hypothesis, and suggests that

> the presence of a Cuban business sector does nothing to depress employment opportunities among immigrant men. Low-skilled and relatively recent Cuban immigrants fare no differently than white high school graduates in the likelihood of holding a job...the employment niche occupied by Miami's Cubans is not particularly impressive. Working Cubans are a good deal less likely than low-skilled whites to hold adequate jobs, which in turn generates a wide gap between Cuban men and comparable white natives. (Waldinger, 2001b, p. 104)

Further, on Cubans who are recent arrivals, he suggests that they

> are about as likely as their Mexican, West Indian and Dominican counterparts elsewhere to be adequately employed, a finding hard to reconcile with the notion that Miami offers Cubans a distinct mode of entry into the US economy. (Waldinger, 2001b, p. 105)

The above does not detract from the remarkable role played by Cuban entrepreneurs in the transformation of Miami. It compares very favourably with most international comparison of refugee outcomes. It is quite unusual, for example, for an immigrant refugee group to capture local political power within a generation. This is all the more remarkable given the particularly difficult circumstances faced by different waves of Cuban refugees. The Marielitos were demonised and discriminated against for their colour, their poverty and perceived or actual sexual orientation. Yet they managed with little official assistance, indeed in the teeth of opposition by both Anglos and the established Cuban community, to make or earn a living.

One graphic illustration of economic 'success', is that the Cuban ethnic enclave has outstripped available supplies of co-ethnic labour for low-paid sector employment. In part this is driven by the ageing of the Cuban population in the United States, a decline in the size of households and second-generation resistance to entry into the niche sectors, if alternatives are available. In itself, this is not unusual, and can be found in the experiences of other immigrant groups and the histories of other ethnic communities. One significant factor in this instance arises from the unusually high demand for labour created by the vibrant economy of Miami. This is sucking immigrant workers into Miami and the wider Florida economy, and increasingly entrepreneurs from other Hispanic groups and from a wide geographical area which has added to the previous flows of refugees from Central America during the 1980s. According to current US Census material, out of the total of 206,047 Hispanic or Latino-owned enterprises in Miami, a minority, 94,960 are Cuban owned. Of firms with employees, however, most are Cuban-owned, and these accounted for 62 per cent of employment and 65 per cent of the payroll (see Table 4.5, prev. cit.).

A surge of immigration from other Hispanic groups over the past decade – from Central and South America, as well as north-east US states such as New York and New Jersey – has relegated Cuban-Americans to a minority status in Florida's Hispanic community. Cubans are just 31 per cent of the state's 3.2m Hispanics: less than the combined total of people of Mexican and Puerto Rican origins (Chaffin, 2004, p. 12).

These trends are likely to continue, since Cubans in the state tend to be older and have fewer children and are not likely to be replenished by new waves of boat-people in the immediate future. These demographic trends are even more pronounced in Miami–Dade County region. Puerto Ricans are the largest non-Cuban group, accounting for 18 per cent of the state's Hispanics. One consequence – since Puerto Rico is a US territory – is that they are eligible to vote, and this is beginning to challenge the entrenched political machinery built by the political exiles, which tied the Cuban community to the far-right in the Republican Party (Chaffin, 2004, p. 12).

The evolution of Cuban enterprise in Miami points to an economy which began as an ethnic economy. Due to its exceptional spatial concentration and density it also became a political enclave, constructed, in part, in the image of the political exiles. The Cuban ethnic enclave economy is being transformed today into an immigrant enclave economy, as Cuban entrepreneurs and workers become part of a more diverse society composed of different Hispanic immigrant groups and typified by greater ethnic interspersion in the labour force: a trend that is laying the basis for future vertical as well as horizontal patterns of association.

The above has optimistic implications for one cost which is apparent in most ethnic economies and appears in an exaggerated form in the Cuban Hispanic enclave. This is the loss of structural autonomy by individuals and social groups, or the loss of 'weak ties', to use Portes' term for this condition. Arguably, this loss might be a necessary condition of dense relations and social capital processes which, in this instance, originated in the over-defensive social posturing adopted by the initial group of political exiles. Portes (1995, p. 259) argues that density in ethnic networks 'is not incompatible with weak ties'. Yet the Hispanic community in Miami, unlike Los Angeles, perhaps, has paid a heavy price for its lack of cultural heterogeneity and dominance of the economic and political enclave by a revanchist solidarity, which reinforced homogeneity (or assumed homogeneity) and demanded community compliance in the anti-communist project.

In Los Angeles 'Hispanic' is a code-word for downward social mobility associated with social-economic indicators which are lower than those for Black Americans. Many also have to live with the fear of deportation. In this we see the role of the political–institutional framework in the racialisation and ethnic channelling of immigrants into particular sectors and occupations. Agriculture and many industries and services would find it difficult to continue in their present form without Mexican Hispanic immigrant labour. Without Mexican women workers,

Los Angeles would not be the largest concentration of garment production in the United States, making it (after Chicago) the second largest concentration of manufacturing employment in the United States. In the above we see a recognisable pattern of Hispanic adaptation. At the same time this pattern, driven by the political–institutional framework, creates differences which intersect with, cut across and reinforce existing differences based in ethnicity. Social and economic indicators reveal that more significant differences exist in both Miami and Los Angeles between Hispanics who are foreign-born but naturalised and Hispanics who are foreign-born but non-citizens, than any attributes we may associate with variations in Hispanic ethnicity. This is at odds with analyses by Portes *passim* which in offering explanations for difference, point to the social capital and cultural endowment of particular ethnic groups and sub-groups as critical to the development of a benign ethnic enclave economy.

The conclusions remain critical of dire predictions about Hispanic migration in Los Angeles and its perceived consequences for native workers. These theories purport to show that Hispanic immigrants are 'stealing' jobs which rightly belong to 'native' workers, exaggerate differences inside the US working class and also ignore, as Light et al. (1999) argue, the role of jobs created by immigrant-owned enterprises in the economy of Los Angeles or, as Saxenian (1999) noted in the case of Asian enterprise in Silicon Valley, in the wider Californian economy. Neither do these theories account for the possibility that financial crises, economic restructuring, sectoral realignments and occupational changes are taking place in the entire industrial world and unlikely, therefore, to be the result of local variation.

The proposition that Mexican Hispanic immigrants are responsible for increasing unemployment amongst African Americans through a substitution or displacement effect, legitimised xenophobia and placed California centre-stage in the resurgence of American nativism. The Sensenbrenner HR 4437 bill was largely targeted at Hispanic migrants. It was passed by the House of Representatives and proposed to criminalise the estimated 12 million undocumented workers in the United States and to apply the felony statute to anyone who helps them, whether family member, labour organiser or member of the clergy. Undocumented workers who have been working in the United States (for decades in cases) would be defined, if they are lucky, as transient 'guestworkers'. The idea of a temporary work programme or guestworker system as an answer to irregular migration, in which eligible workers paying a fee would be granted temporary renewable visas, was pushed by the Bush administration in 2004 and it was this more than anything else which prompted the May Day protests in 2006. Ilias et al. (2008, pp. 757–758) noted that many older migrants with memories of the *Bracero* temporary work programs experienced that 'despite safeguards written into guest worker laws, in practice the *Bracero* programs were associated with a host of human right abuses'. They suggest that such systems institutionally create 'parallel societies', 'in which natives and low-income newcomers live in the same country but share little else'.

Opposition to HR 4437 galvanised the largest mobilisation in the history of the United States, and on May Day 2006 more than two million immigrants or perceived immigrants and their supporters demonstrated in what was the largest mass protest in US history. In California the protest had the aspect of a state-wide general strike and in Los Angeles alone an estimated one million people marched under the banner 'A Day Without Immigrants' (Moctezuma, 2006). CNN reported that an estimated 400,000 marched in Chicago, where the largely Hispanic crowd was joined by illegal Irish and Polish workers. One revealing insight into Hispanic political adaptation was that unlike the mobilisations against Proposition 187 in the State of California targeting undocumented Mexican migrants a decade earlier, the most common flag visibly carried on the May Day protest was not the Mexican flag but the flag of the United States, and many of the protestors presented themselves, not inaccurately, as 'Hispanic Americans'.

5
Polish Migration and Enterprise in the European Union: Between the Old and the New

Introduction

The chapter presents a critical review of the academic and institutional research on migration and emergent enterprise among migrants from Poland and the other seven eastern and central European states which formalised their membership of the European Union in June 2004. These countries are sometimes referred to as the European Union Accession 8 (A8) states and consist of Poland, the Czech Republic, Estonia, Hungary, Latvia, Lithuania, Slovakia and Slovenia. Bulgaria and Romania were admitted to the European Union in January 2007. The migrant flow from the A8 countries, primarily Poland, made up the second largest wave of migration to the United Kingdom since the French Huguenots in the sixteenth century and was significantly higher than immigration from the New Commonwealth countries during the 1950s and 1960s. A8 migrants provided a significant new source of labour for the United Kingdom before the recession. What is less clear, however, is the extent to which and they ways in which they are incorporated in the small enterprise sector and ethnic economies. This chapter identifies change and continuity in the incorporation of 'old' and 'new' migrant groups in the United Kingdom. As with New Commonwealth migration in the United Kingdom and Turkish guest-workers in Germany, Polish migrants were very much seen in instrumental terms as a labour market response to shortages in the workforce. However, unlike many 'old' Turkish and New Commonwealth migrants, the 'new' migrants, as EU citizens, did not experience similar lack of political rights and restrictions to travel. As a result of EU enlargement and partly due to the availability of cheap transport, Polish migrants made more frequent return visits home when compared to the historical experiences of most other migrants groups, and this made them even more aware and responsive to the opportunity structure available both in the United Kingdom and Poland. The chapter argues that one key factor in understanding Polish and A8 migration is the extent to which the political–institutional framework has facilitated a recognisable but selective pattern of independent, circular migration by large numbers of young men and women from eastern and central Europe. The primary purpose is to consider the theoretical implications of globalisation 'from above' and to offer a critique of analyses by the new geography of migration and the globalisation 'from below' thesis which purport to show that irregular migration and participation in informal labour markets are defining characteristics of contemporary migration.

Theoretical implications of Polish and A8 migration

The migration of A8 workers and entrepreneurs in the European Union raises a number of challenging questions which appear at odds with much of the literature produced by the 'new' geography of migration or the globalisation 'from below' thesis. In much of this literature (see Chapter 3), conflict between migrants and the institutional framework, 'irregular migration' and human trafficking, underpinned by informal labour markets, appear as general characteristics of migrant labour market incorporation. These analyses have focussed on issues such as irregular migration and the social and political issues which can become linked to it, the development of new models of migration to explain the transformation of southern European countries from labour exporters to major importers of labour today, and providing explanations for the incorporation of diverse immigrant groups into informal labour markets (Berggren et al., 2007; Campani, 2007; King, 1993, 2000, 2001; Light, 2000; Sassen, 1991). They provide useful insights on changes taking place in the pattern of migration in both Europe and the United States, but appear less convincing in offering an explanation for institutional variation within the European Union towards different groups of migrants. Migrants are made up of diverse groups who are institutionally dealt with in different ways. Frequently this is influenced by factors such as the gender and nationality of the migrant, their legal status and the significance of their particular skills and the trades, sectors and sub-sectors in which they might be employed.

As we saw in Chapter 3, analyses of migration by the new geography of migration and the globalisation 'from below' thesis assume that 'irregular migration' and participation in informal labour markets are essential and general characteristics of contemporary migration which brings migrants into conflict with the state. As we shall see, these analyses have conceptual problems in explaining the case of A8 migration. In this case migration was facilitated by states in the form of a selective EU enlargement. Cosmopolitanism and globalisation 'from above' is not a new phenomenon in the history of migration in Europe. Much of the post-war labour migration to Western Europe was facilitated by states (Castles and Kosack, 1973). Whilst historically unprecedented freedom to move is a feature of EU enlargement, the selective incorporation of A8 and other migrants in the EU countries cautions against sweeping generalisations and indicates that immigration policy-making in the European Union is both enabling and disabling in a relationship between EU convergence on one hand and national variation on the other. An important explanation for national variation lies in the role of periodic moral panics about migration. Much of the 'debate' about migration in Europe has been shaped by xenophobia and current variations such as Islamophobia. Favell (2008) located one source for national variation in European Union member states' policy on immigration in the role of anti-immigrant politicians who used the 'threat' of open doors eastwards, for example in the 'ugly French debate about the "Polish plumber" during the EU constitutional vote in May 2005' when a 'handful' of plumbers, compared to the much larger number heading for the United Kingdom, were seized on by the right as 'proof' of the 'invasion by hordes from the East' (Favell, 2008, p. 703). Bauder and Semmelroggen (2009, p. 1) in considering the language used in Parliamentary debates on migration in the *Bundestag* between 2002 and 2006, identified two key narratives: Muslim migration as 'threat' and migration as economic utility.

Bahna (2008) similarly noted that before Accession, analyses of migration from the eight Central and Eastern European (A8) countries by the old Member States were shaped by the fear of an expected (and subsequently actual) large wave of labour migration and difficult-to-predict migrant intentions. This led to the introduction of special rules targeting these migrants in the form of negotiated transition periods, which in 12 out of the 15 old Member States saw the temporary closing of labour markets. In fact, only three Member countries (the United Kingdom, Ireland and Sweden) opened their labour markets to workers from Eastern Europe. Subsequently, southern Cyprus also gave priority to EU citizens and the recruitment of Polish nurses, followed by construction- and tourism-related workers (Thomson, 2006, pp. 8, 16). The United Kingdom introduced a temporary work scheme, the Workers Registration Scheme (WRS) as a means of managing migration from the A8 countries. Sweden played a small marginal role, accounting for only 1.6 per cent of migrant employment in the immediate post-accession period (May to September 2004) compared to the United Kingdom and Ireland. At the same time as opening the door for Polish migrants, the United Kingdom closed its door on most Bulgarian and Romanian workers until 2011. Restrictions on these workers were introduced as soon as these countries joined the European Union and their numbers were limited to about 20,000 (Bahna, 2008, p. 849).

In discussing the role of A8 and in particular Polish migration to the United Kingdom, there are many parallels which can be drawn with the guestworker polices adopted by the Federal Republic of Germany. In both cases labour transfer was the intended purpose of the policy. The experience of A8 migration, however, is more complex than that of Turkish guestworkers. Much of the research indicates that that A8 migration is made up of diverse groups who migrate for different purposes and whose perspectives change over time, often as a reflection of the ageing process itself as well as the economic circumstance they find themselves in. The literature also indicates that the constitution of families and a growing stake in the host society are processes taking place amongst these new migrant groups. A particularly strong and perhaps initial defining feature of A8 migration manifested itself in a very modern form of circular labour migration by large numbers of young people linking, in particular, the United Kingdom and Poland. The retention of very close links with home – a necessary precondition for transnational community analyses – appears as an extraordinary strong force amongst A8 migrants.

Whilst a number of factors influence the development of patterns of migration, in the case of circular labour migration two factors appeared to be of particular practical and strategic significance. The migration was facilitated by the availability of cheap transport, but more a critical factor was the role played by the political–institutional framework in the form of (selective) European Union enlargement. This gave migrants from member states (theoretically, if not always practically) political rights not apparent in the experience of other migrant groups such as Arab migrants in France, Turkish migrants in Germany, or groups defined by the European Union as Third Country Nationals (TCNs), in what Thomson (2006) refers to as the 'new hierarchy' of labour created by an enlarged European Union. This is most clearly revealed in the experience of foreign domestic workers in the European Union, where the overwhelmingly majority are classified as TCNs and in whose case migration is anything but 'irregular', with short-term contracts used to ensure a transient migrant labour force (Ehrenreich and Hochschild, 2003; Panayiotopoulos, 2005).

Castles (2006, p. 742) asked whether EU enlargement and circular migration signal the return of the guestworker system. Whilst answering in the negative, 'there is no question of a general return to guestworker policies' it is also argued that 'some current approaches do share common features with past guestworker programs'. The growth of the Temporary Migrant Worker Programs (TMWPs) is cited as an example. Germany makes extensive use of TMWPs, such as clauses in the 2000 'Green Card' scheme for 20,000 ICT specialists which did not allow for family reunions and long-term residency. The largest TMWP is the seasonal worker program set up in 1991 which provides workers on 'up to' three month contracts in agriculture, construction and catering, mainly from Central and Easter Europe and which in 2001 accounted for 278,000 workers. Of these, 85 per cent came from Poland (Castles, 2006, pp. 749–750). The United Kingdom has also introduced elements of guestworker policy in its attempt to manage migration through a permit system based on employer needs. The Seasonal Agricultural Workers Scheme (SAWS) allows young people to work in the United Kingdom for a maximum of three months. Most recruits also came from Poland (Castles, 2006, p. 752). Agriculture is a key area of employment. Whilst foreign-born workers make up 12.1 per cent of the United Kingdom's labour force, during peak months in seasonal agriculture they provide up to 80 per cent of labour (Somerville and Sumption, 2009, p. 11). In the United Kingdom, Reports from the UK Parliamentary Environment, Food and Rural Affairs Committee and the UK Agricultural and Allied Workers Union estimated that there were 3000 agents providing the agricultural sector with casual labour needed by the fruit and vegetable sector at peak picking times. In the last ten or fifteen years this has become big business and some gangmasters employ up to 2000 people, looking primarily to Eastern and Southern Europe for sources of labour (Bell, 2002).

In explaining the labour market position of Polish migrants, Eade et al. (2007, p. 31) suggest that 'recent Polish immigrants have mainly found employment in low paid jobs' and that fewer, when compared to other migrant groups, are in professional and managerial positions. A not unusual experience is presented in the example of Polish workers employed by the Dawn Pac meat-packing plant near Llanelli in South Wales, which is a supplier for Marks & Spencer. The UNITE union claimed that shifts were regularly abandoned at short notice with workers having in some cases to walk the 15 miles back to Llanelli. The union also claimed that when employees found their own housing or transport rather than use that of CSA Recruitment (the agency which provided the labour), they found their work suddenly dried up. CSA charges £200 to bring workers to the United Kingdom and gets workers to sign a 'zero-hours deal' when they arrive in the United Kingdom, after a 36-hour coach trip. This means 'hours can change without notice' (Rees, 2007, p. 3).

In a study carried out on behalf of the Enfield Citizens Advice Bureau, North London, Warhaftig and Wierzbicka (2007, p. 3) found that Polish immigrants, whilst more likely to be in the greatest need of assistance, were also the least visible and the most difficult to make contact with. They found the concept of an 'underclass' characterised by the lowest levels of language skills, the poorest accommodation, the worst types of employment, and the lowest rates of pay, to be useful in explaining the position of a significant section of the migrants. Employment, they pointed out, is likely to be at below the minimum wage, with no contracts, no employment protection, and migrants worked without the benefit of employer liability insurance, and in places that do not comply with Health and Safety legislation. The employees themselves not only have no employment protection but are often subject to harassment and other kinds of discriminatory behaviour from their employers. This situation is reinforced by the fear of possible reprisals – loss of employment, and frequently the loss of accommodation as well.

Drinkwater et al. (2006, pp. 14, 21) identify a labour diaspora in the high concentration of A8 migrants in construction (the 'Polish builder phenomenon') and similarly ask 'has enlargement produced a guestworker type of system, dominated by temporary migration?' At the same time they also remarked on the growing indication that many recent Polish migrants are unsure of how long they would stay but that a significant proportion expected to work in the United Kingdom for a long period. Castles (2006, p. 743), writing on the demise of the guestworker system in Germany during the 1970s recession, asked: 'Why did many [Turkish] migrant workers turn into permanent migrants?' In offering an answer to the question Castles pointed to two factors which appear as particularly relevant to discussion about young Polish migrants today:

First, migrants' objectives were linked to the life cycle: young single workers originally intending to stay for a few years, but as they grow older and established families, their plans change. Second, the recession was much worse in Turkey and North Africa than Europe, so there were economic incentives to stay (Castles, 2006, p. 743).

History rarely, if ever, repeats itself in the same way and in comparing Turkish and Polish migration, one critical difference appears in the presence or absence of political rights and citizenship which underpin migrant 'mixed embeddedness' (Kloosterman and Rath, 2001; Kloosterman et al., 1999; Rath, 2000, 2002). Polish migrants, through EU enlargement, have acquired rights which are still not extended to Turkish migrants, who in many cases have spent 30 years of their lives on a production line, or to their children, most of whom were born and raised in Germany. Indeed, in the stalled negotiations on Turkey's accession to the European Union, one condition was that Turkish nationals resident in Germany would be treated as Third Country Nationals (Panayiotopoulos, 2008). The more secure arrangements facing Polish migrants in the United Kingdom laid the basis for a circular migration inconceivable for Turkish guestworkers in the Federal Republic of Germany. Circular labour migration, as a concrete and selective form of politically driven transnationalism facilitated by EU enlargement, needs to be clearly understood, partly in order to qualify some of the triumphalism associated with cosmopolitanism, such as Bahna (2008) who writes that,

> The paradigm of immigration and integration, in particular, becomes redundant in the face of the emergent, regional-scale, European territorial space. Within this, European citizens – old and new – can move freely against a wider, transnational horizon that encourages temporary and circular migration trends, and demands no long-term settlement or naturalisation in the country of work. (Bahna, 2008, p. 706)

A8 transnationalism parallels the discussion by Glick-Schiller (2003, p. 105) about 'transmigrants': 'persons who, having migrated from one nation-state to another, live their lives across borders, participating simultaneously in social relations that embed them in more than one nation-state'. Somerville and Sumption (2009, p. 11), similarly pointed to a 'pattern of circular migration from Eastern Europe' which established itself in the United Kingdom between 2004 and 2007 and which saw an estimated half of A8 migrants arriving in 2004 having returned home at least once. Ryan et al. (n.d.) in commenting on the extent to which recent Polish migrants, the largest group of new migrants to Britain with over half of registrations under the WRS (see Home Office, 2007b), are developing new patterns of migration, observed patterns which 'reflect neither the permanent settlement of past generations nor the extreme transience of the past decade' (Ryan et al., 2009, p. 2). They pointed to a situation in which A8 migrant expectations were shaped by the view that their 'new legal status and the ability to claim citizenship rights could promote more prolonged stays and greater permanence', [and that] 'borders are easier to cross, thus facilitating more back and forth movement' (Ryan et al., 2009, pp. 52, 61). This hybrid migrant formation, which developed under a specific set of political circumstances, had important social dimensions. It saw the reconfiguration of family relations in the form of transnational networks made up of diverse inter-generational relationships, which meant that 'whilst many migrants may arrive in Britain alone, they are often involved in complex family networks and relationships both in Britain and back home in Poland' (Ryan et al., 2009, p. 65).

Family formation raises challenging questions for analyses which regard Polish and other A8 country migrants as short-term transients (Wallace, 2002), or predominantly male (Kepinska, 2004). Fihel et al. (2006) alluded to the 'temporariness' of these migrants and Morokvasic (2004) described them as 'transnational commuters'. Early analyses focussed on young, single people migrating without dependents – since these were the people migrating. An important dimension of this was the feminisation of migration in the form of independent female migration by young women. Ryan et al. (2009, p. 62) note that by 2007 nearly half of all workers registered with the WRS were women, most of them young and with no dependents. They do strike a note of caution, however, in that the predominance of young single people in WRS registrations 'may not accurately represent the range and diversity of migrants coming to Britain'. One illustration they provided, which reflects on family reunion and family formation, is the experience of Polish Sunday Schools, which indicates that '10 years ago these schools were closing because there were not enough children to keep them running but within the last 10 years, things have changed dramatically with a massive enrolment of Polish-born children' (Ryan et al., 2009, p. 67).

Between the old and the new: Polish migration in the United Kingdom

Warhaftig and Wierzbicka (2007, p.3) in a study for the Citizens Advice Bureau in the North London borough of Enfield on the issues faced by East European migrants, found little significant impact on the Social Security system. However, within local education, the number of children at Enfield schools has increased by 69 per cent over the previous three years. They remarked on the lower visibility of migrants in Enfield, when compared to other London Boroughs. Polish migrants still tended to gravitate towards existing communities in West and North-West London. This might enable them to make use of support networks for finding work, and the social space based around the churches, as well as restaurants and social centres. Within Enfield the relatively low level of East European presence is evidenced by the absence of delicatessens and speciality food shops in the borough. The research, surprisingly, perhaps, found no Polish or East European restaurants in the boroughs of Enfield, Haringey and Waltham Forest, in North-East London. One indication of distribution is the newspaper 'Polish Express' which has a print run of 50,000 copies and a claimed readership of 250,000, with 4000 delivery points nationally. Of the delivery points across London, it does not have any in Enfield, compared to five in Waltham Forest. six in Haringey and 36 in Acton/Ealing, West London.

A8 migration has raised new questions about the relationship between 'old' and 'new' migrants in the United Kingdom. Kyambi (2005) makes the distinction between 'new' and 'settled' immigrant groups, with new immigrants defined as foreign-born people who arrived after 1990 and who tend to be younger and are drawn from a much wider number of countries than settled immigrants who arrived in most cases (such as the New Commonwealth migrants) long before 1990. An important contributing factor for the wider distribution of migrants was that as a result of the break-up of Yugoslavia during the 1990s and subsequent wars in the Gulf, Afghanistan and the Great Lake region in Africa, the world became a more dangerous place, leading to displacement and an increase in the number of people seeking refuge. Past migrants to Britain originated in a relatively small number of ex-colonial countries, whilst recent migrants have been drawn from a wider range of countries beyond the Commonwealth and Western Europe. The number of people born in Poland, other Eastern European countries, the former Yugoslavia, Sierra Leone, Somalia, Iraq, Turkey and South America, has increased sharply, whilst those born in the traditional migrant groups, such as the Caribbean and Ireland, have decreased. 'New' immigrant groups are playing a more significant role in Britain's demography. Of the United Kingdom's 2.2m population increase between 1991 and 2001, just over half (1.14m) was made up of persons born abroad and the remainder by natural population increase. Of those born abroad, who made up 7.5 per cent of the total population in 2001 and 5.8 per cent in 1991, 'new' immigrants accounted for just over half the immigrant population increase in 2001, compared to one-third in 1994 (Kyambi, 2005). What flows from these trends is the observation that the frequently used categories of white, black and Asian for describing ethnic groups have become more inadequate at capturing the increased diversity of Britain's immigrant population.

Whilst there are key elements of continuity in old and new migration such as in the role of economic objectives in decision-making, there are also significant differences between them. Considerably fewer members of the old New Commonwealth migrant groups arrived in the United Kingdom as refugees. Amongst the A8 migrant groups family reunions appear to play a much smaller role. This is reflected in ONS statistics (Office for National Statistics, 2009b, p. 2), which indicate that 68 per cent of A8 migrants came to the United Kingdom with the expressed purpose of working, compared to 28 per cent of migrants from India and 9 per cent of migrants from Bangladesh and Pakistan. In contrast, 71 per cent of migrants from Bangladesh and Pakistan migrated for the purpose of accompanying, reuniting or forming families, compared to only 21 per cent of migrants from the EU A8 countries (see Table 5.1). In terms of help received in migration, relatively more migrants from the A8 countries (19%) cited the help of private employment offices/agencies than migrants from India (at 4%) or Bangladesh and Pakistan (at 5%). Migrants from both old and new groups cited 'friends' as the main source of help. At the same time the largest proportion in all migrant groups was in the 'no help was received' category (Office for National Statistics, 2009b, p. 5) (see Table 5.2).

Significant differences appear amongst old and new migrant groups in their level of education and human capital formation. Amongst new migrant groups much of the investment in human capital was undertaken in the home country. Few A8 migrants migrate for the express

Table 5.1 Main reason for coming to the United Kingdom for foreign-born people: By country of birth (selected groups) (per cent)

	EU14*	EUA8**	India	Bangladesh & Pakistan
Employment	45	68	28	9
Study	20	10	14	10
International protection	0	1	1	3
Accompanying family/ Family reunification	13	11	32	45
Family formation	8	2	18	26
Other	13	7	7	6

Notes: *Poland, the Czech Republic, Estonia, Hungary, Latvia, Lithuania, Slovakia and Slovenia; **Term used in UK statistics to describe countries which were the existing members before enlargement, Austria, Belgium, Denmark, Finland, France, Germany, Greece, Holland, Italy, Luxembourg, Portugal, Republic of Ireland, Spain and Sweden.

Source: Office for National Statistics (2009b), p. 2.

Table 5.2 Main help received in finding current job or setting up business in the United Kingdom: By country of birth (per cent)

	EU14	EUA8	India	Bangladesh & Pakistan
Public employment office	3	5	4	5
Private employment office	11	19	9	6
Relatives/friends	19	29	20	29
Migrant/ethnic organisations	0	2	0	1
Other help	9	9	11	10
None – no help received	58	35	55	49
Total	100	100	100	100

Source: Office for National Statistics (2009b), p. 5.

purpose of study relative to other groups. An analysis of where new and old migrant groups gained their highest qualification shows that amongst A8 migrants 85 per cent had already completed higher education in their own countries (Office for National Statistics, 2009b, p. 4). Amongst migrants from India – at 42 per cent and Bangladesh and

Pakistan at 56 per cent – their highest qualification was gained in the United Kingdom (see Table 5.3).

The arrival of large numbers of 'ready-made' EU A8 university graduates is a strong feature of the new migration and one which highlights a significant contradiction: that between the high level of human capital formation amongst many of the migrants on one hand and the low level of earnings and remuneration experienced by most of them, even relative to other migrant groups, on the other. In the pre-Accession period, during which the smaller number of migrants from Eastern Europe were more likely to be drawn from sections of the elite, A8 median gross weekly earnings (including overtime) increased significantly from £279 in 1998 (93 per cent of UK median income) to £420 (116.6% of UK average income). In the post-Accession period of 2003–2008, when migration became a mass phenomenon, these income trends went into sharp reverse. By 2008, A8 median income stood at £290: 66.5 per cent of the UK average income of £438 (Khan, 2008b, p. 2). These were the lowest weekly wages for any migrant group. The only other comparable group were migrants from Bangladesh and Pakistan at £292 per week (see Table 5.4).

Table 5.3   Where the highest qualification was gained by country of birth: United Kingdom (per cent)

	EU14	EUA8	India	Bangladesh & Pakistan
In the UK	55	14	42	56
Outside the UK	44	85	58	43
No Answer	1	1	0	1

Source: Office for National Statistics (2009b), p. 4.

Table 5.4   Median gross weekly earnings* for full-time employees by country of birth for country groups: United Kingdom (£s)

	1998	2003	2008
Total	300	360	436
UK	298	358	438
EUA8	279	420	290
Australia & New Zealand	392	529	577
Pakistan & Bangladesh	200	250	292

Note: *Earnings include overtime.

Source: Khan (2008b), p. 2.

Polish migrants in the UK labour market

Polish migration to the United Kingdom did not begin with Poland's Accession to the European Union. Jordan's (2002) study of Polish migrants in London during the pre-Accession period revealed significant 'irregular' migration and a group of migrants who 'have little contact with the settled community in London' and who were described as 'risk-tolerant' and 'enterprising' (Jordan, 2002, p. 4). A common theme after the collapse of the Stalinist regime appeared in the taking up of temporary work abroad by sections of the elite who took advantage of fewer restrictions to overseas travel. These migrants were identified as 'acquisitive', 'intelligent, motivated and adaptable' migrants for whom migration was a kind of economic mobility appropriate in the age of globalisation which 'seldom involves resettlement, or the movement of whole families' and implied only an instrumental accommodation to the host society (Jordan, 2002, pp. 2–3). It is of note that half of the 25 undocumented workers interviewed by Jordan were university or college graduates (Jordan, 2002, p. 7). For other migrants the experience was one of living in multi-occupancy 'Polish houses' and finding work in London through friends, mainly in the garment and cleaning industries which employed mainly women and also in the building industry, which was a main employer for men. In the case of the garment industry, most were working for Turkish Cypriot entrepreneurs (Jordan, 2002, p. 11).

Many of the worst stereotypes about the Polish community owe their origins to the experiences of the migrants in the pre-Accession period, during which remaining undetected was a key objective of irregular and undocumented migrants. These material circumstances in the absence of solidarity can form the basis for compliance, mistrust and even, in some cases, malevolence towards co-ethnic fellow workers. Drinkwater et al. (2006, p. 8) noted that these circumstances were a strong feature of the pre-Accession period, which in 1996 saw Polish nationals ranked third amongst those most likely to being identified for illegal entry. During 2001–2003 they were the group most likely to be refused entry to the United Kingdom. Stereotypes about Polish migrants under these circumstances produced statements such as

> Poles in London engage in unrestrained competition, including informing to the authorities on each other, in order to get each other's jobs. Every service, every amenity, has a price. They exploit

each other mercilessly. They cannot be relied on to keep promises. (Jordan, 2002, p. 4)

Gryzmala-Kazlowska (2005, p. 687) also argued that circumstances of irregular migration in the pre-Accession period lent themselves to compatriot exploitation and that 'Poles who have regular status in Belgium have been deriving substantial benefits from the presence of undocumented Polish workers'. Some of the research indicates that Polish migrants were perceived by other migrant worker groups as compliant (Datta et al., 2006). Erdemir and Vasta (2007) also pointed to ethnic compliance and compatriot exploitation as 'a recurring theme' amongst Turkish irregular migrants in London, indicating that this type of behaviour may not be the property of any given ethnic group but rather a common outcome in a hostile institutional environment.

Accession in 2004 saw the removal of legal barriers to travel and work and led to a radical transformation in the Polish migrant population in the United Kingdom. One aspect was the arrival of larger than expected numbers of migrants. This is illustrated in conservative predictions by Dustmann et al. (2003), which projected A8 net migration in the region of 5000 to 13,000 per year, whilst the Home Office et al. (2006) enumerated 427,000 A8 migrants in the United Kingdom up to June 2006. In terms of social composition many of the migrants were young workers, plumbers, welders, packers and office workers, but a large number were also young men and women freshly out of college, who like their counterparts in other European countries migrated looking for foreign experiences as well as the ability to earn wages higher than they could at home. This youth exodus, facilitated by a succession of right-wing conservative governments only too happy to expel potentially troublesome unemployed and well educated young people, made up a significant part of the initial wave of migration and was indicated by the collapse of the club scene in Poland's University towns. In Lublin, the owner of one (empty) club, commenting on the 'missing clubbers', said that 'the nightlife has died. Everyone left. The bands that played here and the people who listened to them, they're all gone' (Ciensky, 2007). The student/youth dimension of outward migration is indicated in analyses of the UK Labour Force Survey data, which examined the labour outcomes of current A8 labour migrants in the United Kingdom compared to previous flows as well as with other recent migrant groups in the United Kingdom, and which found that 'the majority of post-enlargement migrants from accession countries have found employment in low paying jobs, despite some (especially Poles) having relatively high levels of education' (Drinkwater et al., 2006, p. 3).

The management of A8 migration, despite the rhetoric of free movement, includes restrictions on A8 migrants not applied to other groups of workers. Before Polish and other A8 migrants are allowed to work, they must register with the Home Office Worker Registration Scheme (WRS). They must also re-register if they change jobs, addresses or their marital status. No other workers have to do this. Paradoxically, for the same reasons, WRS statistics are useful in that they allow us to review at local level the distribution of national groups defined in terms of nationality rather than country of birth, as is the case with Census data; the statistics also give information on hours worked and hourly pay. One major deficiency is that the WRS excludes the self-employed. This is important, since the right of establishment in the European Union allows self-employed citizens of the European Union (including A8 citizens) to move to another state in order to establish their business with fewer restrictions, and this was widely used by A8 migrants (Bauere et al., 2007, pp. 7–8).

WRS registrations for the period May 2004 to December 2006, monitored by Bauere et al. (2007, p. 8), saw a total 508,407 registrations, of which 42.3 per cent were by women. Over 93 per cent had no dependents with them and 82.5 per cent were between the ages of 18 and 34. They noted that the WRS and work permit system served different occupational niches. During 2005 most A8 migrants (82%) registered with the WRS occupied lower-skilled jobs, whereas the majority of work permit approvals (89%) were for people taking up managerial, professional and associate positions. What is evident from WRS registrations is the channelling of A8 migrants into a narrow range of sectors with just three: administration, management and services, hospitality and catering and agriculture accounting for most registrations (66.5%) (see Table 5.5).

The sectoral dynamics of employment shaped the geographical distribution and concentration of A8 migrants: the demand for cleaners and restaurant workers in Westminster, London, for example, or agricultural labourers in Boston, South Holland and Fenland, was a critical factor in explaining why these areas are amongst the UK local authorities with the highest number of A8 migrants per thousand of the total population (see Table 5.6). Registered A8 nationals were paid on average between £4.50 and £5.99 per hour. Polish migrants made up the largest group and accounted for 64.4 per cent (327,538 people) of the total A8 registrations. In the ten local authorities where A8 migrants

Table 5.5 Workers Registration Scheme: A8 citizens registered by industry in the United Kingdom, 2004–06*

Industry	Number	Per cent
Administration, management, services	186,043	36.6
Hospitality and catering	96,522	19.0
Agriculture	55,179	10.9
Food processing	25,428	5.0
Health and medical services	24,003	4.7
Retail and related services	21,244	4.0
Transport	13,781	2.7
Financial services	1,429	0.3
Computer services	1,236	0.2

Note: *Between May 2004 and December 2006.
Source: Bauere et al. (2007), p. 17.

Table 5.6 A8 citizens registered per thousand of population: Top ten United Kingdom local authorities, 2004–06*

Authority	Numbers	Total A8
City of London	2,700	293.5
Boston	5,643	97.3
Westminster	15,021	61.5
Northampton	10,279	52.7
South Holland	4,018	49.5
Peterborough	7,110	44.5
Fenland	3,441	39.5
East Cambridgeshire	3,072	39.1
Herefordshire, County of	6,755	37.8
Dungannon	1,871	36.9
Total	508,487	8.4

Note: *Between May 2004 and December 2006.
Source: Bauere et al. (2007), p. 8.

were most concentrated Polish migrants represent 90 per cent or more of the total A8 population (Bauere et al., 2007, pp. 11, 18). Drinkwater et al. (2006, p. 9) noted that of WRS applications made to work in the United Kingdom between May 2004 and June 2006, almost 62 per cent of applicants were by Polish nationals. One significant variation they point to between A8 migrants and other immigrant groups is that only 14 per cent of A8 migrants lived in London compared to over 40 per cent of all immigrants. The highest concentration for A8 migrants was in rural East Anglia.

One concrete measure of the growing cultural diversity in the United Kingdom is in the allocation of National Insurance numbers (NINos) which are needed in order to be able to work legally and to claim benefits and tax credits. During the 12 months to September 2008, 720,000 NINos were allocated, with foreign nationals from the A8 countries accounting for 37 per cent of all registrations. The largest allocation, of 210,000, was for migrants from Poland. The second largest category was for Indian nationals, who in 2002 constituted the largest category issued with NINos (see Table 5.7). Statistics provided by the Department for Work and Pensions and the Home Office show that of the National Insurance allocations to the end of March 2008, 80 per cent were for people between the ages of 18 and 34, and that the London region accounted for 37.2 per cent of allocations. Out of the 706,000 registrations for 2006–07 only 20,000 – or 2.9 per cent – were claiming Jobseeker's Allowance, Incapacity Benefit or Income Support (Department for Work and Pensions, 2008).

The distribution of NINos and related material indicates significant variation in the purpose of migration between A8 and other migrant groups. Office for National Statistics data show that 68 per cent of those born in the A8 countries and now resident in the United Kingdom moved for work purposes, compared with less than one-third (31%) of all people born overseas (Office for National Statistics, 2009a). The

Table 5.7 Top National Insurance number recipients in the United Kingdom (000s, rounded)

2002		2007–08	
Country	Recipients	Country	Recipients
India	22	Poland	210
Australia	18	India	50
South Africa	17	Slovakia	27
Pakistan	16	Pakistan	25
France	14	Australia	24
Philippines	11	Romania	22
Spain	10	France	21
Germany	9	Lithuania	20
Afghanistan	8	Germany	17
Rep of Ireland	7	Italy	15

Source: Department for Work and Pensions (2008).

Table 5.8   Working age employment rate by selected country of birth: United Kingdom (per cent)

	Male			Female		
	1998	2008	Change 1998–08	1998	2008	Change 1998–08
United Kingdom	78.6	78.6	−0.1	68.9	72.9	3.1
India	74.5	82.3	7.8	53.7	56.8	3.1
Poland	49.2	93.7	44.5	30.6	78.5	47.9
Pakistan	58.7	74.8	16.1	13.5	15.9	2.4
Bangladesh	56.9	70.9	14.0	11.5	20.3	8.7
Nigeria	69.9	86.5	15.2	51.3	70.3	19.0
Ghana	77.6	80.7	3.1	42.0	65.5	23.5
Jamaica	67.7	66.1	−1.6	64.8	73.8	8.9
Turkey	53.0	67.7	14.7	19.0	30.6	11.6
Lithuania	NA	84.1	NA	NA	80.7	NA

Note: Working age defined as 16–59 for females and 16–64 for males;
NA Estimate cannot be provided due to insufficient sample size.

Source: Khan (2008a), p. 7.

incorporation of A8 migrants as labour migrants is indicated in the large proportion of Polish migrants who are of working age. In 1998 less than half of Polish-born migrant males in the United Kingdom were of working age, and this was the lowest rate of any comparable male migrant group. By 2008, and under the impact of mass migration, the proportion of males of working age increased to 93.7 per cent (the highest of any migrant group). Amongst women, in 1998, 30.6 per cent and in 2008, 78.5 per cent were of working age (see Table 5.8). These figures demonstrate the rapid transformation and social re-composition of the Polish community from a collection of pensioners and war veterans to a group with the highest employment rate amongst all immigrant and ethnic minority groups.

Research from the Centre for Research on Nationalism, Ethnicity and Multiculturalism (CRONEM) suggests that migration from Poland introduces more complexity than projections about transience and a return to the guestworker system. CRONEM points to a highly complex set of migration patterns which reflect the ease of mobility within the European labour market and fluidity between seasonal, long-term and undecided duration migrants. Over a fifth (22%) of respondents in the research identified themselves as seasonal migrants and one-third said that they intended to stay for less than two years. Seasonal and short-term migrants tended to be young (less than 24) and were disproportionately concentrated in big cities like London and worked in sectors such as construction or the hospitality/catering industries. Around 30 per cent said they did not know how long they would be staying in the United Kingdom and another 15 per cent said they wanted to stay in the United Kingdom permanently. Nearly 30 per cent said they intended to bring their families and children over, or that their families are already in the United Kingdom. Most of these were in the 35–45 age group. Over 64 per cent were registered with the WRS (CRONEM, 2006).

Similarly, in trying to explain the diversity and novelty contained in the Polish migrant experience, Eade et al. (2007, pp. 33–36) have constructed a typology of how Polish migrant workers understand their socio-economic position within London's labour market. They call the first group *Storks*: circular migrants who employ commuting strategies and are found primarily in low-paid occupations (such as catering, construction, domestic work), or are seasonal workers such as farmers commuting to London building sites, or students working in the London catering industry during the summer months to pay tuition fees in Polish universities. The second group are *Hamsters*: aim-orientated migrants, who treat their move as a one-off act to acquire capital to invest in Poland; this group tends to cluster in particular low-earning occupations. Third, there are the *Searchers*: migrants who keep their options deliberately open and are primarily made up of young and ambitious migrants found in a range of occupational positions from low-earning to highly skilled and professional jobs. Their position is characterised by 'intentional unpredictability'. The fourth and final group is the *Stayers*, 'those who have been in the United Kingdom for some time and intend to remain for good' and are most strongly associated both with 'strong social mobility ambitions' and awareness of the existence of social class. Eade et al. (2007, p. 36) suggest that *Hamsters* and *Storks* see their social class position in relation to Poland, converting their London earnings into Polish currency and assets, whilst *Searchers* and *Stayers* relate their class position to society in the United Kingdom. Proximity is a significant factor in the above, with 80 per cent of respondents making frequent visits to Poland, ranging from 3 to 12 times a year. Eade et al. (2007, p. 40) also note that when respondents commented on the multi-racial nature of London, 'almost all believe that London's diversity would be impossible in Poland'.

The incorporation of migrants is shaped in part by the nature of the local economy, and local studies reveal significant variation in the Polish and A8 migrant experience. Glossop and Shaheen (2009) examined the differential labour market effects of A8 migration countries on the two (contrasting) city economies of Hull (a declining urban centre) and Bristol. The study was conducted during October 2008 and January 2009, a time during which recession and rising unemployment began to limit employment opportunities. During 2004–08, Bristol and Hull were the destinations of 5000 A8 migrants registered with the WRS. A significantly higher proportion, estimated as 25,600 in Bristol and 10,750 for Hull, were allocated NINos (Glossop and Shaheen, 2009, pp. 11–12). The NINos were issued either directly to migrants who lived in Bristol and Hull, or through recruitment agencies which placed workers outside the main urban centre or in rural areas.

In Hull, manufacturing industry was a key area of employment concentration and factory work was easily available. Proximity to rural areas made jobs available in market gardening and food processing plants. A complementary factor was low rents. Many of the migrants intended 'to stay for one to two years' (Glossop and Shaheen, 2009, p. 3). The majority of the migrants were male. In Bristol, the study found that approximately half of migrants worked as process and warehouse operatives or packers, but also in catering as waiters, and as labourers, builders, carers and retail operatives. They found that in contrast to Hull, 'the gender gap has narrowed and women and men migrants were found in equal proportions' (Glossop and Shaheen, 2009, p. 32).

The experience in Bristol points towards a community in formation. In a not unfamiliar process of immigrant adaptation, increased Polish migration between 1997 and 2007 led to 'Polish communities settling around Springbank and Beverley Road, in which they have established shops and restaurants, which have helped to revive run down areas' (Glossop and Shaheen, 2009, p. 12). This has been paralleled by the growth of community associations, support groups and the presence of the Polish Church. Unlike the experience of most labour migrants, the majority of migrants came to Bristol due to the presence of family and friends and for the purpose of family reunions. A particularly high proportion of migrants in Bristol have brought dependents, especially dependents over the age of 17, and approximately 18 per cent of migrants who registered in Bristol between 2006 and 2008 brought their children, partners or both. Most have the intention to stay 'for more than two years' (Glossop and Shaheen, 2009, pp. 13–14). A major problem identified in the study was that migrants were found to be significantly 'under-employed'. Amongst respondents in Bristol, working as packers, waitresses, labourers, carers and shop workers, 45 per cent had a college education and 28 per cent had gone to university. Many were teachers, nurses, and midwives, who faced problems with recognition of foreign qualifications (Glossop and Shaheen, 2009, pp. 21–22). Despite this, in Bristol 'a higher proportion of immigrants are settling in the city compared to Hull' (p. 26).

An indication of the number of East Europeans with children is that 45,252 were claiming Child Benefit, and 22,685 were receiving tax credits during 2006 (Warhaftig and Wierzbicka, 2007, p. 15). The distribution of the more than 60 Polish Saturday schools around the country offering language and cultural lessons to the children of immigrants is a significant indicator of community formation. There are ten of these schools in London but none are in North London. The Ealing Saturday school in West London had doubled in size to over 400 pupils, and in Bristol the increase was larger – from 35 to over 100. Many parents send their children there so that they could easily slip back into the Polish education system if they return home. The Polish schools, mostly run by the Polish Educational Society, are largely financed by the Polish community with very little local government or central government funding (Warhaftig and Wierzbicka, 2007, p. 13).

Classes in formation: Polish enterprises

A8 migrants were primarily seen as young, well educated labour migrants who could be effectively managed by in the United Kingdom through systems such as the WRS. Since the self-employed are excluded from WRS data, it is harder to understand the implications, particularly in Polish migration, of the large number of people who were classified as self-employed. Others became intermediaries and brokers, often in the process of facilitating the employment of fellow migrants. Glossop and Shaheen (2009, p. 23) noted in their study of Bristol that enterprises adopted a system in managing labour whereby 'businesses, notably factories in both cities, employed Polish shift managers with command of the English language to act as intermediaries between management and the workforce'. This lower level of social differentiation between Polish migrants is more explicit amongst the self-employed working on their own account, who became petty employers of co-ethnic migrants. Self-employment is a strong feature of particular industries, such as construction, which became a significant niche for Polish migrant builders, plumbers and carpenters both as workers and entrepreneurs. Other routes into entrepreneurship included acting as cross-border traders, labour agents for domestic workers and in construction, as travel agents, as human smugglers (before Accession) and owning bars and grocery stores.

Drinkwater et al. (2006) noted that Polish migrants, in particular, took advantage of the provision granted by the Europe Agreement of 1991 (ratified in 1994) between the European Union and candidate states that allowed migrants to migrate for the purpose of setting up their own private businesses. The result was a huge increase in those entering via the self-employment route. The Home Office (2003) reported a 156 per cent increase in the number of Poles granted an extension as a person of independent means or as a business person. Many migrants knew that being classified as self-employed was a route into the United Kingdom in the pre-Accession period. Drinkwater et al. noted (2006, p. 11) that there were 'much higher self-employment rates of A8 migrants arriving shortly before enlargement. This is especially true of Poles, since roughly a third of this group with jobs who arrived between 2000 and 2003 are self employed'. During 2003 some 3000 passports were returned by the Home Office to the Polish Consular Office, when irregularities made it impossible to process applications for self-employment visas (Garapich, 2008, p. 742). Many identical and often fictitious 'business plans' were produced for plumbers, carpenters and bricklayers. Most of the 76,000 immigrants in the United Kingdom registered as self-employed during 2006 were Polish.

Participation in the construction industry is a significant employment niche for Polish migrants but also one which saw key changes in the employment status of many of the migrants. Principally these consisted of a move from self-employment to the employment of fellow migrants. The growth in the number of small enterprises and changes in economic status from worker to petty employer is illustrated in the case study presented by Warhaftig and Wierzbicka (2007) of a part owner of an unregistered construction business which operated primarily in North London.

The business commenced trading in 2004 when the border restrictions were first relaxed. Originally the entrepreneur carried out much of the work himself, using other Polish workers with specialist skills as required. They undertook all aspects of home construction work: decorating, laying floors, rewiring, plastering, installation of kitchens, building of bathrooms and shower-rooms, structural alterations and extensions.

The business started off in a small way with quotes in the order of £60 per person per day. Work is now quoted at prices of around £150 per day, which is still highly competitive. Quotes are invariably verbal. Their work all comes from recommendations of previous, highly satisfied clients. It is won on the basis of both the (perceived) quality of their work, and price.

> There are now three Polish workers with the entrepreneur who work on a regular basis, with more added as jobs required. The owner is the only one that speaks English, and all work, changes, and alterations therefore have to be channelled though him. The workers are paid when there is work, and if not working, do not engage with the social security/benefits services. The plumbers, whilst experienced, do not have any UK recognised qualifications. Similarly, the electricians have learnt their trade whilst on the job, have no awareness of the UK regulations and none of the work is signed off by the local authorities in accordance with current regulations. (Warhaftig and Wierzbicka, 2007, p. 16)

Polish builders were very much the public face of A8 migration and many households in the United Kingdom benefited from having good quality work done for less than they expected to pay, in many cases after frustrating inquiries to local builders. Problems began to emerge, however, with the image of the hard-working (and compliant) Polish builder under the impact of mass migration. As more homeowners began to employ more builders, many more of whom came from rural areas in Poland, not all were found as compliant or competent as the initial flow of pre-accession migrants. Articles appeared in the UK press which reported that 'there are signs that some of the skilled workers of three years ago have been replaced by inexperienced, unqualified compatriots'. In one example, the homeowners found that the original builder had returned to Poland for a holiday, but asked three fellow countrymen, straight off the coach, to take on the job. The homeowners found the new builders leaving rubbish everywhere, frequently disappearing (to other jobs), taking 'excessive tea breaks' and were treated with contempt and insolence to boot. That the 'Poles were catching the British disease', became a recognisable feature of discussion and perhaps a proxy indicator of the growing confidence of Polish builders who began to more clearly understand the value of their work (Chittenden and Tchorek, 2007).

Elrick and Lewandowska (2008) pointed to the role of Polish agents, for whom brokerage is a form of enterprise. Their study examined a significant labour diaspora involving the employment of Polish women migrants in Germany in the elderly care sector as live-in carers. The migrant women came from two clusters of villages: one from the eastern part of Poland, with most migrants going to Italy and the other from the western part of Poland, previously German-governed Silesia, where a significant number are ethnic Germans and hold German passports, going to Germany. They pointed to the scissors effect of high unemployment in Poland and an increasing number of elderly persons in Germany where of the estimated 1.8 million persons over the age of 60 in need of care, two-thirds are nursed at home. Of these, two-thirds are cared for by relatives and one-third by professional nurses. Live-in carers 'are a welcome alternative to professional nurses for relatives in search of care for family members'. Both Germany and Italy offer subsidies to relatives acting as carers, but the recipients are 'often tempted to use this money to employ cheap migrant labour instead of doing the care work on their own' (Elrick and Lewandowska, 2008, p. 720).

After EU enlargement, labour recruitment agencies mushroomed all over Poland. Most agencies were not officially registered and operated both in Poland and the receiving countries. The role of agents is that of knowledgeable brokers of scarce information in asymmetrical migrants networks. At the time they earned a commission for placing people of up to 350 euros (Elrick and Lewandowska, 2008, p. 722–723). As with construction, agents are a necessary organisational feature of the employment of foreign domestic workers (Panayiotopoulos, 2005). Elrick and Lewandowska (2008, p. 723) note that agents are especially necessary in the domestic elderly care sector due to the precarious and short-term nature of the employer–employee relationship. They pointed to the radical transformation of social relations by the 'migrant business' as one where agents deriving from groups of previous migrants made use of embedded migrant networks to recruit and transport migrant workers often consisting of 'friends from the place of origin and distant family members'. In the process 'they change from being intermediaries who give information for free, to agents who now charge their fellows and family members' (Elrick and Lewandowska, 2008, pp. 724, 726). Garapich (2008, p. 740) found, in a study of a group of 40 immigration advice officers, that some developed into 'respectable business ventures' whilst others turned out to be run by human smugglers and organised groups providing migrants with false documents.

Garapich with reference to 'fixers and brokers' (Cohen, 1997, p. 163) pointed to the key role of immigration advisors and job brokers, but also the ethnic media, shops, travel agents, money offices, bars were migrants meet, and the larger number of wage-workers and self-employed carpenters, plumbers and bricklayers, as lying at the heart of Polish transnationalism. Within this nexus the observation is made that the combined effects have 'unintentionally resulted in an extraordinary development in the associational, civic, cultural and social life of the Polish migrants in the United Kingdom' (Garapich, 2008, p. 411). More significantly, Garapich points to a process of social and economic differentiation in an immigrant community as one where

> a group of immigration advisors emerged who quickly [in the years 2000–04] transformed the observable patterns of economic and labour behaviour of migrants in their ethnic economic niche. Most of these advisors began as low-key, back-door, one-person businesses, often with a single telephone number and private visits at home... Within a couple of years some of them emerged as very important social brokers, employers and leaders active in the local Polish community. (Garapich, 2008, p. 741)

The underpinning of Polish transnationalism by emergent economic agents is explored by Miera (2008) in a study of the structure and strategies of Polish migrant entrepreneurs in Berlin. During the pre-Accession period emergent entrepreneurs used their personal mobility to benefit from differences in purchasing power between Germany and Poland in the form of cross-border trade. Progressively they became labour recruiters of transnational workers in sectors such as construction and cleaning. This laid the basis for the growing Polish community as a market involving grocers, cafes and travel agents. A number have been extending to Poland enterprise activities initiated in Germany. The community is made up of about 30,000 registered Polish nationals, 100,000 ethnic Germans from Poland (so-called *Aussiedler*) and a number of undocumented migrants. Most of the migrants arrived after the opening of the borders in 1988. In 1988 only 95 Polish enterprises existed in Berlin, but by 1990 their number had increased to 331, mainly concentrated in construction, services, hotels and catering (Miera, 2008, pp. 754, 758).

Miera (2008, p. 754) argues that the enterprise development strategies adopted by Polish entrepreneurs 'differ from those of other migrants functioning as entrepreneurs in large cities' as discussed in the international literature (Light and Gold, 2000; Rath, ed., 2002). Typically, a so-called 'ethnic economy' emerges and ethnic niches are identified, which may act as points of entry into a mainstream economy. 'There is little evidence of such a process amongst the Polish migrants in Berlin'. Miera suggests that they do not form a dense 'ethnic economy' but rather adopt strategies which have been shaped by the highly mobile and transnational nature of Polish migration and networks. Since the opening of the Polish border in 1987–88 hundreds of thousands of Polish travellers have repeatedly made short visits and rapid transactions in currency and goods by Polish 'tourists'. No visas were required for stays of up to 31 days. An aspect of this was to sell subsidised Polish and East German goods in the West German markets, in particular that of Berlin. In construction and cleaning, whether as a worker or self-employed, a feature of informal labour markets was that 'many kept their household in Poland and travelled back and forth' (Miera, 2008, p. 762). Most Polish firms owned construction firms employing men; domestic cleaning firms employing women were small or very small and were active at the 'lower end of the subcontractor chain' (Miera, 2008, p. 763).

The key point made by Miera (2008, p. 766) is that the 'permeability' of the border in both directions contributed to the high mobility of migrants (which may partly account for the variation in this pattern of migration) and that this has been shaped by specific historically evolved German-Polish institutional relations. Miera's (2008, p. 755) argument that the development of migration between Poland and Germany was a function of formal and informal bilateral political–institutional arrangements which tolerated the creation of 'social spaces beyond boundaries through repeated or circular migration across borders' has acquired even more significance in the context of an enlarged European Union.

From accession to recession: The impact of the recession on Polish migrants in the United Kingdom

During the first quarter of 2008 the number of A8 migrants registered to work in the United Kingdom by the Home Office fell by almost 15 per cent when compared to 2007. Amongst Polish migrants this fell by 20 per cent. It was the fourth quarter in succession that registrations by workers from the A8 countries had experienced a year-on-year decline (Taylor, 2008b). Prior to Christmas 2009, travel agents reported that many Polish customers 'were buying one-way tickets home'. The UK Polish-language weekly *Goniec Polski* estimated that during the first quarter of 2009, 10 per cent of the UK Polish migrant population returned to Poland, and that another 10 per cent were also thinking of doing so. Many Polish-owned businesses acting as brokers and employment agencies shut down (Warrell, 2009). *Access*, a firm which finds jobs for skilled Polish technicians in the United Kingdom, saw a

40 per cent decline in income by 2008 and other recruitment agencies reported similar trends (Guthrie, 2008).

The recession raised new issues for migrants generally and Polish migrants in the United Kingdom specifically. As labour migrants, many are likely, other things being equal, to find it more difficult to find jobs. This is the first recession since the population changes experienced by the United Kingdom over the past decade, which saw substantial growth in the immigrant population but also fundamental shifts in the composition of immigrant inflows, as EU enlargement dramatically increased the number of Eastern European migrants working in the United Kingdom. Somerville and Sumption (2009, pp. 6–7), asking whether the recession will reduce immigrant inflows and encourage A8 return migration, noted that 'at the time of recession, immigration issues pose challenges for integration in communities and for good relations in society'. They also caution against seeing migration decisions as solely governed by economic concerns.

An illustration of the impact of the recession was the xenophobic backlash during 2008–09 in the United Kingdom, which saw wild-cat strikes in oil refineries, power stations and gas terminals which, whilst ostensibly over economic demands encompassed in the slogan 'British jobs for British workers', also send a powerful political message of exclusion to immigrants and people perceived as immigrants. The message was given even more potency when Gordon Brown, the Labour Prime Minister (at the time), used the slogan. During February 2008 workers at Total's Lindsey refinery walked out. In May 2009 the liquefied natural gas terminal in Milford Haven, west Wales, saw a walk-out by hundreds of construction workers against the employment of 50 Polish workers by a contractor. This action spread to Aberthaw power station in South Wales, Fiddlers Ferry power station in Widnes, Cheshire and the ConocoPhillips Humber refinery in north Lincolnshire. Management were accused of breaking local agreements requiring contractors to maximise use of local labour at Milford Haven (Briscoe and Groom, 2009). One irony in these disputes is that many, if not most, of the strikers themselves have at one time or another worked abroad.

In trying to assess whether the impact of recession and xenophobia has led to a returnee movement amongst Polish migrants in the United Kingdom it is important to understand the extent to which key decisions made by migrants revolve around the issues of finding work and at the right price. Pay is influenced by a range of factors, not least in the supply of and demand for labour both in the United Kingdom and Poland. An important dimension of this was the significant labour market changes and increased employment opportunities available in Poland in the immediate pre-recession period. One consequence of mass outward migration from 2004 onwards was that labour scarcity became a significant factor in the Polish economy, with an increasing number of firms citing this as a barrier to growth. During 2007 the number of Polish businesses citing the lack of skilled workforce as a barrier to growth had risen from 28 per cent to 43 per cent compared to 2006 (Taylor and Wagstyl, 2007). Similar trends became apparent in the public sector, with rising numbers of vacancies for teachers and social workers. For some the opportunity structure in Poland improved. This was influenced by declining unemployment rates from 25 per cent in 2004 to 10.5 per cent during the first quarter of 2008. Labour shortages of construction workers to build facilities for the 2012 European Football Championship were reported in the Polish media (Ciensky, 2008). In this situation average monthly wages in Poland increased by 39 per cent during July 2008 with a yearly average increase of 12 per cent. In the public sector wage rises were higher than the average. Graduate migrants began to look at the possibilities of private and public sector professional employment in Poland as an alternative to low-paid and low-esteem work in the United Kingdom (Taylor, 2008b).

Another critical influence on the opportunity structure available to labour migrants appeared in the changing exchange rate between the UK pound and the Polish zloty, and the implications this has for remittances sent by the migrants to their families in Poland. The declining exchange rate for the pound contributed towards a scissors effect between rising wages in Poland and the declining value of remittances from the United Kingdom. A survey by Britain's largest Polish speaking radio station (Polish Radio London) found that almost 40 per cent of migrant Polish workers would seriously consider returning home if the exchange rate fell to four zlotys to the pound. During May 2008 the pound was worth 4.20 zlotys, compared with more than seven when Poland joined the European Union in 2004. During June 2009 the pound was equivalent to 5.3 zlotys (Taylor, 2008b). Michael Dembinski, Head of Policy at the British Polish Chamber of Commerce, estimated that migrants typically needed to send £500 a month to justify working in the United Kingdom. Four years ago this would have bought 3565 zlotys. Today it is worth just over 2100 zlotys, a fall of 40 per cent. At the same time, however, most financial transfer institutions and official statistics (calculating in sterling), such as *Onemoneymail*, established by BGZ bank to manage money transfers between Britain and Poland, did not detect any significant decline in remittances that might indicate larger numbers were returning home (Taylor, 2008b). A not unreasonable note of caution in interpreting these trends is that as Polish migrants' knowledge of the UK labour market improved over time and, more importantly, as their workplace seniority increased, so many were finding better-paid employment not captured in official statistics.

A major impact of the recession was to reduce the number of new migrants. Office for National Statistics (2009a) data show that work applications (WRS) from the A8 countries fell by 47 per cent during the first three months of 2008, from 53,000 to 29,000 when compared to the previous period. Polish applications fell from 36,000 to 16,000. This striking decline in WRS applications suggests that migration patterns from the A8 countries are shaped by the actions of relatively mobile migrants who can respond quickly to changing economic circumstances. By summer 2008 the United Kingdom saw the lowest number of migrants from eastern and central Europe since accession in 2004. The Department for Work and Pensions reported that the number of National Insurance (NI) numbers allocated to foreign nationals seeking work rose by just 4 per cent in the 12 months to the end of March 2008. This was the smallest increase since figures were first published in 2002–03. Polish workers still accounted for 28.6 per cent of NI allocations. However, sectors such as construction, hotels, restaurants and retail shops, which drove migration to the United Kingdom, reduced employment. Vacancies in construction where about 10 per cent of the estimated 2m workers are migrants declined by 13 per cent during May–July 2008 when compared to the previous three months (Taylor, 2008b, 2009).

A novel dimension of the recession was that native workers began to act as labour market substitutes for A8 migrants in unskilled jobs as the recession was forcing British workers into tough low-paid jobs that had been the preserve of A8 migrants. Paul Whitehouse, Chair of the Gangmasters Licensing Authority, was quoted as saying 'We're starting to see many British people in some of the places we go to, which we haven't seen before, a lot of people are having to take whatever work they can. These are basic minimum wage jobs, pack-houses, sorting out potatoes on lines, that kind of thing'. This was the first time the agency had seen this trend since it was set up in 2006. Linda Wuttke, from The Workshop, an agency in Cambridgeshire, said 'It just happened recently. It's what I'd call older, middle-aged people who have been in work for 10, 15, 20 years in one place and now with the climate as it is, they are made redundant and willing to take on anything' (Pickard, 2009, p. 5).

The impact of the recession was to introduce more uncertainty amongst Polish migrants resident in the United Kingdom. By December 2008, as the full impact of the economic downturn and rising unemployment became apparent, many migrants began to think more seriously about the possibility of returning home, and not for the usual reasons of Christmas and New Year. The number of people from Eastern Europe leaving the United Kingdom had already more than doubled in the year to September 2008. In the 12 months to September 2008, 56,000 people from the A8 countries, a relatively small number, left the United Kingdom (Boxell, 2009). An increased number were making inquiries about statutory benefits such as Jobseeker's Allowance. To be eligible, applicants need to have worked in the United Kingdom for a 12-month period of continuous employment. Again, whilst the numbers applying for benefits were small they were indicative of the circumstances facing the migrants: in 2008, 13,600 migrants from the A8 countries applied for income-related benefits, up from 12,200 in 2007 and 6287 in 2006. More than half of the claims were from Polish workers (Sherwood, 2009). The circumstances for migrant decision-making became yet more complicated as the pound made a rally against the zloty during 2009 and also as the outlook for the Polish economy, which whilst still positive, had weakened as the recession began to also have an impact on the economies of eastern and central Europe. One result was that many UK-based Poles who had planned to leave were still sitting tight, feeling trapped in uncertainty Many were returning home but even more were determined to ride out the economic downturn in the United Kingdom in the face of possibly even worse economic prospects back home (Guthrie, 2008).

During the first three months of 2009, applications for work registration permits from the A8 countries continued to fall to their lowest level since accession in 2004. Home Office data similarly showed that the total number of people coming to the United Kingdom from Eastern Europe to work had fallen to the lowest level since 2004. New Polish Workers Registrations declined even further to 12,480 during the period of January to March 2009 (Boxell, 2009; Home Office, 2009). In commenting on these trends, Border and Immigration Minister Phil Woolas said,

> Today's figures show that immigration levels are balancing as more Eastern Europeans are now leaving the UK to return home. This suggests that rising incomes in post Soviet Eastern Europe, in the long term can only be beneficial for the UK. (Home Office, 2009)

Glossop and Shaheen (2009, p. 1) point to conflicting evidence about the impact of recession-induced return migration and note that in their studies of Hull and Bristol there had been no mass return by migrants from either city in response to the recession, so far. They noted that in Bristol 'there is greater evidence of settlement than Hull where workers are mainly channelled into factory work by recruitment agencies', and that

> A8 movements are widely perceived to be circular (meaning that they travel back and forth from their home country, and stay for different lengths of time), this study found that semi-permanent communities (those staying for more than two years) are also beginning to form. The research found no evidence of a 'mass exodus' in response to recession in Bristol or Hull. (Glossop and Shaheen, 2009, p. 15)

The above was confirmed in estimates made by the Polish government. By September 2009, the plans put in place by the government during the onset of the recession, in the expectation of a mass return home, proved unnecessary. The Warsaw-based Centre for International Studies found that whilst, as UK figures confirm, the number of migrants leaving Poland had fallen significantly, 'the economic crisis has not caused – at least so far – mass returns' and that 'only a small proportion of migrants are returning to Poland' (Ciensky, 2009, p. 11). Those who were coming home permanently tended to be drawn from professional occupations.

The impact of recession on Polish migrants in the United Kingdom indicates a complex set of relationships involving different groups of migrants. One general factor in explaining unemployment trends between migrants and native workers, however, is that the immigration system is geared to selecting the most employable people, both in terms of skills and human capital. Also, migrants are hired in sectors where there are labour shortages. These are important countervailing tendencies which partly explain why unemployment may increase more amongst native workers when compared to foreign workers. Indeed during the first quarter of 2009 the number of British-born workers in employment fell by 451,000 or 1.8 per cent, whilst amongst the foreign-born jobs rose by 129,000, or 3.5 per cent during the same period. This disguises the possibility that a significant proportion of the unemployed migrants might have returned home. They were not available for statistical purposes (Briscoe and Groom, 2009). Glossop and Shaheen (2009, pp. 15, 24) suggest that an important part of the migrant perspectives was that most perceived that 'it was easier to find a job in the United Kingdom during the recession than it was in countries such as Poland'.

Conclusions

This chapter, in examining the key factors which have shaped migration from Poland to the United Kingdom, concurs with much of the literature surveyed, that the relationship between sympathetic policy-making and proximity created the basis for circular and seasonal migration as a specific form of transnationalism. At the same time, the chapter has described different groups of migrants with differing objectives for migration. Some were short-term guestworkers (labour migrants), whilst others long-term migrants with families. A large section was part of a student and youth exodus which combined work with gaining life experiences. The many graduates amongst the migrants accounted for the high levels of human capital formation amongst Polish and A8 nationals. There are also important differences between groups who arrived at different points in time, such as during the pre- and post-Accession periods, or before and after the current recession, and who at these points faced different problems and opportunities. There are also significant differences in the perspectives of migrants which reflect on the ageing process itself. More difficult to understand, perhaps, are processes in formation both in the development of Polish migrant communities and also in the social and economic differentiation taking place inside these communities. The development of small enterprises in the form of labour agents, self-employed builders who become petty employers, entrepreneurs who act as community leaders, the owners of grocery shops, bar-rooms and travel agents, indicates the social re-composition of Polish migrants. In a not unusual migrant story, many of the entrepreneurs/petty capitalists have emerged from the ranks of labour migrants.

The chapter has suggested that Polish migration and the relationship between the old (New Commonwealth) and the new (Eastern European) migration raises new and novel questions about cultural diversity in the United Kingdom Perhaps it is worth reflecting in this respect, on the conclusions drawn by Alba and Nee (2003) about ethnic competition theories applied to analyses of Polish and other migrant flows into the United States during the late nineteenth century. They argued that the advance of Polish, Italian, Slavic and Jewish migrants did not come at the expense of the descendents of even earlier arrivals from Northern and Western Europe. An important contextual explanation was provided in the effects of economic growth and the post-war boom which vastly expanded employment opportunities in urban America.

The primary purpose of the chapter has been to offer a theoretical critique of the 'new' geography of migration and the globalisation 'from below' thesis. The chapter, in pointing to the extensive management of Polish and A8 migration, concludes that both theories are woefully inadequate at explaining this example of globalisation 'from above' and the selective process of cosmopolitanism sponsored by the political–institutional framework in the form of European Union enlargement. The chapter identified, in the case of Polish migration, the development of circular migration as the most concrete form of transnationalism, one made possible by sympathetic policy-making. Other examples of this are the estimated one to two million British and German old age pensioners living in Southern Spain and the Algarve (Gustafson, 2008). What we need to explain, however, and which needs further investigation is the selectivity in the behaviour of the institutional framework. At the same time as historically unprecedented freedom to move by EU workers, Third Country Nationals, second and third generation Turkish migrants and their children in Germany, refugees deported from Italy to concentration camps in Libya or incarcerated with their children in UK prisons are amongst the most evident examples of the repressive functions of immigration controls by the same member states. The UK government, in the *Five-Year Strategy for Asylum Seekers and Immigration*, envisages, for example, that selective A8 migration will replace unskilled migrants from outside Europe (Home Office, 2005a, p. 13; Home Office, 2005b). Primarily, this implies a decoupling from New Commonwealth migration. The deduction that Polish and A8 migrants are benefiting in a project for a White, Christian, Europe, whilst crude, might not be a completely inaccurate description of migration policy intentions in the United Kingdom.

Much of the discussion of Polish migration in the United Kingdom, such as that concerning the role of the Workers Registration Scheme, is framed to present managed migration as an economic benefit to the receiving country. At the same time, evidence also points to fluidity and contingency in migration regimes. In part this fluidity is driven by the changing social and economic circumstances facing migrants, policy-makers and, in particular, what is happening to sectoral employment in areas most relevant to the employment of migrants. More substantially than is perhaps recognised in the literature, migration regimes are also driven by the way that national and regional political systems rank migrants in enabling and disabling ways. The chapter concludes that the primary functions of managed migration and immigration controls may well not be economic at all, and are not driven by concern about what happens to workers, whether native or foreign-born, but rather serve to underpin the exercise of selection and regimentation in the political and social construction of national and regional identities.

6
Conclusion: Winners and Losers

Introduction

The material in the previous chapters examined the relationship between ethnicity migration and enterprise and showed how human agency, in the form of ethnicity, can be used to invoke economic action and how social relations, often grounded in the experience of migration, can influence the way ethnic minority entrepreneurs mobilise capital and labour in order to produce goods and services. At the same time we also see that the political–institutional framework and the market environment influences, perhaps to an even greater extent, the incorporation of ethnic minorities into labour markets, as wage-workers, self-employed or petty employers, albeit in qualitatively different ways. Frequently this appears in the form of immigration rules and naturalisation policies and periodic drives against the informal economy which bring many ethnic workers and entrepreneurs into conflict with the regulatory framework and various branches of the state. This is common enough in the histories of workers and entrepreneurs in the Hispanic American community in the United States and the Turkish communities in Germany and the Netherlands. It is also revealed, perhaps, in the current moral panic about Muslims and 'terrorism' and the Chinese diaspora and 'irregular migration' in Europe and the United States. At the same time, we saw, in contrast, how the same political–institutional framework facilitated the highly structured incorporation of labour migrants from the recent European Union accession states to the United Kingdom.

The concluding chapter points to a number of common weaknesses in analyses of ethnicity and ethnic minority enterprise presented by transnational thinking and the enclave-economy thesis. In these analyses there is a tendency to ignore the role of the state and the implications of its actions. They say very little about the relationship between class and ethnic resources in the development of minority enterprises, nor do they consider the economic differentiation taking place between them. More generally they do not consider how the social stratification of ethnic communities may influence economic action. In much of the literature on ethnicity and enterprise, it seems as through we are presented with generalities about ethnic minorities, as either protean heroes of grass-roots capitalism, as is the tendency in eulogies of Cuban entrepreneurship in Miami and more generally the Chinese diaspora, and/or as an exploited proletarian reserve army exemplified by the incorporation of Hispanic migrant labour in centres such as Los Angeles, in the histories of Turkish guestworkers in Germany or in more recent Polish migration to the United Kingdom. Whilst, as we have seen, this is a caricature of the migrant experience, a major weakness in transnational thinking is the tendency to ignore the implications of variation in institutional behaviour towards different groups of migrants and ethnic minorities (sometimes the same group in different historical circumstances), or to explain the selectivity of this process and to fully account for its consequences.

In transnational thinking the economic development of ethnic minorities is decoupled from wider political and cultural processes in society concerning citizenship, the right of black and ethnic minorities to take part in shaping their own cultural development or the need to defend these rights in the current political backlash against multiculturalism.

Since analyses of the political–institutional framework are not an important focus in transnational research it says little, therefore, about the political incorporation of ethnic minorities and their ability or inability to influence political systems as others people do. This is revealed in significant differences between members of the same ethnic group who are foreign-born and naturalised, and those who are foreign-born but non-citizens. As we saw in the comparison between the Hispanic communities in Miami and Los Angeles, legal status might be a more significant indicator of difference than anything associated with variations on Hispanic identity. To repeat, Hispanic non-US citizens in either of the two cities, whilst more likely to be self-employed, are also twice as likely in Miami and three times as likely in Los Angeles to be living below the poverty line or to be a member of a family living in poverty than Hispanics who have been naturalised (see Table 4.3, prev. cit.). One conclusion about much of the poverty facing urban America is that if all foreign-born Hispanics became US citizens this would, other things being equal, make serious inroads into the structure of poverty in the United States. At the same time, however, we also know from studies of 'illegal' employment, that in the migrant experience, 'the context of reception does not necessarily make clear distinctions between so-called "legal" and "illegal" migrants' (Ahmad, 2008, p. 853). Informal labour markets can be quite impervious to the legal status of workers they employ.

Major criticisms of ethnic enclave economy theories are that they ignore the role of social and economic difference inside ethnic communities and the relationship between ethnicity and social categories rooted in race, gender, legal status and class. In much of this analysis it is as though social categories are disembodied and social groups are collapsed into aggregate ethnic categories. More significantly, since we are often examining processes in formation, both transnational thinking and the ethnic enclave thesis fail to explain how difference emerges and how social stratification is reproduced inside ethnic communities. At one level social differentiation manifests itself in the emergence, often from the ranks of wage-workers, of people working on their own account as self-employed or as petty employers. A co-related process appears in the economic differentiation of ethnic enterprise and the emergence, frequently from the ranks of the many self-employed and petty employers, of a class of larger and more economically powerful enterprises with more clearly delineated capitalist characteristics, such as recruiting labour from the open labour market and making use of the commercial lending sector.

Ethnic and class resources

The relationship between class and ethnicity has been revealed in a number of ways in the case study material. We saw the argument by Light and Gold (2000, p. 97) that Cubans in Miami built a bigger and more successful ethnic economy by making use of their superior class resources, including human capital formation, when compared to other Hispanic groups and Haitian refugees. Similarly, Barth's research of the Swat Pathan, which pioneered analyses of ethnicity and ethnic 'boundary making', can be seen as a study which was as much about class as ethnicity. He showed how Swat society was also an extremely polarised society, with on one hand the landlord class of *Khans* and on the other their dependent sharecropping tenant farmers, coming from *Gujar*, *Ajar* and *Khoistani* peoples marginalised by elite conquests in the sixteenth century. The division between them was analogous to the caste system in India, with separate mosques and graveyards (Barth, 1959). The analysis by Abram Leon (1998) of the ethnicisation of occupations, skills and trades which appeared historically and in the incorporation of the Jewish masses in the Pale and Russia in the form of a 'people-class' and the extent to which these ideas can be equally applied to analyse contemporary patterns of migrant and ethnic minority labour market incorporation in the heartlands of Europe and North America, provided particularly challenging but familiar questions about the transformation of wage-workers and self-employed artisans into incipient ethnic capitalists.

Whilst the economics of ethnicity need to be contextually understood, a number of recurring themes appear in the emergence of ethnic minority enterprise which suggest a relationship between class and ethnic resources available to a class of ethnic entrepreneurs. It is not unusual for ethnic, and in particular recently arrived migrant, communities to be characterised by a relative abundance of labour but limited supplies of capital. Whilst subsequent flows of migrants can be curtailed by a tightening of immigration rules, which can result in labour shortages that may be compounded by second-generation resistance to entering the 'niche' sectors of the mothers and fathers, a more general problem in the initiation of firms is a shortage of start-up capital, complicated by the unwillingness of the commercial banking sector to lend without collateral. For this reason, ethnic self-employed and small enterprises are found disproportionately in sectors which have lower costs to entry and are labour-intensive (requiring less capital and more labour, relative to other sectors), and this is a key factor in explaining the tendency for many enterprises to 'crowd-around' particular sectors and sub-sectors. Ethnic minority entrepreneurs attempt to compensate for capital scarcity by making use of ethnic ties and networks. A considerable body of evidence points to initial privileges enjoyed by ethnic entrepreneurs, which substantially derive from their greater social integration in the ethnic economy and which are used both in the mobilisation of capital and labour. The emergence of ethnic enterprises in the garment industry has been frequently linked in the wider literature to near-monopoly access by the entrepreneurs to co-ethnic female labour, often involving family members (Anthias, 1992; Green, 2002; Panayiotopoulos, 1996; Phizacklea, 1990; Zhou, 2002).

Longitudinal studies of minority enterprise in the United States observe a historical transition by many entrepreneurs from a first-generation dependence on ethnic resources and peer-group based lending from friends, relatives and informal Rotating Savings and Credit Associations (ROSCAS) established by co-workers and fellow migrants, to a subsequent generation use of class resources, reflected in collateral-based lending and access to the commercial banking sector (Light, 1972; Light and Gold, 2000). Light and Gold (2000, p. 102) describe the resources available to any ethnic entrepreneur as involving a relationship between class and ethnic resources. Class resources can be either material or cultural. Ethnic resources are the 'socio-cultural and demographic features of the whole group which coethnic entrepreneurs actively utilize in business or from which their business passively benefits' and which 'contribute to entrepreneurship independent of class'. However, they also argue that

> a defining feature of class resources is universality. Class resources lack distinctive ethnic or cultural character. The bourgeoisie of Finland possesses them just as does the bourgeoisie of Taiwan. Every bourgeoisie possesses the same class resources 'but not necessarily the same resources in the same quantities.' [And that], 'ethnic and class resources need not be of equal importance. In some mixed cases, class resources predominate; in other mixed cases, ethnic resources predominate; in others ethnic and class resources are of equal importance'. (Light and Gold, 2000, pp. 102–103)

The relationship between class and ethnic resources in the development of enterprise and the extent to which ethnicity and class can also act independently of each other points to significant areas for further exploration and debate. The market, however, is quite impervious to how a commodity is produced or what relative proportions of ethnic or class resources have been used in its production. It trades primarily in the form of price competition, including as we saw, ironically, in a network involving the production of fake designer goods. Yet in most of the analyses of ethnicity and economic action that have been examined, there is little recognition of price competition or any other form of competition between entrepreneurs. This is at odds with studies of ethnic minority participation in, for example, a cut-throat industry like the women's fashion-wear sector. If co-ethnic entrepreneurs are brothers, then, to paraphrase Marx, they are also brothers at war. Often this war appears in a relationship between strategies of accumulation and economic differentiation at the higher end and the informalisation of production and a reduction in costs of production at the lower end. Frequently this involves the use of extensive systems of subcontracting, often grounded in the idiom of ethnicity, but which, as with subcontracting elsewhere, have the economic function of expelling marginal and institutional costs (Munck, 2007; Panayiotopoulos, 1996, Panayiotopoulos and Dreef, 2002; Schierup, 2007).

Ethnic enclave economy theories ignore social and economic differentiation inside ethnic communities

Much of the discussion about the ethnic enclave economy thesis has focussed on proving or disproving the benign effects of a concentrated ethnic economy in which ethnic entrepreneurs employ co-ethnic workers. The thesis argues that workers and entrepreneurs in the enclave receive earnings/returns to human capital similar to those they would receive in the open labour market, and that the enclave represents an effective vehicle for upward mobility among ethnic minorities and, in particular, amongst recent migrant groups (Garapich, 2008; Portes and Jensen, 1989; Zhou, 1992; see also Kitching et al., 2009). A major criticism of this line of inquiry is that a necessary precondition for evaluating the effects of the ethnic enclave economy is that we need to understand how ethnic communities are socially stratified. An even more basic condition is that we need to know who the entrepreneurs are and how they change over time. In order to explain 'who benefits' from the ethnic economy we need to explain how members of an ethnic group are differentiated in terms of class, gender, age, race and employment status as well as legal status.

An emerging body of literature points to negative effects of the ethnic enclave economy, particularly on women. Wang (2007, p. 1) argues that amongst the Chinese community in San Francisco, while 'abundant ethnic resources may exist in ethnic neighborhoods and enclaves for certain types of employment opportunities, these resources do not necessarily help Chinese immigrant workers, especially women, to move upwards along the labor market hierarchy'. In addition, men and women show 'distinct labor market concentration patterns', with most women 'concentrated in semi- or low-skilled jobs' such as clerks, cashiers, waitresses and food preparation, with sewing machinists being the second largest concentration (Wang, 2007, pp. 23–24).

Pedace and Rohn (2008, pp. 16–18), drawing from US Census material, suggest that that 'the enclave has negative effects on wages for Mexican, Central American, West Asian and East Asian workers' while, peculiarly, 'having an insignificant impact on the wages of other groups'. The research points to 'significant negative effects' for women in these groups. The above challenges the common argument that the ethnic enclave provides an explanation for the 'economic success' of Cuban enterprise in Miami, for example.

Most analyses of ethnic economies or ethnic enclave economies, whether pessimistic or optimistic, ignore the internal economic differentiation of ethnic minority enterprises in terms of purpose, size and labour input. Many are small, survival-orientated enterprises in the 'niche' sectors which depend on family labour (newsagents, take-aways, grocery stores), but others, as in the garment or information technology industries, may be large employers and recruit labour with the necessary skills from a range of ethnic groups available in the local and international labour markets. A significant number operate as micro-multinational companies and engage in international outward processing. Some describe this as a process of 'breaking out' of the ethnic economy. At the other end of the enterprise spectrum, the precarious status of entrepreneur is itself frequently an emergent and submergent phenomenon characterised by high levels of entry and exit. The above points to significant variation within immigrant economies and suggests that it would be unwise to make generalisations about an 'essential' ethnic enterprise (typically in the form of the 'family firm') (Altinay and Altinay, 2008; Panayiotopoulos, 2008; Panayiotopoulos and Dreef, 2002; Rutherford and Blackburn, 2000).

Economic differentiation influences relationships with the market and the institutional framework, and it is here that the impact of differentiation is at its most significant. Ethnic manufacturers, wholesalers, contractors and retailers relate to the market at different levels of the production cycle, are subject to different outcomes and adopt different strategies to cope with market fluctuation. The same broad polarity can be applied in relationships with the banking sector, branches of the state, and, in particular, with local government. The beneficiaries of institutional support are more likely to be entrepreneurs who are the most economically powerful and who are also the most politically embedded, whilst in contrast, the contractors, subcontractors and the multitude of self-employed are the least likely to receive institutional support and the most likely to feel the wrath of the state, typically for not conforming to relevant legislation on taxation and labour standards. One important dimension of differentiation is the way it influences business mobility, transnational positioning and relations with the political–institutional framework. In many respects the 'most' globalised entrepreneurs tend to be those with the greatest economic power and connectivity not simply with ethnic minority communities, but also with the dominant institutions of the host society.

The book has argued that the differentiation of ethnic minority enterprise has critical implications for how entrepreneurs respond to changes in the market and institutional environment, how they manage their enterprises and in how they relate to the production process. The experience of ethnic minority participation in the North London garment industry and elsewhere, indicates that differentiation has typically represented a move away from a pattern of many small Cut Make Trim (CMT) contractors and towards one of fewer manufacturers. A much smaller number have become considerable owners of property (Panayiotopoulos, 2006; Panayiotopoulos and Dreef, 2002). This process, along with the informalisation of production and its negative impact on labour rights, has been a significant experience of Cypriot participation and informed conclusions in early research about the community as an 'achieving' minority, which more recent ethnic entrants in the garment sector (in New York, Berlin, Paris and Amsterdam) might 'emulate' (Waldinger et al., 1985, p. 587).

The size and complexity of the enterprise may determine the physical form in which the proprietor takes part in the enterprise. In small workshops, restaurants, take-aways and small taxi firms, the entrepreneur frequently works side-by-side with other shop-floor workers. In larger workshops the proprietor may give up manual working and specialise in commercial, marketing and other functions, which may detach the entrepreneur from the establishment and from the common experience of physical labour. Material that points to the role of non-co-ethnic labour, such as in Cypriot, Jewish or Korean-owned factories, typically through the employment of women homeworkers from various ethnic groups, raises one major issue. If an employer no longer sweats side-by-side with other workers, of whom an increasing proportion may come from an ethnic group different from that of the employer, then the claim to a common identity based on common ethnic origins and experience, which may unite the employer and the worker, is considerably weakened. This trend can become amplified in emergent enterprises, which employ larger numbers of workers and within which family workers constitute a smaller proportion of the labour force.

In much of the analysis of ethnic minority enterprise little regard is shown to how entrepreneurs often emerge from the ranks of wage-workers, or how they manage their day-to-day activities, how they organise the production of goods and services, the nature of the labour regime, and how they make sense of the changes taking place around them in their new-found roles as self-employed or petty employer. Whilst for a wage-worker to become an ethnic employer is not unusual in the circumstances described, it does imply a transformation in social relations of revolutionary proportions both in how the worker-now-employer relates to labour and markets and also in their world view. A class of ethnic capitalists who have risen from the ranks of workers may translate (to paraphrase Gramsci, 1971), into one where amongst small employers, the ethnic migrant 'man in the mass' contains two consciousnesses: vestiges of his/her artisanal, or working class origins (or what may be seen as a theoretical consciousness), and on the other, his/her actual practical consciousness as a petty or larger employer. In this sense, the emergent entrepreneurs may be seen as the bearer of two consciousnesses, or of one contradictory consciousness.

Nowhere is this contradictory consciousness more apparent than in attitudes towards trade unions. A study of Cypriot contractors in the London garment industry showed that most of the entrepreneurs had risen from the ranks of wage-workers and many were previously members of trade unions. Sixteen (out of 78) specified that they were members in the home country and two actually held full-time positions in Communist-led trade unions. Some continued membership of English trade unions and 13 specified previous membership in the United Kingdom: three were shop stewards and one was a District Official. When the question was asked, 'Is there a trade union here?', the answer in 77 out of 78 cases was negative, with a typical response consisting of, 'what, for fifteen people?'. When the question was asked 'What do *you* think of trade unions?', many entrepreneurs (particularly amongst the 'first' generation immigrant group) saw them in a positive light. It was illustrative that at one left-wing meeting, seven respondents were present and the meeting was advertised in three factories with, in two, the poster prominently displayed on the employer's office door (Panayiotopoulos, 2006, p. 223).

The emergence of a class of ethnic employers from the ranks of migrant wage-workers in sectors such as the garment industry, construction, catering and taxi-driving can be seen as a concrete manifestation of the reproduction of class society. Much of the evidence suggests that the status of ethnic employer is an emergent and submergent phenomenon, characterised by high levels of entry and exit. Evidence from studies of ethnic minority entrepreneurs in the Parisian garment industry (Morokvasic et al., 1990, p. 167) suggests that the ambiguity of the contractor's status is such that the contractor 'may be literally employer and employee at the same time' and that 'some immigrants regularly shift from one status to another several times a year'. *Le système Sentier* is characterised by high rate of firm turnover (failures) (Green, 2002). Similar patterns are found amongst Polish, Hispanic, Turkish and Chinese entrepreneurs at the low end of sectors such as construction, the fast-food industry, fashion-wear and accessories manufacture, the private care service sector or labour agents.

One cautionary note is that the complexity of an increasingly differentiated milieu makes it difficult to draw overarching conclusions. Another suggestion from sectoral studies of ethnic minority enterprise is that the restructuring of sectors such as retailing, catering and sub-sectors of the garment industry, such as the women's fashion-wear sector, may be a more critical factor in the incorporation of ethnic minority groups, the differentiation of enterprise and the modification of economic behaviour, than characteristics associated with any single immigrant or ethnic group. This introduces a note of caution to the assumption that an optimistic or pessimistic causal connection exists between enterprise, work norms, practices and the ethnic origin of entrepreneurs and workers employed by them. This sectoral and structural observation challenges basic assumptions held by the new economic sociology which underpins transnational and ethnic enclave thinking.

More significantly, perhaps, economic differentiation is influenced and in many ways structured by the political–institutional and market environment facing ethnic minority entrepreneurs. The example of Amsterdam shows the fragility of this. One tentative conclusion from the European experience is that cities characterised by a protracted presence of ethnic communities which have civil rights somewhere near the average, may be more likely to enjoy the conditions necessary for the development of sustainable ethnic minority-owned enterprises. The diverse experiences of entrepreneurs suggest the need to reconsider the relationship between economic differentiation and how this influences the way entrepreneurs manage their enterprises and relate to the market and institutional environment in which they operate. These questions are excluded in assumptions made about relatively homogeneous (and compliant) ethnic economies or ethnic enclave economies.

Transnational thinking ignores the role of the state and assumes permeable borders

Transnational thinking and the globalisation 'from below' thesis operate as though the state does not exist, or if it does, its effects can be easily circumvented. It assumes permeable borders. Yet it is often through the actions of the political–institutional framework that we see how ethnic and racial groups are ranked for exclusion or inclusion in extensive but selective systems of immigration controls and managed migration. Waldinger (2008, p. 24) makes the observation that transnationalism 'is a rare condition' and that settled immigrants, possessing secure legal status, are more likely to engage in those cross-border activities seen as indicators of transnationalism. In a similar vein, Waldinger and Fitzgerald (2004, p. 1179), drawing from US material, argue that transnational theories ignore the 'interaction of migrants with states and civil society actors in both sending and receiving countries'. They point to the 'absence of any concerted effort to analyse the relationship between immigrant transnationalism and receiving states'. Portes (2009, p. 9) concedes that immigrants most likely to take part in transnational activities 'are not the most recent arrivals, but those better established and with more solid economic positions in the host country'. This process of selectivity in the ethnic migrant experience is illustrated in the example of Polish migration to the United Kingdom as a manifestation of politically induced globalisation (or, more accurately, regionalisation) driven by European Union enlargement. One consequence has been the emergence of a new hierarchy of labour between European Union citizens and Third Country Nationals (TCNs).

Both the United States and Europe have extensive histories of immigration controls. A running theme in UK immigration policy appears in processes of selectivity. Race, gender, nationality, religion, and the status of migrants as refugees or economic migrants, documented and undocumented migrants, are significant factors in determining entry and the terms of integration. Immigrants from the White Commonwealth countries (Australia, Canada, New Zealand), for example, are many more times likely to be admitted than immigrants from the Black, New Commonwealth countries (Caribbean, Indian sub-continent, Africa). Similarly, UK immigration legislation denied Asian women the right to independent migration for nearly a quarter of a century. The British Government introduced in 1905, for the first time, anti-immigrant legislation (The Aliens Act) which targeted poor Yiddish Eastern European immigrants, who had transformed the East End of London into a centre of Jewish economic, political and intellectual life, rivalling that of New York's Lower East Side. In 1962 the UK Commonwealth Immigrants Act targeted West Indian and Asian immigrants. In 1968 the Ugandan Commonwealth Immigration Act targeted Asian UK passport holders from Uganda.

Throughout these experiences the UK government linked migration policy to economic benefit for the British economy. New Commonwealth migration as a means of managing labour shortages in the post-war boom is a case in point. A contemporary manifestation is in the Home Office (2007a) Report on *The Economic and Fiscal Impact of Immigration*, which was written with Polish migration in mind, produced the calculation that 'a 1 per cent increase in the ratio of immigrants to natives would lead to 0.3 per cent to 0.4 per cent increase in the average earnings for natives'. A counter-report from the House of Lords (2008) Economic Affairs Committee rejected the government case for the benefits of migration to the United Kingdom and concluded that high net immigration has had little effect on income per head in the resident population. Further, it urged the government to set numerical targets for inward migration. Christopher Caldwell (2007, p. 12) commented that '4% of the average weekly non-migrant wage of £395 works out at £1.58', 'roughly the cost of half a pint of beer' and called it 'a pittance'. Similar sentiments were expressed by David Coleman. He priced the value of the economic contribution made by each migrant as equivalent to the price of a Mars Bar. This supply-side discourse which sees migrants and minorities as essentially labour migrants ignores both the demand-side effect of migrants on aggregate demand (as consumers), which drove much of US growth before the current recession, and the employment generation capacity of immigrant/ethnic minority-owned enterprises. It does, however, indicate that 'pricing' the value of a migrant is a complex and subjective affair, which creates messy problems for the institutional framework.

During February 2008 the UK government introduced the new 'points-based immigration' system (pbi) as an attempt to add more economic value to migration. The points-based system is a highly structured attempt designed to stem the flow of low-skilled migrant workers from non-European countries and to give preference to entrepreneurs and skilled professionals. Highly Skilled or 'Tier 1' immigrants, which include entrepreneurs, must score, like other migrants, a minimum of 75 points, calculated on the basis of their age, qualifications, past earnings and experience of studying in the United Kingdom (Home Office, 2006). For example, if for entry one requires 75 points, then 50 can be earned if the migrant is a PhD holder and another 20 if under the age of 27 (see Table 1.3, prev. cit.). In contrast, a migrant from China who is a cook, or a waiter from Bangladesh or a taxi driver from Pakistan will find it nearly impossible to migrate legally to the United Kingdom. Under the new rules, employers recruiting workers from outside the European

Economic Area must be able to show that the job could not have been filled from the existing 'resident labour market'. Migrant workers will have to demonstrate English language competence, have a definite job and enough money (about £800 per month) to support themselves for the first month they are here.

The United States has also has used extensive immigration controls. The first ever anti-immigrant legislation (Immigrant Act 1875) targeted women who worked in bars or were 'prostitutes'. In fact, young Irish women who worked as housemaids and in many cases travelled as independent female immigrants were the first to feel this restriction. The Chinese Exclusion Act (1882) made Chinese labourers inadmissible, and this was extended in 1888 for 20 years (with a clause for a further 20 years to 1928). It was not repealed until 1943, in favour of meagre quotas (literally hundreds) which continued until 1965. Following the assassination of President William Mackinley by a freelance anarchist in 1901, the Immigration Act (1903) prohibited entry to 'polygamists' and 'anarchists' Legislation in 1907 (The Gentlemen's Agreement) severely limited Japanese immigration. The Immigration Act (1917) imposed literacy tests for admission which virtually barred all Asian immigrants from entry. The National Quota Law (1921) limited immigration of each nationality to 3 per cent of the number of foreign-born of that nationality living in the United States in 1910. This was extended in the National Origins Act (1924) which set annual quotas for each nationality at 2 per cent of that nationality living in the United States in 1920 (Tichenor, 2002, pp. 3–5). These laws were used to limit the number of Jewish refugees fleeing Nazi Germany and admitted to the United States. Many German Jews faced 'double barriers', with on the one hand US consuls (responsible for processing applications) demanding evidence of economic self-sufficiency and on the other Nazi officials preventing immigrants from removing money and other assets from Germany. Tichenor (2002, p. 151) writes that 'the State Department's Visa Bureau and consular officials were especially resistant to Jewish refugees and often did use their discretion to target European Jews for harsh treatment'.

The National Origins Act, which for over forty years operated a racially selective mechanism in structuring immigration policy, was abandoned in 1965 and this laid the basis for 'new wave' migration from Asia, South and Central America. The advocates of less restrictive immigration policies point to the contribution made by immigrants towards aggregate demand and in human capital formation. One-third of immigrants to the United States since 1990, for example, had a bachelors degree, or higher. Opponents of immigration put forward the proposition that the 'sweatshop' is making a come-back in the US economy, with large 'waves' of undocumented workers providing the labour force. The consequences of 9/11, however, shifted the balance towards the direction of the social conservatives and the United States has experienced the return of an aggressive American nativism, demanding tough controls against immigrants.

The Patriot Act (2001) is the most pervasive form of control, which targeted Muslim and Arab immigrants and visitors for special attention. In practice, however, its main impact has been felt by Mexican migrants either already in or trying to enter the United States. The extension of surveillance has included bi-optic identification, fingerprinting and photographing of all visa holders arriving in the United States, as well as the personal interview of applicants by US embassy staff. This saw an estimated 23 million visitors to the United States each year affected, with US universities complaining of falling enrolments and loss of competition to European institutions due to the burdensome new regulations. The decision by the then Bush administration to create the Department of Homeland Security, a new federal agency dedicated to preventing terrorism, saw the entire immigration function of the government contained within the new department. This reorganisation is a powerful signal that all immigrants will now be viewed as terrorist threats. Thousands of immigrants lost their jobs when 750,000 letters were sent out immediately after the 9/11 attack by the Social Security Administration to employers, telling them that a Social Security number they had supplied did not match the one on its database. Congress passed a law requiring all airport baggage screeners to be US citizens. Thousands of immigrant workers who had not yet become citizens were fired from jobs which in some cases they had held for many years. The Justice Department started enforcing a little-used, 50-year-old law making it a crime for an immigrant not to report a change of address to the INS within ten days of moving (National Migration Forum, 2002).

It is important to restate the above partly in order to amplify the deficiencies of transnational thinking in its unwillingness to account for the influence of the institutional framework and the actions of states in the political and occupational positioning and repositioning of members of a migrant or ethnic group. The lack of political rights of ethnic minorities in the heartlands of Europe and the United States makes them easier to target. Transnational thinking ignores the role played by the regulatory framework and the naturalisation process and the extent to which the development of sustainable ethnic communities and enterprises is shaped in part by the presence or absence of political rights and citizenship (Kloosterman and Rath, 2000, 2001; Kloosterman et al., 1999; Miera, 2008; Panayiotopoulos, 2008; Rath, 2002). This line of investigation is absent from transnational thinking, since this would imply the re-territoralisation of an approach which has long ago dispensed with territories as cultural and more importantly, political, units of analysis. The influence of the nation-state on the development of ethnicities reveals diverse paths and histories in the incorporation of ethnic minorities. Some of these are clearly stated in immigration and naturalisation policies. Others involve more discrete processes, which are also indicative of the limits of naturalisation. They appear in the way that Turks (whether citizens or not) are widely referred to as 'foreigners' in Germany. In the Netherlands the term *autochtoon* is used to describe native, usually white persons and *allochtoon* to describe members of black, ethnic minority and first or second generation immigrant groups. It is revealing that the words *auto* and *allon*, have their roots in the Greek words for 'self' and 'other' respectively. Widely used to signify difference in society, academic analyses and in the underpinning institutional behaviour, these terms and associated territorially based descriptions may be as important as, if not more important than, the legal status of members of ethnic and racial minority groups.

Conclusions: Towards an understanding of multiculturalism 'from below'

This book critically assesses fundamental assumptions made by ethnic competition theories and ethnocultural approaches about homogeneous communities in the use of ethnicity to invoke economic action. It points to both optimism and pessimism in the analyses of key ethnic groups in Europe and the United States. The voices of ethnic pessimism are easier to identify. By ethnic pessimism we mean the view that some ethnic groups are 'locked into' particular paths of development, whether in an upward or downward direction. From Huntington's (2004a) 'Hispanic challenge' based on nativist assumptions about the 'parallel lives' led by Hispanics in the United States and projections about second-generation decline, through the Commission Stasi (2003) in France, which drew similar conclusions about young Arabs in the *banlieues*, and the dire predictions made by Trevor Phillips and the Bishop of Rochester about the Muslim community in the United Kingdom, to those who justify war and Islamophobia in the name of the Enlightenment, a frequent common theme is that multiculturalism is leading to segregation. We are, as Grillo (2007, p. 980) argued, seeing a 'European-wide moral panic about "difference"'.

The book concludes, contrary to the claim by ethnocultural approaches and ethnic competition theories that ethnicity defines culture, that in the real world it is frequently the other way round. It is in the culture of everyday life, work and day-to-day learned experiences of conventions and norms which govern the sociability and daily transactions that define us as humans, that the ethnicity of 'being' is itself shaped and re-shaped. By the ethnicity of 'being' we mean processes and manifestations of self-definition which are collectively recognised by members of a group. Ideas about ethnic solidarity held by members of an ethnic migrant group, and particularly by wage-workers who have become entrepreneurs, can be seen as an attempt to construct and reconstruct a conscious explanation of the changing world around them. Gramsci argued (1971, p. 333) that this process should not be seen as 'fixed' or as the cultural property of individuals, classes or ethnic groups. Rather, ideas are a reflection of the relationships between people and the world around them and, as such, 'as the terms of that relationship change, so consciousness itself is thrown into turmoil'.

Out of this 'turmoil' comes the possibility of multiculturalism 'from below'. In this lies a voice for optimism which points to the reproduction of sociability and how working-class people from culturally diverse backgrounds learn to negotiate and re-negotiate cultural boundaries, frequently by being forced to confront issues of common interest which may emerge and recede according to political circumstances, or more mundanely to work together and share common public services which cut across or 'transverse' cultural differences. Multiculturalism from below challenges both the basic assumptions and the dire predictions made by nativists and ethnic pessimists. There are many examples which illustrate, contrary to ethnic competition or enclave economy theories, how culturally diverse people from the same class manage to work together, live together and negotiate their differences. The East End of London, Lower Manhattan in New York and the Sentier garment district in Paris, all areas strongly associated with ethnic enterprises, also show that these enterprises can sometimes act as the basis for intercultural learning. The Parisian garment centre of Sentier saw ethnic minority enterprise laying the basis for a multi-racialism and multi-ethnicity of the poor which challenges the assumptions of ethnic heterogeneity which underpin many ethnocultural approaches. The Sentier is above all a living testament to multiculturalism and toleration between poor and diverse ethnic groups, from which the dominant culture could learn. One example is 'The King of the Sentier', Maxi Librati, son of Moroccan Jews, who 'began with Polish Jewish and Armenian homeworkers; today he works with Turkish, Serbian, and Chinese contractors' (Green, 2002, p. 43). As Nancy Green argued, in the Sentier district, the multi-ethnic nature of many firms' employment, 'reminds us that cultural complicity is not the only framework of labour relations' and that 'network theory may imply *ipso facto* ethnicisation of the history of the garment industry'. One consequence is that internal 'conflicts within ethnic networks have been minimised by optimists' such as, Waldinger, Mohan and Portes. The focus on the co-ethnic workplace (or diaspora) has too often overlooked the 'truly mixed character' of the garment districts (Green, 2002, p. 41).

Much of the contemporary sociological analyses of immigration and ethnicity suggest that, far from ethnicity being a state reflecting ineradicably differences and highly durable cultural traits, ethnicity and its economic arrangements are an emergent and submergent phenomenon. This becomes doubly apparent in studies of ethnic minority and immigrant participation in particular industries. Material from comparative research indicates that the supply of and demand for labour can re-configure the ethnic composition of the labour force in ethnic minority-owned enterprises. This has been the experience of the garment industry in New York and East London, both once dominated by the Jewish community and now by other immigrant and ethnic groups. Edna Bonacich (1973) applied Leon's (1998) argument about the 'end' of the 'people class', that is, an occupationally based ethnicity which advances and recedes in different historical circumstances, to explain these changes. Waldinger noted (in the New York garment industry) that 'in all sizes of firm made it necessary to recruit beyond the owner's kinship network' (Waldinger, 1986, p. 157). Similarly, evidence from London shows a decreasing role for Cypriot wage-workers in Cypriot-owned factories and an expansion in the employment of, in particular, women home workers from other ethnic groups (Panayiotopoulos and Dreef, 2002). Bonacich (1994) noted that in the Los Angeles garment industry the antagonism between contractor and workers takes on interethnic dimensions between Asian contractors and Hispanic women workers. Such situations provide the material conditions for the development, as Ivan Light argues, of an 'immigrant', rather than ethnic enclave, economy.

Ethnicity and multiculturalism as emergent and submergent phenomena, however, need to be qualified. It is too broad to conclude that the tendency in many enterprises experiencing labour shortages to show (as in the example above) a considerable ethnic interspersion in labour recruitment results in the undermining of the occupational basis of ethnicity as a collective identity, for all social strata in an ethnic group. This is subject to variation, not least in the impact of immigration controls and in opportunities available for working-class youth in ethnic communities. The tendency for a significant proportion of workers *not* to be employed by an employer from the same ethnic group, however, poses questions for social embeddedness theories, which see ethnic solidarity as a necessary precondition for ordering workplace relations and in structuring the redistributory functions of enterprise (Portes, Waldinger, passim). This creates problems for a negotiated paternalism, which applies ethnicity (however defined) as the basic unit for classification and analytical purposes. The tendency to reduce analyses of enterprise and ethnic identity to claims associated with a common origin rather than to common experiences which themselves are subject to change, which may sharply diverge between particular sections of the same group, and which more generally may be subject to a tension between the ideal values of a particular community and the everyday life of its constituent members, however defined, needs to be questioned. Stratification analyses pose problems for culturally driven claims to common identities applied in economic action and workplace relations, and in doing so invite questions about 'who benefits' from ethnic minority enterprise.

Glossary of Key Terms and Concepts

Economic differentiation refers to processes which explain the differences in ethnic minority enterprises in terms of purpose, size and labour input: many are small, survival-orientated family enterprises dependent on family labour, whilst others are large employers who recruit labour from a range of ethnic groups, and in some cases operate as micro-multinational companies engaging in international outward processing. Some describe this as a process of 'breaking out' of the ethnic economy (Altinay and Altinay, 2008; Panayiotopoulos, 2008; Panayiotopoulos and Dreef, 2002; Rutherford and Blackburn, 2000).

Ethnicity and ethnic solidarity can be understood as an emergent and submergent phenomenon, based on claims to common origins shared by members of the same group, and manifested in cultural, economic and political arrangements which underpin the economic incorporation of an ethnic group. For practical purposes this appears in the ethnicity of 'being' or 'the untutored and largely unconscious ethnicity of everyday life' (Barth, 1969; Brass, 1991; Fishman, 1980; Portes, 1984; Waldinger, 2000).

Ethnic economy is a semi-autonomous economic system characterised by entrepreneurs hiring co-ethnic workers. The 'ethnic niche' and 'ethnic enclave' are concentrated forms of the ethnic economy: 'ethnic niche' refers to the tendency for workers to concentrate in particular sectors of the economy. 'Ethnic enclave' refers to concentration in particular cities and neighbourhoods (Favell, 2008; Light and Gold, 2000; Light et al., 1994; Uzar, 2007).

Ethnic enclave economy is a particularly dense ethnic economy characterised by ethnic entrepreneurs employing co-ethnic workers. The enclave economy thesis proposes that workers and entrepreneurs in the enclave receive earnings/returns to human capital commensurate with the earnings/returns of immigrants in the open labour market and that immigrant enterprise represents 'an effective vehicle for upward mobility among immigrant minorities' (Garapich, 2008; Portes and Jensen, 1989; Zhou, 1992; see also Kitching et al., 2009; Pedace and Rohn, 2008).

Globalisation 'from below' purports to show that the restructuring of gateway cities in Europe and the United States has been substantially driven by migrants themselves, acting as their own agents, in spite of institutional hostility. Globalisation 'from above' refers to the disabling and enabling effects of the political–institutional framework in the positioning of migrants and members of an ethnic group (see also *transnationalism*) (Henry et al., 2000; Light, 2000; Panayiotopoulos, 2008; Portes, 1997).

Immigrant enclave economy refers to labour force interspersion driven by the supply and demand for labour. Unlike ethnic economies, in which entrepreneurs employ co-ethnics, immigrant economies arise when entrepreneurs employ immigrant workers from a variety of ethnic backgrounds (Green, 2002; Light et al., 1999; Logan et al., 2002; Panayiotopoulos, 1996).

Informal sector refers to a contested concept and the sum total of economic activities not registered for the purposes of GDP within which labour is not protected by any social legislation and is, therefore, cheaper. The concept, associated initially with analyses of Third World urban labour markets, was 'rediscovered' in Europe and the United States during the 1970–1980s recession and subsequently applied to analyses of migration and ethnic minority and migrant enterprise (Erdemir and Vasta, 2007; Gerry, 1987; Jones et al., 2006; Portes, 1994; Portes et al., 1989; Sassen, 1994).

Interculturalism differs from multiculturalism by claiming to recognise that cultural boundaries are not 'fixed' but in a 'state of flux and remaking'. Multiculturalism developed initially as an attempt to change the vertical terms of engagement between ethnic minority groups and the dominant culture. Interculturalism adds a different layer to analyses of cultural understanding by pointing to processes of horizontal negotiation, and modes of intercultural crossing such as and between 'old' and 'new' migrant groups (Kyambi, 2005; Wise, 2007; Wood et al., 2006).

Local economy refers to the structure and traditions of particular urban centres, neighbourhoods, localities, and the role of particular sectors and sub-sectors of the economy within those localities (London Skills Forecasting Unit, 2001; Panayiotopoulos, 1992; Rath, 2002; Sassen, 1995).

Mixed embeddedness refers to the level of integration by immigrant and ethnic minority entrepreneurs to immigrant and ethnic communities *and* to the host society and its institutional framework. The concept relates immigrant social relations and transactions to wider political and economic processes and structures (Kloosterman and Rath, 2000, 2001; Kloosterman et al., 1999; Miera, 2008; Rath, 2002).

Multiculturalism 'from above' is a bureaucratic process involving the politics and policies of recognition, redistribution and representation in which ethnic groups are often reduced to passive participants. Multiculturalism 'from below' involves processes of self-representation and directs our attention towards how culturally diverse people 'reproduce sociality' in everyday life and how membership of different classes shapes emergent forms of multiculturalism (Werbner, 1999; Wise, 2007; Wise and Velayutham, 2007).

Political–institutional framework creates the legal framework for the regulation of enterprises, immigration itself, and the structuring of formal political rights. It can facilitate or constraint, depending on the extent to which immigrant groups have political representation, capacities for political mobilisation and 'mixed' embeddedness (Panayiotopoulos, 2008; Rath, 2000).

Racialisation points to the role played by the state in the ranking of populations through immigration and nationality regulations. The reconstitution of national identities is frequently articulated through concepts of 'race', in which colour remains a key signifier of difference. Through immigration and nationality laws, governments rank human populations into hierarchies of assimilation, in which some groups are regarded as more likely to 'fit in' than others. Once racialised in this way, migrant workers and entrepreneurs come under pressure and in some cases are ethnically channelled to particular 'niches' in the labour market or enterprise spectrum (Carter et al., 1996; Ellis and Wright, 1999; Trimikliniotis, 1999; Schonwalder, 2004).

Small enterprises, the self-employment sector, and the agglomeration of small immigrant-owned enterprises in particular sectors and localities, typically as contractors and subcontractors in difficult-to-monitor production systems, provides the material basis for the ethnic enclave economy thesis (Jones et al., 2006; Light and Roach, 1996; Waldinger, 1986; Watson et al., 2000).

Social capital is described by Portes as 'the capacity of individuals to command scarce resources by virtue of their membership in networks or broader social structures', such as those grounded in ethnicity. Fernandez-Kelly refers to a 'process' which determines access to benefits from social networks, and points to complimentary cultural capital: a repertory of symbols held by all members of an immigrant or ethnic group, which structures social and economic relations (Coleman, 1988; Fernandez-Kelly, 1995; Portes, 1994; Putnam, 1993).

Social embeddedness refers to the level of integration by immigrant entrepreneurs in the market *and* extra-market activities of immigrant workers and communities; much of the literature identifies this as a necessary precondition for enterprise formation and critical in the management of enterprise functions (Granovetter, 1985, 1995; Portes and Sensenbrenner, 1993; Ram et al., 2002; Uzzi, 1996).

Social differentiation points to the reproduction of social stratification inside immigrant and ethnic communities, for example, in the emergence of entrepreneurs from the ranks of wage workers and in the role of ascriptive disadvantage embedded in given social categories and hierarchies: class, gender, race, age and religious affiliation and the intersections between them (Anthias, 1992; Bonacich and Appelbaum, 2000; Eade et al., 2007; Kabeer, 2000; Sampson, 2009).

Transnationalism purports to show that contemporary patterns of migration have resulted in the undermining of the nation-state, leading to the formation of new kinds of diaspora, transnational networks and communities which feel equally at home in receiving and sending countries. The term 'de-territorialised nation-states' has been used to describe ethnic groups who move with ease between cultures and countries, pursuing economic, political and cultural interests that require a 'simultaneous presence in both' (Basch et al., 1994; Cohen, 1997; Morokvasic, 2004; Portes, 1997).

Bibliography

Abdullah, H. (ed.) (2006) *Departures and Arrivals: Turkish Cypriots Who Came to England between 1934 and 1963* (London: Turkish Cypriot Community Association).

Ahmad, A. N. (2008) 'The labour market consequence of human smuggling: "Illegal" employment in London's migrant economy', *Journal of Ethnic and Migration Studies*, 34:6, 853–74.

Alba, R. D. (1999) *Ethnic Identity: The Transformation of White America* (New Haven: Yale University Press).

Alba, R. D. and V. Nee (2003) *Remaking the American Mainstream: Assimilation and Contemporary Immigration* (Cambridge, MA: Harvard University Press).

Aldrich, H. and A. Reiss Jr (1981) 'Continuities in the study of ecological succession: Changes in the race composition of neighbourhoods and their businesses', *American Journal of Sociology*, 81, 846–66.

Aldrich, H., T. Jones and D. McEvoy (1984) 'Ethnic advantage and minority business development', in R. Ward and R. Jenkins (eds) *Ethnic Communities in Business*, 189–210 (Cambridge: Cambridge University Press).

Ali, A. M. (2001) *Turkish Speaking Communities and Education* (London: Fatal Publications).

Altinay, L. and E. Altinay (2008) 'Factors influencing business growth: The rise of Turkish entrepreneurship in the UK', *International Journal of Entrepreneurial Behaviour and Research*, 14:1, 24–46.

Amin, A. (2000) 'Ethnicity and the multicultural city: Living with diversity', *Environment and Planning*, 34, 959–80.

Anderson, B. (2003) 'Just another job? The commodification of domestic labor', in B. Ehrenreich and A. R. Hochschild (eds) *Global Women*, 104–14 (New York: Metropolitan Books).

Anthias, F. (1992) *Ethnicity, Class, Gender and Migration: Greek Cypriots in Britain.* (Aldershot: Avebury).

Arastirmalar, T. and M. Vakfi (2003) *Economic Potential of Turkish Migrant Entrepreneurs in Germany* (University of Essen: Stiftung Zentrum für Türkeistudien).

Atema, J. and P. I. Panayiotopoulos (1995) 'Promoting urban informal enterprises: A case study of the Action Aid-Kenya Kariobangi Savings and Credit Programme', *Papers in International Development* No. 15 (Swansea: Centre for Development Studies).

Avci, G. (2006) 'Comparing integration policies and outcomes: Turks in the Netherlands and Germany', *Turkish Studies*, 7:1, 67–84.

Bahna, M. (2008) 'Predictions of migration from the new member states after their accession into the European Union: Successes and failures', *International Migration Review*, 42:4, 844–60.

Bailey-Todd, A., M. Eckmann and K. Tremblay (2008) 'Evolution of the Los Angeles County apparel industry', *Journal of Fashion Marketing and Management*, 12:2, 260–76.

Barrett, G. A. and D. McEvoy (2006) 'The evolution of Manchester's "curry mile": From suburban shopping street to ethnic destination', in D. Kaplan and W. Li (eds) *Landscapes of the Ethnic Economy*, 193–207 (Lanham, MD: Rowman and Littlefield).

Barrett, G. A., T. Jones and D. McEvoy (1996) 'Ethnic minority business: Theoretical discourse in Britain and North America', *Urban Studies*, 33:4–5, 783–809.

Barrett, G. A., T. Jones, D. McEvoy and C. McGoldrick (2002) 'The economic embeddedness of immigrant enterprise in Britain', *International Journal of Entrepreneurial Behaviour and Research*, 8:1–2, 11–31.

Barry, B. (2001) *Culture and Equality: An Egalitarian Critique of Multiculturalism*. (Cambridge: Cambridge University Press).

Barth, F. (1959) 'Segmentary opposition and theory of games: A study of Pathan Organisation', *Journal of the Royal Anthropological Institute*, 89, 5–21.

Barth, F. (1969) 'Introduction', in F. Barth (ed.) *Ethnic Groups and Boundaries: The Social Organisation of Culture Difference*, 9–38 (London: George Allen and Unwin).

Basch, L., N. Schiller and C. Blanc-Szanton (1994) *Nations Unbound: Transnational Projects, Post-colonial Predicaments and De-territorialized Nation-States* (Langhorne, PA: Gordon and Breach).

Basu, A. (2004) 'Entrepreneurial aspirations among family business owners: an analysis of ethnic business owners in the UK', *International Journal of Entrepreneurial Behaviour and Research*, 10:1–2, 2–33.

Basu, A. and E. Altinay (2002) 'The interaction between culture and entrepreneurship in London's immigrant business', *International Small Business Journal*, 20:4, 371–94.

Basu, A. and E. Altinay (2003) 'Family and work in minority ethnic business in the UK', Joseph Rowntree Trust, *Findings*, No. 13.

Bauder, H. and J. Semmelroggen (2009) 'Immigration and imagination of nationhood in the German Parliament', *Nationalism and Ethnic Politics*, 15, 1–26.

Bauere, V., P. Densham, J. Millar and J. Salt (2007) 'Migrants from central and eastern Europe: Local geographies', Migration Research Unit, University College London. *Population Trends*, 129, 6–19 (London: Office for National Statistics).

Bayar, A. (1996) 'Ethnic business among Turkish immigrants in Europe', *Forum*, 3:4, 1–7.

Becker, H. (1956) *Middlemen Trading Peoples: Germ Plasm and Social Situations*. (New York: Praeger).

Beja, J. and W. Chunguang (1999) 'Un village du Zhejiang à Paris: migration Chinoise', *Hommes et Migration*, 1220, 65–82.

Bell, N. (2002) 'Contribution to the Conference on "Borders on Migration" organised by the Austrian League for Human Rights', Vienna 29–30 October: European Civic Forum.

Benoit, B. (2003) 'Germans wake up to the call of the muezzin', *Financial Times*, 4 November.

Benoit, B. (2004) 'Germany shines the spotlight on its shadow economy', *Financial Times*, 6 February.

Benton, G. and F. N. Pieke (eds) (1998) *The Chinese in Europe* (Basingstoke: Macmillan Press).

Berggren, E., L.-B. Branka, G. Toksoz and N. Trimikliniotis (eds) (2007) *Irregular Migration, Informal Labour and Community: A Challenge for Europe* (Maastricht: Shaker Publishing).

Bilger, V., M. Hofman and M. Jandl (2006) 'Human smuggling as a transnational service industry: Evidence from Austria', *International Migration*, 44:4, 60–93.

Black Information Link (2006) 'Trevor Phillips would be "final nail in CEHR coffin", 4 July. http://www.blink.org.uk/pdescription.asp?key=11964&grp=44

Blackburn, R. and R. Rutherford (1999) *Enterprise for Culturally Diverse Communities* (London: Kingston University).

Bohning, W. R. (1972) *The Migration of Workers in the United Kingdom and the European Community* (Oxford: Oxford University Press).

Boissevain, J. et al. (1990) 'Ethnic entrepreneurs and ethnic strategies', in R. Waldinger, H. Aldrich and R. Ward (eds) *Ethnic Entrepreneurs*, 131–56 (London: Sage Publications).

Bonacich, E. (1972) 'A theory of ethnic antagonism: The split labour market', *American Sociological Review*, 37, 34–51.

Bonacich, E. (1973) 'A theory of middleman minorities', *American Sociological Review*, 38, 583–94.

Bonacich, E. (1994) 'Asians in the Los Angeles garment industry', in P. Ong, E. Bonacich, I. Light and C. Wong (1976) 'Korean immigrants: small business in Los Angeles', in E. Gee (ed.) *Counterpoint: Perspectives on Asian Americans*, 437–49 (Los Angeles: Asian American Studies Center, UCLA).

Bonacich, E. and R. Appelbaum (eds) (2000) *Behind the Label: Inequality in the Los Angeles Apparel Industry* (Berkeley: University of California).

Bonacich and L. Cheng (eds) *The New Asian Immigration in Los Angeles*, 137–63 (Philadelphia: Temple University Press).

Bonacich, E. and J. Modell (eds) (1980) *The Economic Basis of Ethnic Solidarity: Small Business in the Japanese American Community* (Berkeley: University of California).

Booth, W. (1998) 'One nation, indivisible: Is it history?', *Washington Post*, 22 February.

Boulange, A. (2004) 'The hijab, racism and the state', *International Socialism*, 102, 3–26. http://www.socialistreviewindex.org.uk/ijindex.htm

Boxell, J. (2009) 'Recession spurs migrant workers to leave', *Financial Times*, 21 May.

Boyes, R. (2004) 'Germans fear Islamic unrest', *The Times*, 17 November.

Brass, P. R. (1991) *Ethnicity and Nationalism* (London: Sage Publications).

Briscoe, S. and B. Groom (2009) 'Overseas workers more able to keep jobs', *Financial Times*, 20 May.

Cabinet Office (2002) *Ethnic Minorities in the Labour Market* (London: ABI Associates). http://www.abi.co.uk/reports.htm

Caldwell, C. (2007) 'No easy answers on immigration', *Financial Times*, 21 October.

Camarota, S. and A. McArdle (2003) *An Examination of State Residing Foreign Born by Country of Origin in 1990 and 2000* (Washington, DC: Center for Immigration Studies).

Campani, G. (2007) 'Irregular migration and trafficking: Controversial concepts and changing contexts in Southern Europe', in E. Berggren et al. (eds) *Irregular Migration*, 66–84 (Maastricht: Shaker Publishing).

Carling, J. (2007) 'Unauthorised migration from Africa to Spain', *International Migration*, 45:4, 3–37.

Carmichael, S. and C. V. Hamilton (1967) *Black Power: the Politics of Liberation in America* (New York: Random House).

Carter, B., M. Green and R. Halpern (1996) 'Immigration policy and the racialization of migrant labour: The construction of national identities in the USA and Britain', *Ethnic and Racial Studies*, 19:1, 135–57.

Carter-Pokras, O. et al. (2008) 'Health status of Mexican-origin persons: Do proxy measures of acculturation advance our understanding of health disparities?', *Journal of Minority Health*, 10, 475–88.

Castles, S. (2000) *Ethnicity and Globalisation: From Migrant Worker to Transnational Citizen* (London: Sage Publications).

Castles, S. (2004) 'Why migration policies fail', *Ethnic and Racial Studies*, 27:2, 205–27.

Castles, S. (2006) 'Guestworkers in Europe: A resurrection?', *International Migration Review*, 40:4, 741–66.

Castles, S. and G. Kosack (1973) *Immigrant Workers and Class Structure in Western Europe* (Oxford: Oxford University Press).

Ceccagno, A. (2003) 'New Chinese migrants in Italy', *International Migration*, 41:3, 187–213.

CEEDR (2000) *Greater London Enterprise Strategies: Final Report* (London: Middlesex University Business School).

Centre for Research on Nationalism, Ethnicity and Multiculturalism (CRONEM) (2006) *Polish Migrant Survey Results*. Commissioned by the BBC, Newsnight, 4 July.

Chaffin, J. (2004) 'Florida's new Hispanics', *Financial Times*, 13 April.

Chin, C. B. N. (1998) *In Service and Servitude: Foreign Female Domestic Workers and the Malaysian 'Modernity Project'* (Columbia: Columbia University Press).

Chin, K. (1999) *Smuggled Chinese: Clandestine Immigration to the United States* (Philadelphia: Temple University Press).

Chin, K.-S., I.-J. Yoon and D. Smith (1996) 'Immigrant small business and international economic linkage: A case of the Korean wig business in Los Angeles, 1968–1977', *International Migration Review*, xxx: 2, 485–510.

Chittenden, M. and K. Tchorek (2007) 'Poles catch British disease', *Sunday Times*, 16 September.

Chu, D. C. and J. Huey-Long Song (2008) 'Chinese immigrants' perceptions of the police in Toronto, Canada', *International Journal of Police Strategies and Management*, 31:4, 610–30.

Ciensky, J. (2007) 'Sorry, Polish party is over. Gone West', *Financial Times*, 30 January.

Ciensky, J. (2008) 'Poles go home to greener pasture', *Financial Times*, 1 January.

Ciensky, J. (2009) 'Downturn puts paid to Polish mobility', *Financial Times*, 16 September.

Clark, W. (2003) *Immigrants and the American Dream: Remaking the Middle Class*. (New York: The Guildford Press).

Cohen, A. (1974) 'The lesson of ethnicity', in Abner Cohen (ed.) *Urban Ethnicity*, ix–xiii (London: Tavistock Publications).

Cohen, R. (1994) *Frontiers of Identity: The British and the Others* (London: Longman).

Cohen, R. (1997) *Global Diasporas: An Introduction* (London: UCL Press).

Coleman, J. (1988) 'Social capital in the creation of human capital', *American Journal of Sociology*, 94:S95-120.

Cologna, D. (2005) 'Chinese immigrant entrepreneurs in Italy: Strengths and weaknesses of an ethnic enclave economy', in E. Spaan et al. (eds) *Asian Migrants and European Labour Markets*, 262–77 (London: Routledge).

Commission Stasi (2003) *Commission de Réflexion sur l'Application du Principe de Laïcité dans la République*.

Constant, A., Y. Schachmore and K. F. Zimmerman (2003) 'What makes an entrepreneur and does it pay? Native men, Turks and other migrants in Germany', Bonn Institute for the Study of Labor, Discussion Paper No. 940.

Craig, G. (2005) *At a Turning Point? The State of Race Relations in Kingston upon Hull* (University of Hull: Centre for Social Inclusion and Social Justice).

Crawley, H. and M. J. Hickman (2008) 'Migration, postindustrialism and the globalized nation state: Social capital and social cohesion re-examined', *Ethnic and Racial Studies*, 31:7, 1222–44.

Cummings, S. (1980) 'The unique legacy of immigrant economic development', in S. Cummings (ed.) *Self-Help in Urban America*, 5–32 (Washington, DC: Kennikat Press).

Datta, K., C. McIlwaine and S. Evans (2006) *Work and Survival Strategies among Low Paid Migrants in London* (University of London: Department of Geography).

Davidson, N. (1999) 'The trouble with "ethnicity"', *International Socialism*, 84, 3–30. http://www.socialistreviewindex.org.uk/ijindex.htm

Davis, M. (1992) *City of Quartz: Excavating the Future in Los Angeles* (London: Vintage).

Day, J. C. (1996) *Population Projections of the United Sates by Age, Sex, Race, and Hispanic Origin 1995 to 2050*. P25–1130 (Washington, DC: US Government Printing Office).

Denton, N. and D. Massey (1989) 'Racial identity among Caribbean Hispanics: The effect of double minority status on residential segregation', *American Sociological Review*, 54:5, 790–808.

Department for Work and Pensions (2004) 'Regulations to protect benefit system and welcome workers', Press Release, 30 April.

Department for Work and Pensions (2008) *National Insurance Number Allocations to Adult Overseas Nationals Entering the UK 2007/8*. http://www.dwp.gov.uk/asd/asd1/tabtools/nino_allocations_0708.pdf

Dinmore, G. (2009) 'Treviso lion's roar echoes in immigration debate', *Financial Times*, 4 March.

Dobbs, M. and R. T. Hamilton (2007) 'Small business growth: Recent evidence and new directions', *International Journal of Entrepreneurial Behaviour and Research*, 13:5, 296–322.

Dombey, D. (2004) 'Ankara accepts deal after war of nerves', *Financial Times*, 18 December.

Drinkwater, S., J. Eade and M. Garapich (2006) 'Poles apart? Enlargement and the labour market outcomes of immigrants in the UK', *IZA Discussion Paper*

No. 2410. http://www.iza.org/index_html?lang=en&mainframe=http%3A//
www.iza.org/en/webcontent/publications/papers/topdownloads%3Fdate%3D
2006/11/01&topSelect=publications&subSelect=papers

Dumont, A. (2008) 'Representing voiceless migrants: Moroccan political transnationalism and migrants' organizations in France', *Ethnic and Racial Studies*,
31:4, 792–811.

Dustmann, C., M. Casanova, P. Fertig and C. Schmidt (2003) *The Impact of EU
Enlargement on Migration Flows*. Home Office Report 25/03. London: Home
Office. http://www.homeoffice.gov.uk/rds/pdfs2/rdsolr2503.pdf

Eade, J., S. Drinkwater and M. Garapich (2007) *Class and Ethnicity – Polish Migrants
in London*. Centre for Research on Nationalism, Ethnicity and Multiculturalism,
Research Report for the RES-000-22-1294 ESRC project. http://www.esrcsociety
today.ac.uk/esrcinfocentre/viewawardpage.aspx?awardnumber=RES-000-22-
1294

Eaglesham, J. (2009) 'Minister defends his comments about "sinister" ONS',
Financial Times, 5 March.

Ehrenreich, B. and A. R. Hochschild (eds) (2003) *Global Women: Nannies, Maids
and Sex Workers in the New Economy* (New York: Metropolitan Books).

Ellis, M. and R. Wright (1999) 'The industrial division of labour amongst immigrants and internal migrants to the Los Angeles economy', *International
Migration Review*, 33:1, 26–54.

Elrick, T. and E. Lewandowska (2008) 'Matching and making labour demand
and supply: Agents in Polish migrant networks of domestic elderly care in
Germany and Italy', *Journal of Ethnic and Migration Studies*, 34:5, 717–34.

Enneli, P., T. Modood and H. Bradley (2005) *Young Turks and Kurds. A Set of
'Invisible' Disadvantaged Groups* (York: Joseph Rowntree Foundation).

Erdem, K. and R. A. Schmidt (2008) 'Ethnic marketing for Turks in Germany',
International Journal of Retail and Distribution Management, 36:3, 212–23.

Erdemir, A. and E. Vasta (2007) *Differentiating Irregularity and Solidarity: Turkish
Immigrants at Work in London*. Centre on Migration, Policy and Society,
Oxford, Working Paper No. 43. http://www.compas.ox.ac.uk/fileadmin/files/
pdfs/WP0742-Vasta.pdf

Evans, Y. and A. Smith (2004) *Creative Destruction: De-industrialisation or a
'Fashion Capital for the Creative Industries' in London?* Paper prepared for the
conference Clothing Europe: Comparative Perspectives on Trade Liberalisation
and Production Networks in the New European Clothing Industry, University
of North Carolina, Chapel Hill, 15–16 October.

Fallers, L. (1967) *Immigrants and Associations* (The Hague: Mouton Press).

Favell, A. (2008) 'The new face of East-West migration in Europe', *Journal of
Ethnic and Migration Studies*, 34:5, 701–16.

Fernandez, G. A. (2007) 'Race, gender and class in the persistence of the Mariel
stigma twenty years after the exodus from Cuba', *International Migration
Review*, 41:3, 602–22.

Fernandez Kelly, P. (1995) 'Social and cultural capital in the urban ghetto:
Implications for the economic sociology of immigration', in A. Portes (ed.)
The Economic Sociology of Immigration, 213–47 (New York: Russell Sage
Foundation).

Fernandez-Kelly, P. and A. Garcia (1989) 'Informalisation at the core: Hispanic
women, homework, and the advanced capitalist state', in A. Portes, M. Castells

and L. Benton (eds) *The Informal Economy: Studies in Advanced and Less Developed Countries*, 247–64 (London: Johns Hopkins Press).

Fihel, A., P. Kaczmarczyk and M. Okolski (2006) *Labour Mobility in the Enlarged EU* (Warsaw: University of Warsaw, Centre of Migration Research). http://www.focus-migration.de/EU_Expansion_and_the.1201.0.html?&L=1

Finney, N. and L. Simpson (2009) *Sleepwalking to Segregation? Challenging Myths About Race and Immigration* (London: Policy Press).

Fishman, J. (1980) 'Social theory and ethnography', in P. Sugar (ed.) *Ethnic Diversity and Conflict in Eastern Europe*, 84–97 (Santa Barbara: ABC-Clio).

Foot, P. (1968) *The Politics of Harold Wilson* (Aylesbury: Penguin).

Garapich, M. P. (2008) 'The migration industry and civil society: Polish immigrants in the United Kingdom before and after EU enlargement', *Journal of Ethnic and Minority Studies*, 34:5, 735–52.

Geddes, A. (2003) *The Politics of Migration and Immigration in Europe* (London: Sage Publications).

Gerry, C. (1987) 'Developing economies and the informal sector in historical perspective', *The ANNALS of the American Academy of Political and Social Science*, 493, 101–19.

van Geuns, R. (1992) 'An aspect of informalisation of women's work in a high-tech age: Turkish sweatshops in the Netherlands', in S. Mitter (ed.) *Computer-Aided Manufacturing and Women's Employment: The Clothing Industry in Four EC Countries*, 125–37 (London: Springer-Verlag Press).

Glanz, R. (1976) *The Jewish Woman in America: Two Female Immigrant Generations 1820–1929* (2 Vols) (New York: Ktav).

Glasgow, D. (1980) *The Black Underclass: Poverty, Unemployment and Entrapment of Ghetto Youth* (San Francisco: Jossey-Bass Publishers).

Glazer, N. (1983) *Ethnic Dilemmas 1964–1982* (Cambridge, MA: Harvard University Press).

Glazer, N. (1997) *We Are All Multiculturalists Now* (Cambridge, MA: Harvard University Press).

Glazer, N. and D. Moynihan (1970) *Beyond the Melting Pot: The Negroes, Puerto Ricans, Jews, Italians and Irish of New York City* (Cambridge, MA: MIT Press).

Glazer, N. and D. Moynihan (1975) 'Introduction', in N. Glazer (ed.) *Ethnicity*, 1–26 (Cambridge, MA: Harvard University Press).

Glick-Schiller, N. (2003) 'The centrality of ethnography in the study of transnational migration: Seeing the wetlands instead of the swamp', in N. Foner (ed.) *American Arrivals*, 99–128 (Santa Fe, NM: School of American Research Press).

Glossop, C. and F. Shaheen (2009) *Accession to Recession: A8 migration in Bristol and Hull* (London: Centre for Cities). http://www.centreforcities.org/assets/files/Accession%20to%20Recession%20.pdf

Gokturk, D. (1999) 'Turkish delight – German fright: Labour and migration', *Working Paper* No. WPTC-99-01 (London: ESRC, Transnational Communities Programme). http://www.transcomm.ox.ac.uk/working_papers.htm

Golash-Boza, T. and W. Darity (2008) 'Latino racial choices: The effects of skin colour and discrimination on Latinos' and Latinas' racial self-identification', *Ethnic and Racial Studies*, 31:5, 899–934.

Goldenberg, S. (2002) 'Greatest wave of migrants drives US engine', *Guardian*, 3 December.

Graham, R. (2003) 'French secularism unwraps far more than headscarves in the classroom', *Financial Times*, 21 December.

Gramsci, A. (1971) *Selection from the Prison Notebooks of Antonio Gramsci* (London: Lawrence and Wishart).

Granovetter, M. (1985) 'Economic action and social structure: The problem of embeddedness', *American Journal of Sociology*, 91:3, 481–510.

Granovetter, M. (1995) 'The economic sociology of firms and entrepreneurs', in A. Portes (ed.) *The Economic Sociology of Immigration: Essays on Networks, Ethnicity and Entrepreneurship*, 128–65 (New York: Russell Sage Foundation).

Greater London Authority (GLA) (2008) *ONS Ethnic Group Population Estimates: Mid-2006, Data Management and Analysis Group Briefing 2008–15* (London: GLC).

Green, N. (2002) 'Paris: A historical view', in J. Rath (ed.) *Unravelling the Rag Trade: Immigrant Entrepreneurship in Seven World Cities*, 29–47 (Oxford: Berg Publishers).

Grillo, R. (2003) 'Cultural essentialism and cultural anxiety', *Anthropological Theory*, 3:2, 157–73.

Grillo, R. (2007) 'An excess of alterity? Debating difference in a multicultural society', *Ethnic and Racial Studies*, 30:6, 979–98.

Gryzmala-Kazlowska, A. (2005) 'From ethnic cooperation to in-group competition: Undocumented Polish workers in Brussels', *Journal of Ethnic and Migration Studies*, 31:4, 675–97.

Gumble, A. (2002) 'A decade on LA South Central still smoulders', *Independent*, 30 April.

Gustafson, P. (2008) 'Transnationalism in retirement migration: The case of North European retirees in Spain,' *Ethnic and Racial Studies*, 32:3, 451–75.

Guthrie, J. (2008) 'Polish migrant workers feel the chill', *Financial Times*, 20 December.

de Haas, H. and R. Plug (2006) 'Cherishing the goose with the golden eggs: Trends in migration from Europe to Morocco 1970–2005', *International Migration Review*, 40:3, 603–34.

Haberfellner, R. (2003) 'Austria: Still a highly regulated economy', in R. Kloosterman and J. Rath (eds) *Immigrant Entrepreneurs. Venturing Abroad in the Age of Globalisation*, 213–32 (Berg, Oxford: Berg Publishers).

Hall, S. (1996) 'Who needs "identity"?, in S. Hall and P. du Gay (eds) *Questions of Cultural Identity*, 1–17 (London: Sage Publishers).

Hamilton, G. (1978) 'Pariah capitalism: A paradox of power and dependence', *Ethnic Groups*, 2: 1–15.

Harris, A., K. Jamison and M. Trujillo (2008) 'Disparities in the educational success of immigrants: An assessment of the immigrant effect for Asian and Latinos', *The ANNALS of the American Academy of Political and Social Science*, 620:12, 90–114.

Harris, N. (2002) *Thinking the Unthinkable. The Immigration Myth Exposed* (London: I.B. Tauris).

Hart, K. (1973) 'Informal income opportunities and urban employment in Ghana', *Journal of Modern African Studies*, 11, 99–111.

Hartog, J. and A. Zorlu (1999) *Turkish Confection in Amsterdam: The Rise and Fall of a Perfectly Competitive Labour Market* (Amsterdam: Tinbergen Institute).

Hatziprokopiou, P. (2004) 'Balkan immigrants in the Greek city of Thessaloniki: Local processes of incorporation in an international perspective', *European and Regional Studies,* 11:4, 321–38.

Hellerstein, J., M. McInerney and D. Neumark (2009) *Spatial Influences of U.S. Hispanics: Spatial Mismatch, Discrimination, or Immigrant Networks?* CES 09–03 (Washington, DC: Bureau of the Census).

Henry, N., C. McEwan and J. Pollard (2000) 'Globalisation from below: Birmingham post-colonial workshop of the world', *Working Paper, No. WPTC-2K-08* (London: ESRC Transnational Communities Programme). http://www.transcomm.ox.ac.uk/working_papers.htm

Herbert, J., K. Datta, Y. Evans, J. May, C. McIlwaine and J. Wills (2006) *Multicultural Living? The Experience of New Migrants in London.* Paper presented to the Sixth European Urban and Regional Studies Conference, 21–24 September, Roskilde, Denmark.

Hernandez, R. (2002) *The Mobility of Workers under Advanced Capitalism: Dominican Migration to the United States* (New York: Columbia University Press).

Hewitt, R. (2005) *White Backlash and the Politics of Multiculturalism* (Cambridge: Cambridge University Press).

Hillmann, F. (1999) 'A look at the "hidden side": Turkish women in Berlin's ethnic labour market', *International Journal of Urban and Regional Research*, 23:2, 267–82.

Hillmann, F. (2000) 'Are ethnic economies the revolving doors of the urban labour markets in transition?', Paper presented to the Conference on The Economic Embeddedness of Immigrant Enterprise, Jerusalem, 18–20 June.

Hillmann, F. and H. Rudolph (1997) *Redistributing the Cake – Processes of Ethnicisation in the Food Sector of Berlin.* Berlin: WZB-Discussion Papers, No. 97–101.

Hintjens, H. (2001) 'When identity becomes a knife', *Ethnicities*, 1:1, 25–55.

Home Office (2003) *Control of Immigration: Statistics 2003* (London: Home Office). http://www.archive2.official-documents.-co.uk/document/cm63/6363/6363.htm

Home Office (2005a) *Five-Year Strategy for Asylum and Immigration, Controlling Our Borders: Making Migration Work for Britain.* Command 6472 (London: Home Office). http://www.ukba.homeoffice.gov.uk/sitecontent/documents/aboutus/reports/fiveyearstrategy/

Home Office (2005b) *Improving Opportunity, Strengthening Society* (London: Home Office).

Home Office (2006) *A Points-Based System: Making Migration Work for Britain.* Command 6741 (London: Home Office). http://www.homeoffice.gov.uk/documents/command-points-based-migration

Home Office (2007a) *Accession Monitoring Report, May 2005–December 2005.* (London: Home Office). http://www.rpo.gov.pl/pliki/12230402940.pdf

Home Office (2007b) *The Economic and Fiscal Impact of Immigration.* Command 7237 (London: Home Office/Department for Work and Pensions). http://www.official-documents.gov.uk/document/cm7237/7237.pdf

Home Office (2009) *Fewer Workers Coming from Eastern Europe.* News Release 20 May. http://www.homeoffice.gov.uk/about-us/news/fewer-workers-eastern-europe

Home Office et al. (2006) *Accession Monitoring Report May 2004–June 2006*. A joint report by the Home Office, the Department for Work and Pensions, the HM Revenue and Customs and the Office of the Deputy Prime Minister (London: Home Office).

Hondagneu-Sotelo, P. (2001) *Domestica: Immigrant Workers Cleaning and Caring in the Shadows of Affluence* (Berkeley: University of California Press).

Hondagneu-Sotelo, P. and E. Avila (1997) ' "I am here, but I'm there": The meanings of Latina transnational motherhood', *Gender and Society*, 11:5, 548–71.

Hood, M. (1998) 'Fuzhou', in L. Pan (ed.) *The Chinese Overseas*, 33–5 (Surrey: Curzon Press).

House of Lords (2008) *The Economic Impact of Immigration* (London: The Stationery Office). http://www.publications.parliament.uk/pa/id200708/ldeconaf/82/82.pdf

Huang, S., S. Brenda, A. Yeoh and T. Lam (2008) 'Asian transnational families in transition: The liminality of simultaneity', *International Migration*, 46:4, 3–13.

Huntington, S. M. (2004a) *Who Are We?* (New York: Simon and Schuster).

Huntington, S. M. (2004b) 'The Hispanic challenge', *Foreign Policy*, March–April.

Husbands, C. (1994) 'Crises of national identity as the "new moral panics": Political agenda setting about definitions of nationhood', *New Community*, 20, 191–206.

Hutchinson, J. and A. D. Smith (eds) (1996) *Ethnicity* (Oxford: Oxford University Press).

Ilias, S., K. Fennelly and C. M. Federico (2008) 'American attitudes towards guest worker policies', *International Migration Review*, 42:4, 741–66.

Institute for Migration and Ethnic Studies (IMES) (1998) *Immigrant Businesses in Manufacturing: The Case of Turkish Businesses in the Amsterdam Garment Industry* (Amsterdam: University of Amsterdam).

Inter-American Development Bank (2006a) *Remittances*. Background Paper, 13 March.

Inter-American Development Bank (2006b) 'Migrant remittances from the United States to Latin America to reach $45 billion in 2006', Press Release, 18 October.

International Labour Office (ILO) (1972) *Employment, Incomes and Equality: A Strategy for Increasing Productive Employment in Kenya* (Geneva: ILO).

James, C. L. R. (1980) *Black Jacobins: Toussaint L'Ouverture and the San Domingo Revolution* (London: Alison and Busby).

Jansen, M., J. Spronsen and S. Willemsen (2003) *Immigrant Entrepreneurship in the Netherlands*. Zoetermeer: Scientific Analysis of Entrepreneurship and SMEs, Research Report No. H200304.

Jenkins, R. (1984) 'Ethnic minorities in business: A research agenda', in R. Ward and R. Jenkins (eds) *Ethnic Communities in Business: Strategies for Economic Survival*, 231–8 (Cambridge: Cambridge University Press).

Jiang, J. (1968) 'Towards a theory of pariah entrepreneurship', in G. Wijeyewardene (ed.) *Leadership and Authority: A Symposium*, 147–62 (Singapore: University of Malaya Press).

Jones, T., M. Ram and P. Edwards (2006) 'Shades of grey in the informal economy', *International Journal of Sociology and Social Policy*, 26:9–10, 357–73.

Jordan, B. (2002) 'Migrant Polish workers in London: Mobility, labour markets and the prospects for democratic development', Paper presented to the conference on Beyond Transition: Development Perspectives and Dilemmas, Warsaw, 12–23 April. http://www.case.com.pl/dyn/servFile.php?plik_id=71598

Josephides, S. (1987) 'Associations amongst the Greek Cypriot population in Britain', in J. Rex, D. Jolly and W. Czarina (eds) *Immigrant Associations in Europe*, 42–62 (Aldershot: Gower).

Josephides, S. (1988) 'Honour, family, and work: Greek Cypriot women before and after migration', in S. Westwood and P. Bhachu (eds) *Enterprising Women: Ethnicity, Economy and Gender Relations*, 34–57 (London: Routledge).

Kabeer, N. (1994) 'The structure of revealed preference: Race, community and female labour supply in the London clothing industry', *Development and Change*, 25, 307–31.

Kabeer, N. (2000) *The Power to Choose: Bangladeshi Women and Labour Market Decisions in London and Dhaka* (London: Verso).

Kaufman, M. T. (1998) 'Stokely Carmichael, rights leader who coined 'Black Power' dies at 57', *New York Times*, 16 November. http://www.interchange.org/Kwameture/nytimes111698.html

Kepinska, E. (2004) *Recent Trends in International Migration: The SOPEMI Report for Poland*. University of Warsaw, Institute for Social Studies, Working Papers No. 53. http://www.focus-migration.de/Poland.2810.0.html?&L=1

Khan, K. (2008a) *Employment of Foreign Workers: Male and Female Labour Market Participation* (London: Office for National Statistics). http://www.statistics.gov.uk/articles/nojournal/MFMigAug08.pdf

Khan, K. (2008b) *Employment of Foreign Workers: Focus on Earnings* (London: Office for National Statistics). http://www.statistics.gov.uk/downloads/theme_labour/EmpofForeignWorkersEarningsNov08.pdf

Kindleberger, C. (1967) *Europe's Post-War Growth. The Role of Labour Supply* (New York: Harvard University Press).

King, D. (2000) *Making Americans. Immigration, Race and the Origins of the Diverse Democracy* (Cambridge, MA: Harvard University Press).

King, R. (ed.) (1993) *The New Geography of European Migrations* (London: Belhaven-Wiley).

King, R. (2000) 'Southern Europe in the changing global map of migration', in R. King et al. (eds) *Eldorado or Fortress: Migration in Southern Europe* (Liverpool: Liverpool University Press).

King, R. (ed.) (2001) *The Mediterranean Passage: Migration and New Cultural Encounters in Southern Europe* (Liverpool: Liverpool University Press).

Kitching, J., D. Smallbone and R. Athyde (2009) 'Ethnic diasporas and business competitiveness: Minority-owned enterprises in London', *Journal of Ethnic and Migration Studies*, 35:4, 689–705.

Kloosterman, R. (1996) 'Mixed experiences: Post industrial transition and ethnic minorities on the Amsterdam labour market', *New Community*, 22:4, 637–53.

Kloosterman, R. (2000) 'Immigrant entrepreneurship and the institutional context: A theoretical exploration', in J. Rath (ed.) *Immigrant Businesses. The Economic, Political and Social Environment*, 90–106 (Houndmills: Macmillan).

Kloosterman, R. and J. Rath (eds) (2001) 'Immigrant entrepreneurs in advanced economies: Mixed embeddedness further explored', *Journal of Ethnic and Migration Studies*, 27:2, 189–202.

Kloosterman, R. and J. Rath (eds) (2002) 'Working on the fringes. Immigrant businesses, economic integration and informal practices', *Marginalisering eller Integration*, 177–88 (Stockholm: NUTEK).

Kloosterman, R. and J. Rath (eds) (2003) *Immigrant Entrepreneurs: Venturing Abroad in the Age of Globalisation* (Oxford: Berg Publishers).

Kloosterman, R., J. van der Leun and J. Rath (1999) 'Mixed embeddedness: (In) formal economic activities and immigrant businesses in the Netherlands', *International Journal of Urban and Regional Research*, 23:2, 252–66.

Koser, K. (2008) 'Why migrant smuggling pays', *International Migration*, 46:2, 3–26.

Krogstad, A. (2004) 'From chop suey to sushi, champagne, and VIP lounge: Culinary entrepreneurship through two generations', *Social Analysis*, 48:I, 196–216.

Kuper, A. (1999) *Culture: The Anthropologists' Account* (London: Harvard University Press).

Kwong, P. (1997) 'Manufacturing ethnicity', *Critique of Anthropology*, 17:4, 365–87.

Kwong, P. (1998) *Forbidden Workers: Illegal Chinese Immigrants and American Labor* (New York: New Press).

Kyambi, S. (2005) *Beyond Black and White. Mapping New Immigrant Communities* (London: Institute for Public Policy Research).

Laczko, F. (2003) 'Europe attracts more migrants from China', *International Organization for Migration*, July, 1–7.

Ladbury, S. (1984) 'Choice, change or no alternative: Turkish Cypriots in business in London', in R. Ward and R. Jenkins (eds) *Ethnic Communities in Business: Strategies for Economic Survival*, 105–25 (Cambridge: Cambridge University Press).

Lam, J. (2000) 'They are still treating us like criminals', *Socialist Worker*, 1 July.

Lawrence, F. (2005) 'The precarious existence of the thousands in Britain's underclass', *Guardian*, 10 January.

Lazaridis, G. (2007) 'Irregular migration and the trampoline effect: "les infirmières exclusives", "quasi-nurses", nannies, maids and sex workers in Greece', in E. Berggren et al. (eds) *Irregular Migration*, 242–54 (Maastricht: Shaker Publishing).

Lee, J. and F. D. Bean (2007) 'Reinventing the color line: Immigration and America's new racial/ethnic divide', *Social Forces*, 86:2, 561–87.

Leon, A. (1998) *The Jewish Question. A Marxist Interpretation* (Mexico City: Ediciones Pioneres). http://www.marxist.de/religion/leon/index.htm

Leung, M. W. H. (2002) 'From four-course Peking duck to take-away Singapore rice. An inquiry into the dynamics of the ethnic Chinese catering business in Germany', *International Journal of Entrepreneurial Behaviour and Research*, 8:1–2, 134–47.

Levi-Strauss, Claude (1967) *The Scope of Anthropology*, Inaugural Lecture, Chair of Social Anthropology, College de France, 5 January 1960 (London: Jonathan Cape).

Light, I. (1972) *Ethnic Enterprise in America: Business and Welfare among Chinese, Japanese and Blacks* (Berkeley: University of California Press).

Light, I. (2000) 'Globalisation and migration networks', in J. Rath (ed.) *Immigrant Businesses. The Economic, Political and Social Environment*, 162–81 (Basingstoke: Macmillan Press).

Light, I. and S. J. Gold (2000) *Ethnic Economies* (San Diego: California Academic Press).

Light, I. and M. F. Johnston (2009) 'The metropolitan dispersion of Mexican immigrants in the United States 1980–2000', *Journal of Ethnic and Migration Studies*, 35:1, 3–18.

Light, I. and V. Ojeda (2002) 'Los Angeles: Wearing out their welcome', in J. Rath (ed.) *Unravelling the Rag Trade: Immigrant Entrepreneurship in Seven World Cities*, 135–50 (Oxford: Berg Publishers).

Light, I. and E. Roach (1996) 'Self-employment: Mobility ladder or economic lifeboat?', in R. Waldinger and M. Bozorgmehr (eds) *Ethnic Los Angeles*, 193–214 (New York: Russell Sage Foundation).

Light, I., R. Bernard and R. Kim (1999) 'Immigrant incorporation in the garment industry of Los Angeles', *International Labour Review*, 33:1, 5–25.

Light, I., G. Sabach, M. Bozorgmehr and C. Der-Martirosian (1994) 'Beyond the ethnic enclave economy', *Social Problems*, 41:1, 65–80.

Locher-Scholten, E. (2003) 'From urn to monument: Dutch memories of World War Two in the Pacific', in A. Smith (ed.) *Europe's Invisible Migrants*, 105–28 (Amsterdam: Amsterdam University Press).

Logan, J., R. Alba and T. McNulty (2002) 'Ethnic economies in metropolitan region: Miami and beyond', *Social Forces*, 72, 322.

London Skills Forecasting Unit (2001) *Ethnic Capital. Shaping London's Local Economies*.

Luk, W. (2009) 'Chinese ethnic settlements in Britain: Spatial meanings of an orderly distribution, 1981–2001', *Journal of Ethnic and Migration Studies*, 35:4, 575–99.

Lutz, H. (2007) 'The "intimate others" – migrant domestic workers in Europe', in E. Berggren et al. (eds) *Irregular Migration*, 226–41 (Maastricht: Shaker Publishing).

Magatti, M. and F. Quassoli (2000) 'The Italian case: Socio-economic characteristics of immigrant businesses in Italy', Paper presented to the Conference on The Economic Embeddedness of Immigrant Enterprise, 18–20 June, Jerusalem.

Magatti, M. and F. Quassoli (2003) 'Italy: Between legal barriers and informal arrangements', in R. Kloosterman and J. Rath (eds) *Immigrant Entrepreneurs. Venturing Abroad in the Age of Globalisation*, 147–72 (Oxford: Berg Publishers).

Manco, U. (2004) *Turks in Western Europe* (University of Ghent: Centrum vor Islam in Europe).

Martin, P. (1994) 'Good intentions gone awry – IRCA and United States agriculture', *ANNALS of the American Academy of Political and Social Science*, 534:1, 44–57.

McKinnon, J. (2003) *The Black Population in the United States* (Washington, DC: US Census Bureau).

Mackintosh, M. (2005) *London: The World in a City. An Analysis of the 2001 Census Result* (London: Greater London Authority).

McConnell, E. D. (2008) 'The US destinations of contemporary Mexican immigrants', *International Migration Review*, 42:4, 767–802.

Mahamdaillie, H. (2005) 'Reply to Trevor Phillips', *Socialist Review*, 301, 12–16. http://www.socialistreviewindex.org.uk/ijindex.htm

Marfleet, P. (2005) *Refugees in a Global Era* (London: Palgrave Macmillan).

Mesthenos, E. and J. Triantafillou (1993) 'Dependent elderly people in Greece and their family carers', in J. Twigg (ed.) *Informal Care in Europe*, 129–51 (University of York: Social Policy Research Unit).

Miera, F. (2008) 'Transnational strategies of Polish migrant entrepreneurs in trade and small business in Berlin', *Journal of Ethnic and Migration Studies*, 34:5, 753–70.

Mitter, S. (1986) 'Industrial restructuring and manufacturing homework: Immigrant women in the UK clothing industry', *Capital and Class*, 27, 37–80.

Moctezuma, A. (2006) 'The Latino civil rights movement', *Socialist Worker* (UK), 13 May.

Modood, T. (2000) 'Anti-essentialism, multiculturalism and the "recognition" of religious groups', in W. Kymlicka and N. Wayne (eds) *Citizenship in Diverse Societies*, 175–95 (Oxford: Oxford University Press).

Mohan, G. (2002) 'Diaspora and development', in J. Robinson (ed.) *Development and Displacement*, 77–140 (Milton Keynes, Open University: Oxford University Press).

Mohan, G. and D. Kale (2007) *The Invisible Hand of South-South Globalisation: Chinese Migrants in Africa*: A Report for the Rockefeller Foundation (Milton Keynes: The Open University).

Morokvasic, M. (2004) 'Settled in mobility: Engendering post-wall migration in Europe', *Feminist Review*, 77, 7–25.

Morokvasic, M. et al. (1990) 'Business on the ragged edge: Immigrant and minority business in the garment industries of Paris, London and New York', in R. Waldinger, H. Aldrich and R. Ward (eds) *Ethnic Entrepreneurs: Immigrant Business in Industrial Societies*, 157–76 (London: Sage Publications).

Munck, R. (2007) 'Irregular migration and the informal market: The "underside" of globalisation or the new form?', in E. Berggren et al. (eds) *Irregular Migration*, 51–65 (Maastricht: Shaker Publishing).

Mung, E. M. and T. Lacroix (2000) 'Context and "economic arrangements" of immigrant enterprises', Paper presented to the Conference on The Economic Embeddedness of Immigrant Enterprise, 18–20 June, Jerusalem.

Mung, E. M. and T. Lacroix (2003) 'France: The narrow path', in R. Kloosterman and J. Rath (eds) *Immigrant Entrepreneurs. Venturing Abroad in the Age of Globalisation*, 173–94 (Oxford: Berg Publishers).

National Migration Forum (2002) 'Immigrants in the crosshairs: The quiet backlash against America's immigrants and refugees', *Backgrounder*, 16 December (Washington, DC: NMF).

Nutter, S. (1997) 'The structure and growth of the Los Angeles garment industry', in A. Ross (ed.) *No Sweat: Fashion, Free Trade and the Rights of Garment Workers*, 113–22 (New York: Verso).

Oakley, R. (1972) *Cypriot Migration and Settlement in Britain,* unpublished D. Phil. Thesis, Oxford University, UK.

O'Connor, S. (2009) 'Downturn deals blow to US immigrants', *Financial Times*, 18 November.

Office for National Statistics (2003) *Ethnic Group Statistics. A Guide for the Collection and Classification of Ethnicity Data*. London: HMSO.

Office for National Statistics (2004a) *2001 Census: Focus on Ethnicity*. London: HMSO.

Office for National Statistics (2004b) *Census 2001: Focus on London*. London: HMSO

Office for National Statistics (2004c) *Minority Self-Employment*. http://www.statistics.gov.uk/cci/nugget.asp?id=463

Office for National Statistics (2006) 'UK population grows to more than 60 million', News Release, 24 August. http://www.statistics.gov.uk/pdfdir/pope0806.pdf

Office for National Statistics (2007a) 'Both UK and foreign-born women contribute to rise in fertility', News Release, 11 December. http://www.statistics.gov.uk/pdfdir/fertility1207.pdf

Office for National Statistics (2007b) *Focus on London* (London: Palgrave).

Office for National Statistics (2009a) 'Latest migration statistics released', News Release, 24 February. http://www.statistics.gov.uk/pdfdir/ppmg0209.pdf

Office for National Statistics (2009b) *Employment of Foreign Workers: Focus on Eurostat Ad Hoc Module*, February. London: HMSO.

Oh, J.-H. (2007) 'Economic incentive, embeddedness, and social support: A study of Korean-owned nail salon workers' rotating and credit associations', *International Migration Review*, 41:3, 623–55.

Ong, P. and A. Valenzuela Jr (1996) 'The labour market: Immigrant effects and racial disparities', in R. Waldinger and M. Bozorgmehr (eds) *Ethnic Los Angeles*, 165–91 (New York: Russell Sage Foundation).

Pai, H.-H. (2004) 'Inside the grim world of the gangmasters', *Guardian*, Special Report, 27 March.

Pai, H.-H. (2007) 'Chinatown's restaurant workers: We are refusing to be scapegoated', *Socialist Worker* (UK), 23 October.

Pai, H.-H. (2008) *Chinese Whispers: The True Story Behind Britain's Hidden Army of Labour* (London: Penguin Books).

Panayiotopoulos, P. I. (1992) 'Local government economic initiatives. Planning, choice and politics: The London experience', *Papers in International Development*, No. 7 (Swansea: Centre for Development Studies).

Panayiotopoulos, P. I. (1996) 'Challenging orthodoxies: Cypriot entrepreneurs in the London garment industry', *Journal of Ethnic and Migration Studies*, 22:3, 437–60.

Panayiotopoulos, P. I. (2000) *Venice*, Personal observation, 12–25 May.

Panayiotopoulos, P. I. (2001a) 'Globalisation and immigrant enterprise', in P. Panayiotopoulos and G. Capps (eds) *World Development*, 98–113 (London: Pluto Press).

Panayiotopoulos, P. I. (2001b) 'The global textile industry: An engendered protectionism', in P. Panayiotopoulos and G. Capps (eds) *World Development*, 192–207 (London: Pluto Press).

Panayiotopoulos, P. I. (2003) *Barcelona and Madrid*. Personal observation, 12–25 April.

Panayiotopoulos, P. I. (2005) 'The globalisation of care: Filipina domestic workers and care for the elderly in Cyprus', *Capital and Class*, 88, 1–36.

Panayiotopoulos, P. I. (2006) *Immigrant Enterprise in Europe and the United States* (London: Routledge).

Panayiotopoulos, P. I. (2007) 'Jobs created by immigrants: Response from Swansea University', Evidence submitted to the Equality of Opportunity Committee

Inquiry into Migrant Workers. Cardiff: National Assembly for Wales http://
www.assemblywales.org/bus-home/bus-committees/bus-committees-
third1/bus-committees-third-eoc-home/bus-committees-third-eoc-inquiry/
bus-committees-third-eoc-mw/bus-committees-third-eoc-mw-writev/bus-
committees-third-eoc-mw020.htm

Panayiotopoulos, P. I. (2008) 'Turkish immigrant entrepreneurs in the
European Union: A political-institutional approach', *International Journal of
Entrepreneurial Behaviour and Research*, 14:6, 395–414.

Panayiotopoulos, P. I. and G. Capps (eds) (2001) *World Development* (London:
Pluto Press).

Panayiotopoulos, P. I. and M. Dreef (2002) 'London: Economic differentiation
and policy-making in the London garment industry', in J. Rath (ed.) *Unravelling
the Rag Trade: Immigrant Entrepreneurship in Seven World Cities*, 49–73 (Oxford:
Berg Publishers).

Pang, C. L. (2000) 'The economic embeddedness of immigrant businesses:
The case of Belgium', Paper presented to the Conference on The Economic
Embeddedness of Immigrant Enterprise, Jerusalem, 18–20 June.

Pang, C. L. (2003) 'Belgium: From proletarians to Proteans', in R. Kloosterman
and J. Rath (eds) *Immigrant Entrepreneurs: Venturing Abroad in the Age of
Globalisation*, 195–212 (Oxford: Berg Publishers).

Parekh, B. (2004) 'Redistribution or recognition? A misguided debate', in S.
May, T. Modood and J. Squires (eds) *Ethnicity, Nationalism and Minority Rights*,
199–213 (Cambridge: Cambridge University Press).

Parekh, P. (2000) *Rethinking Multiculturalism: Cultural Diversity and Political
Theory* (Basingstoke: Macmillan).

Parker, D. and M. Song (2001) 'Introduction', in D. Parker and M. Song (eds)
Rethinking Mixed Race, 1–22 (London: Pluto Press).

Parkes, C. (1998) 'Something stirring in the melting pot', *Financial Times*,
7 June.

Parkes, C. (1999) 'Californians urged to raise a cheer for Asian immigrants',
Financial Times, 3 July.

Parkes, C. (2002) 'Little change in Loss Angeles tinder-box', *Financial Times*,
30 April.

Parsons, T. (1952) *The Social System* (London: Tavistock).

Parsons, T. and N. Smelser (1956) *Economy and Society: A Study in the Integration
of Economic and Social Theory* (London: Routledge).

Pecoud, A. (1999) 'Weltoffenheit Schafft Jobs: Turkish entrepreneurship and
multiculturalism in Berlin', *Working Paper* No. WPTC-01-19 (London: ESRC
Transnational Communities Programme). http://www.transcomm.ox.ac.uk/
working_papers.htm

Pecoud, A. (2001) *Unemployment, Self-employment and Multiculturalism among
German-Turks in Berlin*. Paper presented at the 13th SASE Annual Meeting on
Socio-Economic, University of Amsterdam, 28 June–1 July.

Pecoud, A. (2002) 'Weltoffenheit Schafft Jobs: Turkish entrepreneurship and
multiculturalism in Berlin', *International Journal of Urban and Regional Research*,
26:3, 494–507.

Pedace, R. and S. Rohn (2008) *A Warm Embrace or the Cold Shoulder: Wage and
Employment Outcomes in Ethnic Enclaves* (Washington, DC: Center for Economic
Studies, US Census Bureau).

Penninx, R., J. Schoorl and C. van Praag (1993) *The Impact of International Migration on Receiving Countries: The Case of the Netherlands* (Amsterdam: Swets and Zeitlinger).

Perlmann, J. and R. Waldinger (1997) 'Second generation decline? Children of immigrants, past and present – a reconsideration', *International Migration Review*, 31:4, 893–922.

Personal Social Services Research Unit (PSSRU) (1998) *Demands for Long-Term Care: Projections of Long-Term Care Finance for Elderly People* (Canterbury: University of Kent).

Petros, M. (2005) 'The costs of human smuggling and trafficking', *Global Migration Perspectives*, 31 (Geneva: Global Commission on International Migration).

Pew Hispanic Center (2006) *The Labor Force Status of Short-Term Unauthorised Workers*. Fact Sheet.

Phillips, T. (2004) 'Interview with Trevor Phillips', *The Times*, 3 April.

Phillips, T. (2005) BBC *Breakfast with Frost Interview with Trevor Phillips, Chair CRE*, 22 March. http://news.bbc.co.uk/1/hi/programmes/breakfast_with_frost/

Phizacklea, A. (1990) *Unpacking the Fashion Industry* (London: Routledge).

Pickard, R. (2009) 'Britons take whatever work they can', *Financial Times*, 11 March.

Pieke, F. N. (1998) 'Introduction', in G. Benton and F. Pieke (eds) *The Chinese in Europe*, 1–17 (Basingstoke: Macmillan Press).

Pieke, F. N. (1999) 'The Netherlands', in L. Pan (ed.) *The Chinese Overseas*, 322–7 (Surrey: Curzon Press).

Pieke, F. N. (2002) *Recent Trends in Chinese Migration to Europe: Fujianese Migration in Perspective* (Geneva: International Organisation for Migration).

Pieke, F. N. and G. Benton (1998) 'The Chinese in the Netherlands', in G. Benton and F. Pieke (eds) *The Chinese in Europe*, 125–67 (Basingstoke: Macmillan Press).

Portes, A. (1984) 'The rise of ethnicity: Perceptions among Cuban exiles in Miami', *American Sociological Review*, 49:3, 383–412.

Portes, A. (1994) 'The informal economy and its paradoxes', in N. Smelser and R. Swedbergh (eds) *The Handbook of Economic Sociology*, 426–49 (New York: Princeton University Press).

Portes, A. (1995a) 'Economic sociology and the sociology of immigration: A conceptual overview', in A. Portes (ed.) *The Economic Sociology of Immigration: Essays on Networks, Ethnicity and Entrepreneurship*, 1–41 (New York: Russell Sage Foundation).

Portes, A. (1995b) 'Children of immigrants: Segmented assimilation and its determinants', in A. Portes (ed.) *The Economic Sociology of Immigration: Essays on Networks, Ethnicity and Entrepreneurship*, 248–80 (New York: Russell Sage Foundation).

Portes, A. (1997) 'Globalisation from below: The rise of transnational communities', *Working Paper* No. WPTC-9802 (London: ESRC Transnational Communities Programme). http://www.transcomm.ox.ac.uk/working_papers.htm

Portes, A. (2009) 'Migration and development: Reconciling opposite views', *Ethnic and Racial Studies*, 32:1, 5–22.

Portes, A. and R. Bach (1985) *Latin Journey: Cuban and Mexican Immigrants in the United States* (Berkeley: University of California Press).

Portes, A., C. Escobar and R. Arana (2008) 'Bridging the gap: Transnational and ethnic organisations in the political incorporation of immigrants in the United States', *Ethnic and Racial Studies*, 31:6, 1056–90.

Portes, A. and P. Fernandez-Kelly (2008) 'No margin for error: Educational and occupational achievement among disadvantaged children of immigrants', *The ANNALS of the American Academy of Political and Social Science*, 620:12, 12–36.

Portes, A. and L. Jensen (1987) 'What's an ethnic enclave? The case for conceptual clarity', *American Sociological Review*, 52:3, 768–71.

Portes, A. and L. Jensen (1989) 'The enclave and the entrants: Patterns of ethnic enterprise in Miami before and after Mariel', *American Sociological Review*, 54:3, 929–49.

Portes, A. and D. MacLeod (1996) 'What shall I call myself? Hispanic identity formation in the second generation', *Ethnic and Racial Studies*, 19:3, 523–47.

Portes, A. and R. G. Rumbaut (2001) *Legacies: The Story of the Immigrant Second Generation* (Berkeley: University of California Press).

Portes, A. and J. Sensenbrenner (1993) 'Embeddedness and immigration: Notes on the social determinants of economic action', *American Journal of Sociology*, 98:6, 1320–50.

Portes, A. and A. Stepick (1985) 'Unwelcome immigrants: The labour market experiences of 1980 (Mariel) Cuban and Haitian refugees in South Florida', *American Sociological Review*, 50:4, 493–514.

Portes, A. and A. Stepick (1993) *City on the Edge. The Transformation of Miami* (Berkeley: University of California Press).

Portes, A. and M. Zhou (1993) 'The new second-generation: Segmented assimilation and its variants among post-1965 immigrant youth', *ANNALS of the American Academy of Politics and Social Science*, 530:1, 74–96.

Portes, A. and M. Zhou (1996) 'Self-employment and the earnings of immigrants', *American Sociological Review*, 61:2, 219–30.

Portes, A., M. Castells and L. Benton (eds) (1989) *The Informal Economy: Studies in Advanced and Less Developed Countries* (London: Johns Hopkins Press).

Poutziouris, P. (1998) 'The growth and control dilemma in the family business: The Taramasolada Kings', Manchester Business School: Business Development Centre.

Poutziouris, P. (1999) 'The development of ethnic family business ventures: Lessons for the "breaking-out" strategies of Anglo-Cypriots', Paper delivered to The Conference on Cypriot Society in the Millennium, held at the University of Greenwich, 4–5 December.

Putnam, R. (1993) 'The prosperous community: Social capital and public life', *The American Prospect*, 3:11–17.

Quassoli, F. (1999) 'Migrants in the Italian underground economy', *International Journal of Urban and Regional Research*, 23:2, 212–31.

Raes, S. (2000) *Migrating Enterprise and Migrant Entrepreneurship: How Fashion and Migration Have Changed the Spatial Organisation of Clothing Supply in the Netherlands* (Amsterdam: Het Spinhuis Publishers).

Raes, S., J. Rath, M. Dreef, A. Kumcu, F. Reil and A. Zorlu (2002) 'Amsterdam: Stitched up', in J. Rath (ed.) *Unravelling the Rag Trade: Immigrant Entrepreneurship in Seven World Cities*, 89–111 (Oxford: Berg Publishers).

Ram, M. and T. Jones (1998) *Ethnic Minorities in Business* (Milton Keynes: Open University Business School).

Ram, M., D. Smallbone and D. Deakins (2002) *Access to Finance and Business Support by Ethnic Minority Firms in the UK* (London: British Bankers Association).

Ram, M., D. Smallbone and B. Linneker (2002) *Assessing the Potential of Supplier Diversity Initiatives as a Means of Promoting Diversification among Ethnic Minority Businesses in the UK* (London, Middlesex University: Centre for Enterprise and Economic Development Research).

Ramirez, R. R. and G. P. de la Cruz (2003) *The Hispanic Population in the United States: March 2002* (Washington, DC: US Census Bureau).

Rath, J. (2001) 'A game of ethnic musical chairs? Immigrant businesses and the formation and succession of niches in the Amsterdam economy', in S. Body-Gendrot and M. Martiniello (eds) *Minorities in European Cities*, 26–43 (Basingstoke: Macmillan Press).

Rath, J. (2002) 'Needle games: A discussion of mixed embeddedness', in J. Rath (ed.) *Unravelling the Rag Trade: Immigrant Entrepreneurship in Seven World Cities*, 1–27 (Oxford: Berg Publishers).

Rath, J. and R. Kloosterman (2000) 'Outsiders' business: A critical review of research on immigrant entrepreneurship in the Netherlands', *International Migration Review*, xxxiv:3, 657–81.

Rath, J. and R. Kloosterman (2003) 'The Netherlands: A Dutch treat', in R. Kloosterman and J. Rath (eds) *Immigrant Entrepreneurs. Venturing Abroad in the Age of Globalisation*, 123–46 (Oxford: Berg Publishers).

Rath, J. (ed.) (2000) *Immigrant Businesses. The Economic, Political and Social Environment* (Houndmills: Macmillan).

Rath, J. (ed.) (2002) *Unravelling the Rag Trade: Immigrant Entrepreneurship in Seven World Cities* (Oxford: Berg Publishers).

Rees, C. (2007) 'Report sparks row over Polish staff', *South Wales Evening Post*, 14 December.

Rekers, A. and R. van Kempen (2000) 'Location matters: Entrepreneurs and the spatial context', in J. Rath (ed.) *Immigrant Businesses, the Economic, Political and Social Environment*, 54–69 (Houndmills: Macmillan).

Rex, J. (1996a) 'Multiculturalism in Europe', in J. Hutchinson and A. D. Smith (eds) *Ethnicity*, 241–5 (Oxford: Oxford University Press).

Rex, J. (1996b) *Ethnic Minorities in the Modern Nation State. Working Papers in the Theory of Multi-Culturalism and Political Integration in European Cities* (Basingstoke: Macmillan).

Rex, J. and R. Moore (1967) *Race, Community and Conflict: A Study of Sparkbrook* (London: Oxford University Press).

Rex, J. and S. Tomlinson (1979) *Colonial Immigrants in Great Britain – A Class Analysis* (London: Routledge).

Rhea, J. T. (1997) *Race, Pride and the American Identity* (Cambridge, MA: Harvard University Press).

Robertson, R. (1998) *Identity: Community, Culture, Difference* (London: Lawrence & Wishart).

Robinson, J. (2002) 'Introduction', in J. Robinson (ed.) *Development and Displacement*, 1–18 (Open University: Oxford University Press).

Rose, J. (2004) *The Myths of Zionism* (London: Pluto Press).

Rosenbaum, E. (1996) 'The influence of race on Hispanic housing choices: New York City, 1978–1987', *Urban Affairs Review*, 32:2, 217–43.

Rutherford, R. and R. Blackburn (2000) 'The diversity of ethnic minority small firms: Issues for business support providers', Paper presented at the 23rd National Small Firms Conference, Aberdeen, November.

Ryan, L., R. Sales, M. Tilki and B. Siara (2009)' Family strategies and transnational migration: Recent Polish migrants in London', *Journal of Ethnic and Migration Studies*, 35:1, 61–77.

Sabagh, G. and M. Bozorgmehr (1996) 'Population change: Immigration and ethnic transformation', in R. Waldinger and M. Bozorgmehr (eds) *Ethnic Los Angeles*, 79–107 (New York: Russell Sage Foundation).

Salt, J. (2000) 'Trafficking and human smuggling: A European perspective', *International Migration Quarterly Review*, 38:3, 31–56.

Salt, J. and J. Millar (2006) *Foreign Labour in the United Kingdom: Current Patterns and Trends* (London: Office for National Statistics).

Salt, J. and J. Stein (1997) 'Migration as business: The case of trafficking', *International Migration Quarterly Review*, 35:4, 467–92.

Samers, M. E. (2004) 'The "underground economy", immigration and economic development in the European Union: An agnostic view', *International Journal of Economic Development*, 6:2, 199–272.

Sampson, R. J. (2009) 'Racial stratification and the durable tangle of neighbourhood inequality', *The ANNALS of the American Academy of Political and Social Science*, 621, 260–80.

Sanders, J. and V. Nee (1987) 'Limits of ethnic solidarity in the enclave economy', *American Sociological Review*, 52:6, 745–73.

Santos, M. (1975) *The Shared Space: The Two Circuits of the Urban Economy in Underdeveloped Countries* (London: Methuen).

Sassen, S. (1988) *New York's Informal Economy*. ISSR Working Papers, 4, No. 9.

Sassen, S. (1991) *The Global City: New York, London, Tokyo* (New Jersey: Princeton).

Sassen, S. (1994) 'The informal economy. Between new developments and old regulations,' *The Yale Law Journal*, 103:8, 2289–304.

Sassen, S. (1995) 'Immigration and local labor markets', in Alejandro Portes (ed.) *The Economic Sociology of Immigration: Essays on Networks, Ethnicity and Entrepreneurship*, 87–127 (New York: Russell Sage Foundation).

Sassen, S. (1996) 'New employment regimes in the cities: The impact of immigrant workers', *New Community*, 22, 579–94.

Saxenian, A. L. (1999) *Silicon Valley's New Immigrant Entrepreneurs* (Santa Barbara: Public Policy Institute of California).

Saxenian, A. L. (2006) *The New Argonauts: Regional Advantage in a Global Economy* (Cambridge, MA: Harvard University Press).

Schermenhom, R. A. (1970) *Comparative Ethnic Relations* (New York: Random House).

Schierup, C.-U. (2007) 'Bloody subcontracting in the network society: Migration and post-Fordist restructuring across the European Union', in E. Berggren et al. (eds) *Irregular Migration*, 150–64 (Maastricht: Shaker Publishing).

Schlesinger, A. M. (1992) *The Disuniting of America* (New York: W. W. Norton).

Schlyter, C. (2002) *International Labour Standards and the Informal Sector: Developments and Dilemmas* (Geneva: International Labour Office).

Schonwalder, K. (2004) 'Why Germany's guestworkers were largely Europeans: The selective principles of post-war labour recruitment policy', *Ethnic and Racial Studies*, 27:2, 248–65.

Scott, A. J. (1996) 'The manufacturing economy: Ethnic and gender divisions of labor', in R. Waldinger and M. Bozorgmehr (eds) *Ethnic Los Angeles*, 215–46 (New York: Russell Sage Foundation).

Scott, J. W. (1995) 'Multiculturalism and the politics of identity', in J. Rajchman (ed.) *The Identity in Question*, 3–14 (London: Routledge).

Sen, F. (2002) 'Forty years later: Turkish immigrants in Germany', *Private View*, Spring, 28–35.

Shelley, T. (2007) *Exploited: Migrant Labour in the New Global Economy* (London: Zed Press).

Sherwood, B. (2009) 'Poles apply for benefits as hard times bite', *Financial Times*, 13 April.

Skeldon, R. (2000) *Myths and Realities of Chinese Irregular Migration* (Geneva: International Organisation on Migration).

Smith, A. (2002) 'The new ethnicity classification in the Labour Force Survey', *Labour Market Trends*, 3:657–66,

Smith, D. (2007) 'Migrants ease the inflation pressure', *Sunday Times*, 28 October.

Solomos, J. and L. Back (1995) 'Marxism, racism and ethnicity', *American Behavioural Scientist*, 38:3, 407–20.

Somerville, W. and M. Sumption (2009) *Immigration in the United Kingdom: The Recession and Beyond*. Migration Policy Institute: Equality and Human Rights Commission. http://www.migrationpolicy.org/pubs/Immigration-in-the-UK-The-Recession-and-Beyond.pdf

Spaan, E., F. Hillmann and T. Naerssen (eds) (2005) *Asian Migrants and European Labour Markets* (London: Routledge).

Spaan, E., T. Naerssen and H. Tillaart (2005) 'Asian immigrants and entrepreneurs in the Netherlands', in E. Spaan, F. Hillmann and T. Naerssen (eds) *Asian Migrants and European Labour Markets*, 238–62 (London: Routledge).

Staring, R. (2000) 'International migration, undocumented immigrants and immigrant entrepreneurship', in J. Rath (ed.) *Immigrant Businesses. The Economic, Political and Social Environment*, 162–81 (Houndmills: Macmillan).

Storkey, M. (1993) *Identifying the Cypriot Community from the 1991 Census* (London: London Research Centre).

Storkey, M. and R. Lewis (1997) 'London: A true metropolis', in P. Ratcliffe (ed.) *Ethnicity in the 1991 Census*, 210–25 (London: HMSO).

Struder, I. R. (2003a) 'Do concepts of ethnic economies explain existing minority enterprises? The Turkish speaking economies in London', *London School of Economics Research Papers in Environment and Spatial Analysis Series*, No. 88.

Struder, I. R. (2003b) 'Self-employed Turkish-speaking women in London: Opportunities and constraints within and beyond the ethnic economy', *International Journal of Entrepreneurship and Innovation*, 4:3, 185–95.

Stryker, S. (1959) 'Social structure and prejudice', *Social Problems*, Spring 6, 340–54.

Tana, L. (1998) 'Vietnam', in L. Pan (ed.) *The Chinese Overseas*, 228–33 (Surrey: Curzon Press).

Taylor, A. (2008a) 'Influx raises population close to 61 million', *Financial Times*, 22 August.

Taylor, A. (2008b) 'Britain loses its appeal among Polish jobseekers', *Financial Times*, 22 August.

Taylor, A. (2009) 'Big fall in east Europe job hunters', *Financial Times*, 25 February.

Taylor, A. and S. Wagstyl (2007) 'Poles head for home as wages rise to lure recruits', *Financial Times*, 25 July.

Thomson, M. (2006) 'Migrants on the edge of Europe: Perspectives from Malta, Cyprus and Slovenia', *Sussex Centre for Migration Research: Migration Working Paper* No. 35. http://www.sussex.ac.uk/migration/documents/mwp35.pdf

Tichenor, D. (2002) *Dividing Lines: The Politics of Immigration Controls in America* (Princeton and Oxford: Princeton University Press).

Tomba, L. (1999) 'Exporting the "Wenzhou Model" to Beijing and Florence: Suggestions for a comparative perspective on labour and economic organisation in two migrant communities', in F. N. Pieke and H. Malleo (eds) *Internal and International Migration, Chinese Perspectives*, 280–93 (Surrey: Curzon Press).

Trimikliniotis, N. and M. Fulias-Souroulla (2006) *Mapping of Policies Affecting Female Migrants and Policy Analysis: The Cyprus Case* (Nicosia: Intercollege FeMIPol).

Tumbas, Y. (2003) *Turkish Migrant Entrepreneurs in the EU* (Brussels: Institut Européen de Recherche sur la Coopération Méditerranéenne et Euro-Arabe).

Turkish Research Centre (TRC) (2000) *Turks in the European Union* (University of Essen: TRC).

Turton, D. (2002) 'Forced displacement and the nation-state', in J. Robinson (ed.) *Development and Displacement*, 19–76 (Milton Keynes, Open University: Oxford University Press).

UNFP (2006) *State of the World Population. A Passage to Hope: Women and International Migration.* http://www.unfpa.org/swp/2006/pdf/sowp06-en.pdf

US Census Bureau (2004) 'Census bureau projects tripling of Hispanic and Asian population in 50 years', Press Release, 18 March.

US Census Bureau (2006a) 'Hispanic-owned firms: 2002', *Economic Census, Survey of Business Owners* (Washington, DC: US Census Bureau).

US Census Bureau (2006b) 'Growth of Hispanic-owned businesses triples the national average', Press Release, 21 March.

US Census Bureau (2007) *The American Community – Blacks: 2004.* ACS-04 (Washington, DC: US Census Bureau).

US Census Bureau (2008a) *Los Angeles County, California, Selected Characteristics of the Native and Foreign-Born Populations.* Data Set: 2006–2008, S0501. American Community Survey 3-Year Estimates (Washington, DC: US Census Bureau).

US Census Bureau (2008b) *Miami-Dade County, Florida. Selected Characteristics of the Native and Foreign-Born Populations.* Data Set: 2006–2008, S0501. American Community Survey 3-Year Estimates (Washington, DC: US Census Bureau).

US Census Bureau (2008c) *Los Angeles County, California. Characteristics of People by Language Spoken at Home.* Data Set: 2006–2008, S1603. American Community Survey 3-Year Estimates (Washington, DC: US Census Bureau).

US Census Bureau (2008d) *Miami-Dade County, Florida. Characteristics of People by Language Spoken at Home.* Data Set: 2006–2008, S1603 American Community Survey 3-Year Estimates (Washington, DC: US Census Bureau).

Uzar, F. (2007) 'Social participation of Turkish and Arabic immigrants in the neighbourhood: Case study of Moabit West, Berlin', *Journal of Identity and Migration Studies*, 1:2, 44–66.

Uzzi, B. (1996) 'The sources and consequences of embeddedness for the economic performance of organisations: The network effect', *American Sociological Review*, 61:674–98.

Waldinger, R. (1984) 'Immigrant enterprise in the New York garment industry', *Social Forces*, 32:1, 60–71.

Waldinger, R. (1985) 'Immigration and industrial change in the New York City apparel industry', in M. Tienda and G. Borjas (eds) *Hispanic Workers in the United States*, 323–49 (Orlando: Academic Press).

Waldinger, R. (1986) *Through the Eye of the Needle: Immigrants and Enterprise in New York's Garment Trades* (New York: University Press).

Waldinger, R. (1995) 'The "other side" of embeddedness: A case-study of the interplay of economy and ethnicity', *Ethnic and Racial Studies*, 18:3, 555–80.

Waldinger, R. (1996a) 'Ethnicity and opportunity in the plural city', in R. Waldinger and M. Bozorgmehr (eds) *Ethnic Los Angeles*, 445–70 (New York: Russell Sage Foundation).

Waldinger, R. (1996b) *Still the Promised City? African-Americans and New Immigrants in Post-industrial New York* (Cambridge, MA: Harvard University Press).

Waldinger, R. (1996c) 'From Ellis Island to LAX: Immigrant prospects in the American city', *International Migration Review*, xxx:4, 1078–86.

Waldinger, R. (2000) 'The economic theory of ethnic conflict: A critique and reformulation', in J. Rath (ed.) *Immigrant Businesses. The Economic, Political and Social Environment*, pp. 124–41 (Houndmills: Macmillan).

Waldinger, R. (2001a) 'Conclusion. Immigration and the remaking of urban America', in R. Waldinger, R. (ed.) *Strangers at the Gates: New Immigrants in Urban America*, 308–30 (Berkeley: University of California Press).

Waldinger, R. (2001b) 'Up from poverty? "Race", immigration and the fate of low-skilled workers', in R. Waldinger (ed.) *Strangers at the Gates: New Immigrants in Urban America*, 80–16 (Berkeley: University of California Press).

Waldinger, R. (2008) 'Between "here" and "there": Immigrants cross-border activities and loyalties', *International Migration Review*, 42:1, 3–29.

Waldinger, R. and C. Feliciano (2004) 'Will the second generation experience "downward assimilation"? Segmented assimilation re-assessed', *Ethnic and Racial Studies*, 27:3, 376–02.

Waldinger, R. and D. Fitzgerald (2004) 'Transnationalism in question', *American Journal of Sociology*, 109, 1177–95.

Waldinger, R. and J. Lee (2001) 'New immigrants in urban America', in R. Waldinger (ed.) *Strangers at the Gates: New Immigrants in Urban America*, 30–79 (Berkeley: University of California Press).

Waldinger, R., R. Ward and H. Aldrich (1985) 'Trend report, ethnic businesses and occupational mobility in advanced societies', *Sociology*, 19:4, 586–97.

Waldinger, R., H. Aldrich and R. Ward (eds) (1990) *Ethnic Entrepreneurs: Immigrant Business in Industrial Societies* (London: Sage Publications).

Wallace, C. (2002) 'Opening and closing borders: Migration and mobility in East-Central Europe', *Journal of Ethnic and Migration Studies*, 28:4, 603–25.

Wang, Q. (2007) *How Does Geography Matter in Ethnic Labor Market Segmentation Process? A Case Study of Chinese Immigrants in the San Francisco Area*. CES 07–09 (Washington, DC: US Census Bureau).

Warhaftig, A. and K. Wierzbicka (2007) *East European Immigration and the Effects within the London Borough of Enfield*. A study carried out on behalf of the Enfield Citizens Advice Bureau, April.

Warrell, H. (2009) 'Business goes into reverse at Polish outposts', *Financial Times*, 15 March.

Wassener, B. (2002) 'New laws spur on foreign voters', *Financial Times*, 13 September.

Watson, J. L. (1977) 'The Chinese: Hong Kong villagers in the British catering trade', in J. L. Watson (ed.) *Between Two Cultures: Migrants and Minorities in Britain*, 181–213 (Oxford: Basil Blackwell).

Watson, R., K. Keasy and M. Baker (2000) 'Small firm financial contracting and immigrant entrepreneurship', in J. Rath (ed.) *Immigrant Businesses. The Economic, Political and Social Environment*, 70–89 (Houndmills: Macmillan).

Weber, M. (1958) 'The Protestant sects and the spirit of capitalism', in H. Gerth and C. W. Mills (eds) *From Max Weber*, 302–22 (New York: Oxford University Press).

Weber, M. (1978) 'Ethnic groups', in G. Roth and C. Wittich (eds) *Economy and Society*, Vol. I., 389–95 (Berkeley: University of California Press).

Werbner, P. (1999) 'Global pathways: Working class cosmopolitans and the creation of transnational ethnic worlds', *Social Anthropology*, 7:7, 17–35.

Willems, W. (2003) 'No sheltering sky: Migrant identities of Dutch nationals from Indonesia', in A. Smith (ed.) *Europe's Invisible Migrants*, 33–59 (Amsterdam: Amsterdam University Press).

Williams, C. (2007) 'Small business and the informal economy: Evidence from the UK', *International Journal of Entrepreneurial Behaviour and Research*, 13:6, 349–66.

Wilpert, C. (1993) 'Ideological and institutional foundations of racism in the Federal Republic of Germany', in J. Wrench and J. Solomos (eds) *Racism and Migration in Western Europe*, 67–81 (Oxford: Berg Publishers).

Wilpert, C. (2003) 'Germany: From workers to entrepreneurs', in R. Kloosterman and J. Rath (eds) *Immigrant Entrepreneur, Venturing Abroad in the Age of Globalisation*, 233–60 (Oxford, Berg Publishers).

Wilson, K. and A. Portes (1980) 'Immigrant enclaves: An analysis of the labour market experiences of Cubans in Miami', *American Journal of Sociology*, 86:1, 295–319.

Wimmer, A. (2008) 'Elementary strategies of ethnic boundary making', *Ethnic and Racial Studies*, 31:6, 1025–55.

Wise, A. (2007) *Multiculturalism from Below: Transversal Crossings and Working Class Cosmopolitans*. Paper presented at COMPAS Annual Conference, Oxford, 5–6 July.

Wise, A. and S. Velayutham (eds) (2007) *Multiculturalism from Below: Transversal Crossings and Working Class Cosmopolitanism* (Macquarie University: Centre for Research on Social Inclusion).

Wong, A. (1999) 'Italy', in L. Pan (ed.) *The Chinese Overseas*, 319–21 (Surrey: Curzon Press).

Wood, P., L. Charles and J. Bloomfield (2006) *Cultural Diversity in Britain: A Toolkit for Cross-Cultural Co-operation* (York: Joseph Rowntree Foundation).

World Bank (1989) *Sub-Saharan Africa. From Crisis to Sustainable Growth: A Long-Term Perspective Study* (Washington, DC: Oxford University Press).

World Bank (1994) *Adjustment in Africa. Reforms, Results and the Road Ahead.* A World Bank Policy Research Report (Washington, DC: Oxford University Press).

Wu, B. and V. Zanin (2007) *Exploring Links between International Migration and Whenzhou's Development.* Discussion Paper No. 25, China Policy Institute: University of Nottingham.

Xaba, J., P. Horn and S. Motala (2002) *The Informal Sector in Sub-Saharan Africa.* Working Paper on the Informal Economy (Geneva: International Labour Office).

Yun, G. (2004) *Chinese Migrants and Forced Labour in Europe.* Working Paper No. 32 (Geneva: International Labour Office).

Yurdakul, G. (2006) 'State, political parties and immigrant elites: Turkish immigrant association in Berlin', *Journal of Ethnic and Migration Studies*, 32:3, 435–53.

Yu-Sion, L. (1998) 'The Chinese community in France: Immigration, economic activity, cultural organisation and representations', in G. Benton and F. N. Pieke (eds) *The Chinese in Europe*, 96–124 (Basingstoke: Macmillan Press).

Yu-Sion, L. (1999) 'France', in L. Pan (ed.) *The Chinese Overseas*, 311–17 (Surrey: Curzon Press).

Zeynep, K. (2004) *Stay as You Are! But at What Cost? Multicultural Berlin against Not So Multicultural Germany.* Paper presented to the Conference of Europeanists, 11–13 March, Chicago.

Zhou, M. (1992) *Chinatown: The Socioeconomic Potential of an Urban Enclave* (Philadelphia: Temple University Press).

Zhou, M. (2004) 'Revisiting ethnic minority entrepreneurship: Convergencies, controversies and conceptual advancements', *International Migration Review*, 38:3, 1040–74.

Zhou, M. and J. Logan (1989) 'Returns on human capital in ethnic enclaves: New York and Chinatown', *American Sociological Review*, 54, 809–20.

Zhou, M., J. Lee, J. Vallejo, R. Tafoya-Estrada and Y. Xiong (2008) 'Success attained, deterred, and denied: Divergent pathways to social mobility in Los Angeles' new second generation', *The ANNALS of the American Academy of Political and Social Science*, 620:12, 37–61.

Zhou, Y. (2002) 'New York: Caught under the fashion runway', in J. Rath (ed.) *Unravelling the Rag Trade: Immigrant Entrepreneurship in Seven World Cities*, 113–33 (Oxford: Berg Publishers).

Zinn, H. (1964) *SNCC, The New Abolitionists* (Boston: Beacon Press).

Index